THE TOUCHE ROSS GUIDE
To Personal Financial Management
1984 Edition

W. Thomas Porter, Ph.D., C.P.A.
Touche Ross & Co.

Prentice-Hall, Inc.
Englewood Cliffs, New Jersey

Prentice-Hall International, Inc., *London*
Prentice-Hall of Australia, Pty. Ltd., *Sydney*
Prentice-Hall Canada, Inc., *Toronto*
Prentice-Hall of India Private Ltd., *New Delhi*
Prentice-Hall of Japan, Inc., *Tokyo*
Prentice-Hall of Southeast Asia Pte. Ltd., *Singapore*
Whitehall Books, Ltd., Wellington, *New Zealand*
Editora Prentice-Hall do Brasil, Ltda., *Rio de Janeiro*

Library of Congress Cataloging in Publication Data

Porter, W. Thomas.
Touche Ross guide to personal financial management.
Includes index.
1. Finance, Personal. I. Touche Ross & Co. II. Title.
HG179.P5729 1984 332.024 83-21110
ISBN 0-13-925701-2
ISBN 0-13-925685-7 {PBK}

Printed in the United States of America

THE TOUCHE ROSS GUIDE
To Personal Financial Management
1984 Edition

ABOUT THE AUTHOR

W. THOMAS PORTER, Ph.D., C.P.A., is a partner in the Seattle office of Touche Ross, one of the country's "Big Eight" accounting firms. He is the national director of the firm's personal financial management services. He has organized the seminars Touche Ross conducts across the nation, and has himself instructed the executives of such companies as Boeing, Weyerhaeuser, and Pacific Northwest Bell in personal financial planning and management. Previously he was an accounting professor at the University of Washington, where he still teaches courses in taxation. He was a pioneer in personal financial planning and coauthored in the mid-1970s an earlier book, *Wealth: How to Achieve It*, with Durwood L. Alkire.

That book was selected by major book clubs throughout the country and the favorable feedback from many readers, together with observations from seminar participants and individual clients, formed the basis for this current book.

THE PERSONAL FINANCIAL MANAGEMENT COMMITTEE OF TOUCHE ROSS & CO.

Christopher Carlson
Los Angeles, California

John Connell
Denver, Colorado

Thomas DeLuca
Cincinnati, Ohio

Edward Emering
Chicago, Illinois

Stanford Kauffman
Dallas, Texas

Barry Kessler
New York, New York

Steven Klein
St. Louis, Missouri

W. Thomas Porter
Seattle, Washington

Robert Zobel
Philadelphia, Pennsylvania

To Jerry and Dave

Thanks for your vision, your championing of this project, and your patience.

PREFACE

Nowadays, an earned income of $50,000 or even $100,000 a year offers no guarantee against financial worries or difficulties. We make this observation with great regularity, those of us at Touche Ross who have been conducting executive seminars on personal financial management over the last five years and handling individual counseling for clients for many more years.

Most of the 50,000 executives and professionals who have attended our seminars did so because they felt uneasy about their current financial state or their financial future—and for good reason. Many had incomes that, after taxes, just barely covered their expenditures, and some confessed frankly to being "broke." It is hardly surprising, under such circumstances, that only a few were setting money aside for investments, though most of them doubted that their pensions alone would see them through in retirement. Most had never addressed these issues systematically, and didn't know exactly where to begin in planning their personal finances.

Good planning is an entirely practical matter that cannot take place in the abstract. It has to be based on your particular income and income expectations, your own financial obligations, and your personal life goals and aspirations. Once these have been established and you have learned what can be done and how to do it, you have a valid basis for making the most advantageous decisions on your taxes, investments, insurance, education costs, retirement, and the estate you leave to your survivors. In other words, you will be in control of your own finances.

With this book, we want to extend the same help to you that we offer the participants in our executive seminars and the clients in our individual counseling sessions. We will familiarize you with the planning process as applied to personal finances, and we will give you a structure as well as the basic tools for planning and managing your finances effectively.

If you follow this structure, apply the techniques discussed, and develop your financial plan, you may save more than $2,000 in annual professional fees charged by financial planners to do the same thing for you. You should be able to minimize your income taxes, increase your investment return, realize a comfortable retirement, and transfer your estate at a minimum emotional and financial cost.

By following the step-by-step instructions and using the forms provided, you will develop a comprehensive financial plan to make the things you want more attainable and the future more secure. Otherwise, you can count on dissatisfaction, tension, and insufficient resources to meet your goals.

As you read this book, please bear in mind that it takes into account applicable laws, regulations, rulings, and other determinations as of August 31, 1983; you should consult your professional advisor for any changes subsequent to that date.

W. Thomas Porter

ACKNOWLEDGMENTS

I have received ideas, assistance, and critiques from many partners and staff at Touche Ross, and from many executives and professionals who have attended seminars and who are individual clients.

Special thanks go to David Odegaard, Gerald Gorans, John Connor and Joe Freimuth for their initial support of the project and continued enthusiasm during the writing of the book. Thanks to Ed Ruzinsky and Jim Martin for their efforts in launching the publishing relationship with Prentice-Hall. Thanks also to Vern Dotson, Nicholas Spika, Gerald Padwe, Israel Press, and Ron Brotherton, who read the manuscript and provided many useful comments. I would also like to thank Jeff Knepper for his support of potential software applications of this material, and Carol Congram and Michael Wolff for their effective integration of the book within the Touche Ross organization.

Debby Baxter, Debi Seriales, Anne Secrest, and Loreen Felstet have my special appreciation for their cheerful and skillful typing and related help. Thanks also to Janet Johnson, who contributed significantly in the initial drafts of the manuscript.

Jo Kaufman was just wonderful as a development editor, with tremendous ability to take technical copy and turn it into a clear, succinct, understandable manuscript. She "owned" the book and gave it her utmost love and care.

And finally, my thanks to Ron Ledwith and Tamara Lee at Prentice-Hall, and Bill Porter, Lew Perry, and John Harvey at Lumen Systems Inc.

W.T.P.

CONTENTS

THE TOUCHE ROSS GUIDE
To Personal Financial Management
1984 Edition

1

PERSONAL FINANCIAL PLANNING

The objective of this book is very simple—to help you get better control of your life financially. Money should not be the central concern of one's life, but the management of money is necessary in order to reach lifetime objectives—to provide funds for a home, for schooling and educational travel, for healthful pursuits and other leisure-time activities that broaden one's mind and vision, for creating new employment opportunities, for retiring comfortably.

Life is an incredible journey because it is full of opportunities and *choices*—a choice of what to study, what job to pursue, what hobby to start, whom to marry, what relationship you will have with your family, what community organization to actively participate in, and on and on. Each choice has a *consequence*. A choice once made means a foregone opportunity for a while or permanently. Your choice of a college, a career path, a spouse, where to live, how to live, whether to have children and how to raise them, will affect what future alternatives will be available to you.

Financial planning also involves a series of choices and consequences. One of the countless examples that could be given here is that of a middle-aged couple who consulted us once late in April, after they had completed their tax return. They complained that they paid too much in taxes and had decided they needed a tax shelter (their *choice*). We asked them whether they had ever been in a tax shelter. They said they had. "How did you do?" we asked. They replied, "We lost everything" (the *consequence*). We then asked them for specific and detailed information in order to get a complete picture of their needs and circumstances. From the data they gave us, it became quite clear to us and also to them that the key issue for them was an adequate retirement income. Therefore they did not need a tax shelter, which is usually risky. They needed safe investments that would give a somewhat guaranteed return.

The analysis of choices and consequences is the essence of decision making. To make good financial decisions, you need good information about your financial situation and the options available to you. We recently counseled a professional man who planned on sending his three young children through private school, college, and graduate school. By our calculations, this would cost a total of $1 million, for which, at his 50 percent tax bracket, he would have to earn $2 million. He did not know that the income that will pay for his children's education can be indirectly shifted to his children. Knowing it now will save the family about $750,000 in avoidable income taxes.

To have the financial resources you want in order to reach your goals, you also need *commitment*. You need to commit time and attention to following through on your financial choices. We have often helped clients to identify options that are financially sound. But nothing happens. They always have something else to do that seems more urgent, or they leave all financial planning and whatever actions that may entail for some vague time in the future when there may be nothing more urgent to do. Few of them realize what or how much they stand to lose, but some know it exactly. As an example, take the case of a man whom we advised late in 1981 to change his will so that he could take advantage of new opportunities introduced by the Economic Recovery Tax Act of 1981. When he died early in 1982, his will had not been changed, and his procrastination cost his widow and his children roughly $400,000 in avoidable estate taxes.

Failure to act does not always have such drastic consequences, but the time and attention devoted to planning one's finances and taking the requisite action will generally result in far greater returns or savings than time spent on other, seemingly more urgent tasks.

WHY DO IT?

All of us have read or heard about some wealthy people who pay surprisingly little in taxes. In contrast, most executives and professionals who earn between $50,000 and $100,000 a year pay nearly a third of their income in taxes. After that, little is left for any investments, and those investments are often made on the strength of a sales pitch, a chance conversation at a club or a cocktail party, or some newspaper article. The wealthy make use of experienced financial advisors, who plan their clients' investments carefully and often manage to double them every few years.

Maybe you can't afford the financial advisors that the more affluent can, but you can afford the time and effort to develop your plan as outlined in this book. If you do, you may be able to save between $2,000 and $3,000 in annual professional fees charged by financial planners to do the same thing for you. In addition, you will use your financial resources more effectively.

People who have attended our executive seminars tell us quite often that financial planning has made a greater difference to them than a raise in salary. Whatever objectives they had—travel, cars, boats, buying or remodeling a home, a good education for their children, a comfortable retirement—they either reached or felt more confident of reaching. Once they learned the planning process and understood what was involved, they found the means to increase their net worth and their investments.

HOW TO DO IT

In our seminars, we often ask the question, "How many of you have taken a course in financial planning in college or high school?" Only about 2 percent of the participants say they have. So most people need a way to start, a structure to follow, and methods of organizing financial information, having it readily available, and keeping it up to date. They also need financial planning techniques and ideas for making good choices.

This book will provide both a structure for planning and managing your finances systematically and ideas and techniques to help you accumulate sufficient resources to reach your goals. The book has two basic components: its text and its forms. Between them, they will give you most of the help you need to develop a personal financial plan tailored exactly to your own particular objectives, circumstances, and obligations.

The text covers every important area of personal financial management, explains its function, and shows you how to identify and evaluate your alternative courses of action. It also explains and comments on each of the forms you will be asked to fill in. The forms on which you will list your financial and personal data are at the back of the book, printed on colored paper, detachable, and with prepunched holes, ready for filing in a three-ring binder. We have also provided an extra set of forms for an update of your financial situation.

You may be wondering at this point whether it might not serve your purposes well enough to read the book but not to bother with the forms. If you bought the book just to have something to read, that's fine, but then you will still be lacking the right frame of reference for your financial decisions. If you want to make proper use of your financial resources and the financial options open to you, then fill in the forms. In that process, you will do all of the following:

- Assemble and organize all your financial data and documents
- Calculate your present net worth
- Analyze your present income, expenditures, and insurance coverage
- Project your future needs, income, and expenditures
- Identify your personal and economic objectives and their relative priorities
- Identify the financial strategies for achieving these objectives
- Use your projections to minimize your income tax, select your investments, plan your retirement income, and keep estate taxes to a minimum

The process of financial planning we explain in this text and the forms we have included can be applied to anyone's situation. We have used the process and forms in counseling single people, married couples without children, married couples with children, divorced people, old and young people, the very wealthy and the not-so-wealthy. We may use examples in the book to clarify a point or to illustrate a form. The people in the examples may not be like you. But don't turn off at that point, because the *process* we will be explaining will be relevant to you.

You will apply the process to your situation by completing the forms with *your* data. You will be asked to make some estimates of *your* future. When you make such estimates, do not fret about preciseness or accuracy. Try to come up with reasonable estimates using the information available to you.

YOUR FINANCIAL PLANNER

The end result of completing the forms in this book is "Your Financial Planner." It will contain all your current financial data and make them available as a frame of reference for your future decisions, for periodic review of your goals and your progress, for updating your plan and keeping your data current, and for your survivors in the event of your death.

By preparing Your Financial Planner, you may also save significant annual professional fees charged by financial planners to organize your finances for you. Once you have Your Financial Planner prepared, you can use financial advisors in a much more cost-effective way and can better evaluate their advice.

Physically, Your Financial Planner will be a three-ring binder holding all your filled-in forms, with dividers separating the various types of information. The top of each form specifies in which section of Your Financial Planner to file the form once it has been completed. All you have to do now is to get a three-ring binder for ordinary letter-size (8½" × 11") pages and 14 tabbed dividers for this binder. Printed labels for each of the tabs and for the front and spine of the binder can be found on the first colored page at the back of this book, ready to be cut out and used.

HOW TO PROCEED

Every chapter that follows will tell you why and how specific forms should be completed and how to use the information you prepare. Many chapters will also suggest courses of action to be considered in light of your findings, circumstances, and objectives. We stress your action throughout the book. Any suggested course of action in the book that strikes you as desirable should be listed on the last of the forms, entitled *Your Action Steps*. From this list you will eventually choose the ten action steps you will try to implement this year. We have found that ten action steps are about all a person can implement in one year.

For each of the forms, we don't supply you with just one copy, but with two. The second one should be used for an annual financial checkup, to which we have devoted the final chapter of this book.

Now, are you ready to embark on the interesting process of shaping your finances so as to use, increase, and protect your resources to your own best advantage? In this book, you have all the information you need to get started.

2

FAMILY AND FINANCIAL RECORDS

Eventually, Your Financial Planner will contain all the data that pertain to the planning and management of your financial affairs. In the main, you will be the person who benefits from having all the relevant information in one place—easy to access and easy to update. But you will not be the only one who benefits. Those who survive you will have to pick up where you left off, and you should make that as unproblematic for them as you can. The real sorrow that people feel about someone's death can be accompanied by real irritation when the survivors have to surmount countless difficulties that could easily have been avoided.

What we kept in mind when we designed the three forms you will now be asked to complete was that those who will someday have to take over from you will need all sorts of basic information that you may carry in your head but that they may not carry in theirs.

FORM 1—FAMILY DATA

This form is an easy one—so easy we call it a warm-up. Some of the information to be listed is of the bothersome variety that you frequently look up to complete loan applications, investment partnership agreements, and tax returns, and to update wills. Once you have set it all down in this form, you will know where to find it and never have to go hunting for it again.

If you use advisors, information about your family situation is important. For example, knowing that you have children may trigger the advisor's recommending certain educational financing techniques with significant tax advantages. Another example: If your advisors know that your parents are self-supporting, they may be more concerned about coordinating estate planning among your parents, you, and your children.

FORM 2—FINANCIAL DOCUMENTS

In this paper-mill world we live in, we tend to keep important papers in a variety of "safe" places—in safe deposit boxes, in the desk at home, in the basement or the attic, and at the office. As a result, most of us have spent some anxious moments looking for various important papers, riffling through a mixture of current and obsolete documents, only to find that the one we were looking for was not where we thought it must be.

Save yourself such anxieties in the future by listing your documents and their locations here. You will be doing it at your leisure now, but the next time you need to locate one of these papers, you may well be in a hurry. While you are doing yourself and your survivors this favor, you might also check to see whether some of the documents you have kept have become obsolete in the meantime. If your last will was made out in 1940, you may want to challenge its relevance.

When you complete this form, use the *Additional Description* column for the specifics of the various documents. Beside *Mortgage*, for instance, you might identify the property and the mortgagor. Beside *Life Insurance Policies*, you might identify the insurance company and the policy number.

FORM 3—FINANCIAL ADVISORS

At one of our executive seminars, a participant looked at this form and said, "I don't have all those advisors listed here. Does that mean there is something wrong with me?" Nothing at all was wrong with this person, nor would there be anything wrong with you if you have not used all of these advisors. If you have used some of them, though, and have found them helpful, it would be a good idea to list them here. You yourself may be glad one day that you did—people have been known to forget other people's names and addresses—but the main purpose of compiling this list is to give your survivors some indication of the people who could be consulted and would be conversant with some aspects of your financial affairs.

Once you have completed Form 3, consider these points:

- Make sure your spouse has met all your advisors. A 42-year-old C.P.A. with complicated investment dealings died suddenly a few years ago. Because he was the "professional" in the family, he did all the financial planning. Besides, he was too "young" to die. But he did die young, and his widow spent needless hours unraveling what were now her financial affairs.
- Consider an annual financial checkup meeting with appropriate family members present, together with all or some of your advisors. It's a great way to educate family members on financial planning.
- You should have one advisor you and other family members would turn to in the event of a very important financial decision.

3

YOUR NET WORTH

The overall goal of financial planning is to have enough resources to reach your personal goals. The best overall measure of your financial resources is your net worth.

The process of ascertaining your net worth consists of calculating your total assets and total liabilities and then subtracting your total liabilities from your total assets. It is a fundamental starting point for almost everything in financial planning.

Because it is so fundamental, most people have, at some point in their lives, filled out a net worth statement. If you are one of them, chances are that you did so in order to satisfy a lender's request for financial information. When you do it this time, on Form 4, it will be for your own benefit, to provide you with an essential tool for planning and managing your own finances. You will need it for any one of the following purposes:

- Finding out what your present net worth is.
  You should be more interested in your financial health than your lender is. We would recommend that once a year you check on your financial health and on your progress toward the net worth goal you will be setting yourself, such as an increase of 15 percent.
- Making "what-if" projections.
  You may, for example, want to work out what your retirement funds will be in five years' time if you presently have $100,000 to invest and can put $10,000 in an investment program each year and get a 10 percent return.
- Evaluating your assets.
  Your net worth statement gives you an overall picture of how you have used your assets. It tells you whether most of them are personal assets, such as your residence, car, and furnishings, or investment assets, such as savings, stocks, bonds, and income-producing real estate. It shows you which of your assets you could quickly convert into cash. It shows whether your investments are diversified or concentrated in one or two investment categories.
- Analyzing your liabilities.
  Keeping debt under control is an integral part of good personal financial management.

- Planning or revising your life insurance.
  Generally, the more net worth you have, the less life insurance you will need.
- Estimating estate taxes.
  Your net worth is the starting point for determining your taxable estate and developing an estate plan.

Now we will briefly define total assets and total liabilities.

TOTAL ASSETS

To obtain the amount of your total assets, you add your liquid assets to the value of your investment assets and your personal assets.

LIQUID ASSETS Your so-called liquidity, meaning your financial ability to respond swiftly to emergencies or investment opportunities, is largely determined by the amount of your liquid assets. This amount consists of your cash accounts and short-term investments, such as Treasury bills, savings certificates, and money market funds, and the cash value of your life insurance. Your need for liquidity is influenced by the predictability of your cash income and expenditures, by your employment security, and by your investment strategy.

It is generally held that your liquid assets should roughly equal four to six months' employment income. If you are in an unstable employment situation or about to make a large investment, the amount should probably be greater. If your employment is relatively secure and you anticipate no major cash expenditures in the near future, the amount could be smaller.

INVESTMENT ASSETS These are defined as long-term investments, intended to store up value for major future needs like education costs and retirement. Stocks, bonds, and real estate (other than personal residence or vacation property) are typical investment assets. So are investments in oil and gas and equipment leasing, which usually are made in a limited partnership. Retirement funds, too, are classified as investment assets. These may include Individual Retirement Accounts, Keogh plans, and tax-deferred annuities.

PERSONAL ASSETS Items you acquire for your own or your family's long-term use or enjoyment form part of your personal assets. Typically, they include your private residence and vacation home as well as any cars, boats, art, antiques, and furnishings that you own.

TOTAL LIABILITIES

There are two types of liabilities: short-term obligations and long-term obligations. For the average person, both should be fairly easy to compute.

SHORT-TERM OBLIGATIONS These are defined as all sums that have to be paid within the next twelve months. Thus, they also include whatever amounts are due on long-term obligations within the next twelve months. Typically, these might be consumer credit payments, installment loans, personal loans, accrued income taxes, or borrowings on life insurance.

LONG-TERM OBLIGATIONS Most long-term obligations are incurred for one of two purposes: to finance long-term investments like real estate or oil programs, or to finance the purchase of major personal assets like your residence, your vacation property, or a home computer. Normally, the asset purchased constitutes security for the lender in case you default on the loan. Over time, the value of the investment asset you purchased with borrowed funds may increase, while the amount of your obligation usually decreases. Thus, your equity—the difference between the current value of the asset and the current balance on the loan—usually increases.

BORROWING COSTS The rates of interest you pay on the various moneys you owe are your borrowing costs. Since you will want to minimize the overall amount you pay in interest, you should analyze your interest costs periodically and try to repay the loans with the highest rates of interest first.

FORM 4—STATEMENT OF NET WORTH

Before or while you complete Form 4, you might like to see an example of the completed form. Figure 3-1 shows you this form as it was completed for a family of five: father and mother aged 47 and 43, and their three children aged 20, 19, and 10.

We might here make some generalizations about the net worth of people at various age levels. People in their twenties, thirties, and forties tend to accumulate personal assets—cars, furnishings, homes—and then to trade up and buy a more luxurious car, a larger home, and vacation property. Thus, their total personal assets rise much faster than their total investments. By the time they reach their fifties, most people slow down or stop adding to their personal assets and become more concerned with their investment assets and with their financial security. Thus, the total investment assets of people who are approaching retirement will often exceed the total personal assets.

To calculate your total assets, begin by filling in the first column, *Estimated Current Value*, for each asset you own.

With regard to retirement funds, the last item listed under *Investment Assets*, enter the current value of Individual Retirement Accounts, Keogh plans, or tax-deferred annuities. The current value of employee retirement plans may, however, be difficult to ascertain because the annual information sheet employers provide will often state only what your monthly payments are likely to be when you retire. If so, omit any current value for such programs. It is not as important to estimate the current value of your employee retirement plan for purposes of calculating net worth as it is to know, for retirement planning purposes, what the monthly benefit will be at retirement age. You will use your employee retirement information when we cover retirement planning and your sources of retirement income in Chapter 12.

When you have added up the current value of all your assets and thus obtained the dollar amount of your total assets, compute what percentage of the total each asset item represents, and list that percentage beside the item's current value.

In listing what you owe, any installment loans that extend beyond one year should be divided so that you list the amount due within the next twelve months under *Short-Term Obligations* and the remainder under *Long-Term Obligations*.

List the interest rate you pay for each debt beside its current value.

FIGURE 3-1

File under FINANCIAL PROFILE

Date: February 15

FORM 4 STATEMENT OF NET WORTH

WHAT YOU OWN	CURRENT VALUE (EST.)	% OF TOTAL ASSET VALUE
1 Liquid Assets		
Cash (checking, savings accounts):	$2,100	1%
Short-Term Investments Treasury Bills:		
Savings Certificates:		
Money Market Funds	$24,400	3%
Cash Value of Life Insurance	7,000	1%
TOTAL Liquid Assets	$33,500	5%
2 Investment Assets		
Notes Receivable	$39,800	5%
Marketable Securities Stocks	57,400	8%
Bonds	3,200	1%
Real Estate (investment)	90,000	12%
Tax Incentive Investments	20,000	3%
Other Investment Assets (describe below)		
a. XYZ closely held business	27,000	4%
b.		
c.		
d.		
Retirement Funds	25,400	4%
TOTAL Investment Assets	$262,800	37%

FIGURE 3-1, cont'd.

3 Personal Assets		
Residence	$275,000	39%
Vacation Property	73,000	11%
Art, Antiques	—	—
Furnishings	56,000	8%
Vehicles	____	____
Boats	____	____
Other	____	____
TOTAL Personal Assets	$404,500	58%
TOTAL ASSETS	$700,800	100%

WHAT YOU OWE	CURRENT VALUE (EST.)	INTEREST RATE
4 Short-Term Obligations		
Consumer Credit Obligations	____	____
Borrowings on Life Insurance	$6,300	6%
Installment Loans	____	____
Personal Loans	____	____
Accrued Income Taxes	____	____
Other Obligations (describe below)		
a. ____	____	____
b. ____	____	____
c. ____	____	____
d. ____	____	____
TOTAL Short-Term Obligations	$6,300	____

FIGURE 3-1, cont'd.

5 Long-Term Obligations

Loans to purchase investment assets	$16,000	7.75%
Loans to purchase personal assets	$101,000	8.25%
Mortgage on personal residences	______	___
TOTAL Long-Term Obligations	$117,000	___
TOTAL LIABILITIES	$123,300	

TOTAL ASSETS	$700,800
- TOTAL LIABILITIES	$123,300
= NET WORTH	$577,500

When you have calculated your total liabilities by adding the current values of all your debts, subtract this sum from your total assets in order to arrive at your present net worth.

FORM 5—ANALYSIS OF NET WORTH

Use your figures from Form 4 to complete this form.

- On line 1, enter your total liquid assets.
- On line 2, enter your total short-term obligations.
- On line 3, calculate the excess or deficiency of your liquid assets by subtracting the amount on line 2 from the amount on line 1. Hopefully, the amount on line 3 will be positive. If it is negative, you ought to start building up liquid assets and should definitely stop borrowing short-term.
- Obtain the percentage of your liquid assets excess or deficiency by dividing the amount on line 1 by the amount on line 2. Your target should be a positive figure between 150 and 200 percent. Your liquid assets would thus be 1½ to 2 times greater than your short-term obligations.
- On line 4, enter your total investment assets.
- On line 5, enter your total long-term obligations.
- On line 6, calculate the amount of equity you have in your investments by subtracting the amount on line 5 from the amount on line 4. To compute the percentage of this equity, divide the amount on line 6 by the amount on line 4. If your percentage is less than 20, it is low, and you are significantly borrowing against your investments. If your percentage is greater than 50, it is high, and you may want to consider getting some of your equity out through borrowing. On the other hand, you personally may wish to be debt-free and would therefore be aiming at an equity of 100 percent.
- On line 7, enter your total personal assets.
- On line 8, enter the amount of the loans you have taken for the purchase of personal assets.
- On line 9, calculate the amount of equity you have in your personal assets by subtracting the amount on line 8 from the amount on line 7. Compute the percentage of this equity by dividing the amount on line 9 by the amount on line 7. Many people have a much higher equity in personal assets than in investment assets. If your percentage is less than 20, it is low, and you are leveraging your personal assets. If your percentage is greater than 50, it is high, and you may want to consider borrowing on your equity.
- On line 10, check your computations by adding the amounts on lines 3, 6, and 9 and entering the total. The amount on line 10 should agree with your total net worth as shown at the bottom of Form 4.

USE OF DEBT

One way to increase your assets is to borrow funds. Borrowed funds may be used to purchase personal assets such as furnishings, automobiles, and appliances. Such loans are often called consumer loans and have short repayment periods. Managing consumer debt requires a knowledge of some basic techniques.

Know the safety limit suggested by specialists in consumer debt. They suggest that the average consumer's debt payments (excluding mortgage payments) should not exceed 20 percent of take-home income (after taxes and other payroll deductions). Specialists say a smaller percentage—say 10 percent to 15 percent—is a comfortable debt level; 20 percent gets near the debt overload position for many people.

Another use of debt is to purchase investment assets such as securities and income-producing real estate. In a financial context the use of borrowed money to acquire investment assets is sometimes called *leverage*.

Leverage is used extensively, particularly in real estate transactions. In periods of rising inflation, leverage can be very beneficial. Let us say that in the early 1970s you borrowed $50,000 at 8 percent to purchase a house for rental to others. That borrowing rate was probably based on an inflation rate of 4 percent, giving the lender a real rate of return of 4 percent. Assuming that all your interest expense is tax-deductible, your after-tax cost would be 4 percent, if you were in a 50 percent tax bracket. Although inflation went up during the 1970s, your borrowing costs would have remained steady at 8 percent, but your monthly net rental income would have gone up if you, like all other landlords, increased your tenants' rents. You would therefore have had more than enough to pay back your loan, and even after paying other costs of being a landlord, such as taxes and repairs, you might still have put some cash in your pocket. In addition, the value of your rental house would have risen as inflation went up. That shows why, during the 1970s, the real estate game was the hottest game in town—in every town.

In the meantime, what was known as creative leverage in the 1970s has become creative foreclosure in the 1980s. Why? Some people who entered the real estate game late in the inflationary spiral didn't borrow at 8 percent but at much higher rates. At these rates, their rental income could not cover their high debt payments, taxes, and repairs. In addition, as inflation decreased, property values decreased.

Many financial institutions and investment promoters suggest the use of debt to implement certain investment choices. For example, some suggest reducing equity in your personal residence through refinancing and investing the proceeds elsewhere. When you are considering the use of debt, keep these questions in mind:

1. What will the borrowing cost you annually in after-tax dollars?
   Assume, for example, that your local bank sends you a notice saying it would be happy to refinance your home at 12 percent. If you are in a tax bracket of 40 percent, your after-tax cost would be 60 percent of 12 percent, which is 7.2 percent. Obviously, the lower your tax bracket, the higher your after-tax cost.
2. What is your after-tax return likely to be on the investment you make with the money obtained through borrowing?
   It is a rule of thumb that any investment you make should have the potential to return you twice your after-tax cost. For example, if your after-tax cost on the borrowed money is 8 percent, the investment you make should have the potential for a return of 16 percent after taxes. In other words, since you are taking a risk with borrowed money, you should have the potential of being amply rewarded.

3. What funds will you use to pay off the debt you incur?
   If you choose to invest in something that has great growth potential but little or no cash flow, you need to have some other source of funds to make the monthly payments on the new debt you have incurred. Say you borrow $50,000 at 12 percent for 20 years to purchase real estate; your debt repayments will be almost $6,700 a year, or $558 per month. Granted, you save taxes because of the additional interest deductions, but you still have to come up with $558 per month.

So when you are considering borrowing with the equity in your investment assets, be sure you have a satisfactory answer to each of the three questions above before you take the plunge.

CHOICES AND YOUR NET WORTH

Your net worth is a snapshot of your financial condition at a particular point in time. It is the end result of choices you have made in the past. For example, if you chose to acquire an expensive home and several automobiles, you may have little in the way of investment assets. If you chose to borrow significantly to finance consumer purchases and vacations, you may not have a significant net worth because your debts will be almost as great as your assets.

It is important to look back to understand why your present net worth is what it is, but it is more important to evaluate choices you can make at present to impact your net worth in the future. If you want your net worth to increase, here are some choices you can make:

- Make your investments grow by getting a greater rate of return on your investments. You can improve your rate of return by acquiring more knowledge of investment alternatives, by spending more time in managing your investments, or by selecting an investment advisor to help you manage your investments.
- Increase your investments by putting aside more each year from your current employment income. This can be done by spending less for your current lifestyle or by decreasing your taxes through tax planning.
- Reduce your debt. If you are making monthly payments on your mortgage or other obligations you have, your debt is decreasing and your net worth is growing. Consider accelerating your debt payments; if you do, you will also save significant amounts of interest.

4

YOUR INCOME AND EXPENDITURES

Unless you have inherited assets or married someone with substantial assets, you usually start your adult earning years with little or no net worth. In this situation, there is no magic formula for achieving financial security. What you must do is save. Save some portion of your job income on a systematic basis, invest your savings wisely, and in time your investment assets will be significant. By reinvesting your investment assets so that compounding takes over, you should eventually achieve financial security.

COMPOUNDING

It is easy to make calculations involving compound rates of return when you have the requisite compound interest tables. They let you see what your assets will grow to at various rates of return in a given number of years. The same tables can also be used to predict what income you will need in a given year if you are to stay even with whatever rate of inflation you anticipate.

With the following condensed table, you can project the future worth of an investment you make today. Assume, for instance, that you had $100,000 to invest and could get a return of 10 percent on it. To what sum would a 10 percent compound rate of return increase this investment in ten years?

In Table 4-1, looking at ten years from now in the 10 percent column, you find the factor 2.59. Multiplying $100,000 by 2.59 will then show you that the original investment will grow to $259,000 in ten years at 10 percent compound interest. Similarly, $100,000 invested at 15 percent for ten years has a compounding factor of 4.05, and thus would grow to $405,000 in ten years.

The same table can be used to project the effect that various rates of inflation would have on your expenditures. For example, how much after-tax income will you need in some future year in order to be as well off as you are now? Assume that your present after-tax income is $24,000, and that the annual inflation rate will be 8 percent. In six years, you will need an income of $38,160 after taxes merely to stay at your present standard of living. Or take some specific item like college costs. If at present one year at college costs $5,000, and costs rise at an annual rate of 8 percent, how much

TABLE 4-1
COMPOUND INTEREST

Years From Now	Future Worth of One Dollar with Amount of Return Compounded Annually — Annual Rate of Return				
	6%	8%	10%	12%	15%
1	1.06	1.08	1.10	1.12	1.15
2	1.12	1.17	1.21	1.25	1.32
3	1.19	1.26	1.33	1.40	1.52
4	1.26	1.36	1.46	1.57	1.75
5	1.34	1.47	1.61	1.76	2.01
6	1.42	1.59	1.77	1.97	2.31
7	1.50	1.71	1.95	2.21	2.66
8	1.59	1.85	2.14	2.48	3.06
9	1.69	2.00	2.36	2.77	3.52
10	1.79	2.16	2.59	3.10	4.05
15	2.40	3.17	4.18	5.47	8.14
20	3.21	4.67	6.73	9.65	16.37
25	4.29	6.85	10.83	17.00	32.92

will one year in college cost three years from now? As you can work out, it would cost $6,300.

If you decide that you will take some specific amount from your income each year and add it to your investment capital, Table 4-2 can show you the rewards of regular saving combined with compound interest. Suppose, for example, that you will put $2,000 in an Individual Retirement Account every

TABLE 4-2
GROWTH OF ASSETS FROM SETTING A CONSTANT SUM ASIDE EVERY YEAR

Years From Now	Annual Rate of Return				
	6%	8%	10%	12%	15%
1	1.00	1.00	1.00	1.00	1.00
2	2.06	2.08	2.10	2.12	2.15
3	3.18	3.25	3.31	3.37	3.47
4	4.37	4.50	4.64	4.78	4.99
5	5.64	5.87	6.10	6.35	6.74
6	6.98	7.33	7.71	8.11	8.75
7	8.39	8.92	9.49	10.09	11.07
8	9.90	10.64	11.43	12.30	13.73
9	11.49	12.49	13.58	14.77	16.78
10	13.18	14.49	15.94	17.55	20.30
15	23.27	27.15	31.77	37.28	47.58
20	36.78	45.76	57.27	72.05	102.44
25	54.86	73.10	98.35	133.33	212.79

year at an annual compound interest rate of 12 percent. How much do you think you would have in that account after ten years? How much after twenty years?

As you can see from Table 4-2, you would have $35,100 after ten years. After twenty years, you would have a whopping $144,100.

More complete compound interest tables are included in Appendix I.

FORM 6—INCOME SOURCES

All of us are familiar with earned income, and most of us would agree that it has two somewhat unromantic characteristics. The first is that you must actually work in order to receive it. The second, and this may be worse than the first, is that it is taxed to the hilt, and the hilt here can be as high as 50 percent.

In contrast to that, look at the charms of a sound investment. It generates income for you all day and every day, even if you never get out of bed or spend all your waking hours playing tennis or bridge. Furthermore, the income it produces may be entirely tax-free or only partially taxed, and the gain on selling your whole investment may be taxable at a maximum rate of 20 percent.

Investment income is the key to financial security and independence for many. When your investment income becomes significant, it will allow you to reduce the time you spend working for your money and let you turn to whatever other activities may be important to you.

To complete Form 6, use figures from the last full year for which all data are available. Your best sources of information will be your tax return, paychecks, and monthly statements from banking and investment institutions.

To compute what percentage of your total income you derived from your investment income, divide your investment income by your total income.

FORM 7—BASIC LIFESTYLE EXPENDITURES

Your basic lifestyle expenditures are those that are difficult to avoid without changing your basic standard of living. This form lists the categories that make up most people's basic lifestyle expenditures. The first four—housing, food, clothing, and transportation—account for the largest portion of basic lifestyle expenditures for many Americans.

Your own ideas on which expenditures are basic to your lifestyle and which are discretionary may not entirely coincide with the listings you find on Forms 7 and 8. You should therefore transfer from one form to the other any item that strikes you as wrongly categorized. Contributions to church or charities, for instance, have been listed as basic here, while you may regard them as discretionary expenditures. Conversely, education costs and the support of relatives have here been listed as discretionary, though you may well regard them as basic expenditures.

To complete this form, use figures from the last full year for which all data are available. You can use either monthly or annual amounts, whichever is easier.

You might like to use Table 4-3 to compare your own expenditure patterns with the three predominant spending patterns of families in the United States.

TABLE 4-3
SUMMARY OF ANNUAL BUDGETS FOR A FOUR-PERSON FAMILY AT THREE LEVELS OF LIVING URBAN U.S.—AUTUMN 1981

	Lower Budget		Intermediate Budget		Higher Budget	
	Amount	%	Amount	%	Amount	%
Total Budget	$15,323	100	$25,407	100	$38,060	100
Total Family Consumption	12,069	79	18,240	72	25,008	66
Food	4,545	30	5,843	23	7,366	19
Housing	2,817	18	5,546	22	8,423	23
Transportation	1,311	9	2,372	9	3,075	8
Clothing	937	6	1,333	5	1,947	5
Personal care	379	2	508	2	719	2
Medical care	1,436	10	1,443	6	1,505	4
Other family consumption	644	4	1,196	5	1,972	5
Other Items	621	4	1,021	4	1,718	4
Social Security and Disability	1,036	7	1,703	7	1,993	5
Personal Income Taxes	1,596	10	4,443	17	9,340	25

Note: Because of rounding, sums of individual items may not equal totals.
Source: U.S. Bureau of Labor Statistics. 1981 is the latest year for which data is available.

FORM 8—DISCRETIONARY EXPENDITURES

Discretionary expenditures are those over which you can exercise a good deal of control. It is up to you whether you dine at home or eat out in style and drop a wad. It is your choice whether to throw a canard à l'orange dinner for fifty or a wine and cheese party; and for your vacations you are not strictly obligated to take your family skiing in the Rockies or the Alps. You could take them backpacking or camping in the nearby countryside.

Even though you have quite a lot of control over the amounts you spend on entertainment, vacations, hobbies, and gifts, you will presumably be spending some amount on each of them every year. However, some discretionary expenditures are more discretionary and less regular than others. Most of us would not buy a new car or a new boat every year, nor would we subject ourselves and our budgets to home improvements with such frequency.

Form 8 lists both types of discretionary expenditures: the fairly discretionary and the highly discretionary. With the latter, you should list the average for one year as if the cost were spread over several years. When you complete this form, use figures from the last full year for which all data are available. You can use either monthly or annual amounts, whichever is easier.

FORM 9—INCOME AND EMPLOYMENT TAXES

After the giddy delights of discretionary expenditures, we have now arrived at the bane of modern existence. Please use your most recent tax returns to complete this form.

FORM 10—ANALYSIS OF EARNED INCOME AND EXPENDITURES

A few centuries ago, if you were anybody at all, you did not have to *make* money; you *had* money. The nobles, the heroes and heroines of plays and novels way back then just had it and spent it with carefree abandon. More of this unearned income was sure to come their way soon, either in frequent tax payments from the villages they owned, or in a long-awaited lump sum after the demise of their parents or their rich but childless uncle or aunt. Not only was it possible and acceptable in those days for wealthy aristocrats to live entirely on unearned income; it would have been downright vulgar to do anything else.

It is amazing what a difference a few centuries can make, isn't it? You may not own a single village, let alone several; and your expectations of a huge inheritance, too, may be dim. If that is the case, we strongly advise you to live on your earned income now if you possibly can, and to use all your unearned income as investment capital. We therefore ask you in this form to balance your expenditures only against your earned income, not your total income.

- For item 1, enter your total employment income as shown at the top of Form 6.
- For item 2, use Forms 7, 8, and 9 to obtain the necessary figures.
- For item 3, list the sum total of your three types of expenditures.
- For item 4, subtract your total expenditures from your employment income. Any positive figure that results should be used to help you reach your financial goals.

Next, calculate and list what percentage of your total employment income you have been spending on (a) basic lifestyle expenditures, (b) discretionary expenditures, and (c) taxes. To do so, divide each expenditure by your total employment income. Then arrive at the percentage of excess by dividing the dollar amount on line 4 by the dollar amount on line 1.

INTERPRETING THE RESULTS

Now that you have analyzed your income and expenditures, let's interpret the results and look at the choices you have.

1. How much of your earned income is left for future goals and for investment? In their employment years, people should try to set aside no less than 5—preferably 10—percent of their employment income and invest it. You can increase the amount available for investment by increasing your income and/or by spending less.
2. Can you earn more? Maybe you can make yourself more valuable in the job market by increasing your skills through continuing education courses, or by using your time more effectively, or by focusing on job results rather than the details of the job. The best investment you will ever make is in yourself.

   Can someone else in your family earn more? Perhaps your spouse can work part-time. If your spouse is already working, perhaps he or she can expand the scope of the job. Maybe the answer is career counseling and a new job that will let you use your skills more effectively.

3. Does your federal income tax amount to more than 20 percent of your employment income? If so, something should be done to reduce that tax bite. Chapters 6 and 7 will offer you various suggestions.
4. Do the combined percentages of your basic lifestyle expenditures and your discretionary expenditures come to more than 70 percent? If they do, and your earned income is more than $50,000 a year, then it is likely that you could reduce your expenditures without seriously reducing the quality of your life; and then you could use the difference for making investments.

   Maybe it would make sense to start to simplify your life; to emphasize quality versus quantity; to evaluate your needs versus your wants; and to examine the "instant gratification" lifestyle that usually leads to significant consumer debt, resulting in the need to earn more and more with less and less time to use what we thought we couldn't live without.

   If you need a system to monitor and control your expenditures, here are some useful techniques:

   - Segregate your income and expenditures to assist in record-keeping and control. Deposit all your employment income in an account at your bank or in a cash management account at a brokerage firm. We call this your "income account."
   - Deposit all your investment income in another bank or cash management account, which we will call your "investment account." By doing so, you ensure that all your investment income is reinvested and is compounding.
   - Monthly or semimonthly, transfer from your "income account" to a checking account sufficient funds to handle all planned basic lifestyle expenditures, taxes, and discretionary expenditures for the period.
   - Through the use of this checking account, you have a running total of your expenditures for each period and an indication of what is left to cover the period's remaining expenditures. Make a commitment that the balance can never go below zero in this account before the next transfer from the "income account."
   - Pay for most of your expenditures by check. The use of a checkbook provides a written record of your expenditures for later analysis for tax purposes and an indication of the current balance for control purposes. If you make some payments in cash, save your cash slips or write the amount in a pocket diary to collect information for summarizing your expenditures.
5. If you are contemplating major expenditures like college, extended travel, or home improvements in the course of the next few years, your figures on Form 10 will show you how feasible such plans are under your present circumstances.
6. If you are toying with the idea of taking a cut in employment income in order to gain greater independence or a more stimulating professional environment, these figures will give you some guide to the impact that such a career move might have on your lifestyle.

So analyze your income and expenditure patterns periodically because it helps you to be in control of your finances and highlights the areas in which action ought to be taken.

5

ANALYZING YOUR TAX SITUATION

For many of us, taxes are the fastest rising category of expenditures, and the largest. Taxes influence every phase of personal financial management, from producing and investing your income to your retirement and your estate planning. Much of financial planning is therefore centered on maximizing your after-tax income—the dollars from your earned income and investments that are left after paying taxes and that can actually be spent by you. Most people want to reduce their personal taxes but have not taken the time to obtain the necessary knowledge. Knowing how the tax system works and what tax-planning techniques you can legally use to reduce your taxes will allow you to salvage a great many spendable or investable dollars that would otherwise be swallowed by taxes.

THE CRAZY APRIL GAME

For most Americans, the game commences on April 1, builds to a frenzied rush on April 13, and comes to an abrupt finish at about 11:45 P.M. on April 15, when the tax return is hand-carried to the local postal station. There is much yelling and screaming and frothing at the mouth during the latter stages of the game; even some mad dashes to the local banker to arrange financing to pay for the taxes due. And then, to make matters worse, the taxpayer prolongs the agony by filing for an extension of the date on which he must file his return.

We're not making this up. It's the normal pattern of behavior for too many taxpayers. What makes it worse is that once the tax return is completed, nothing is done to look ahead at the current year's tax situation and to see what tax-saving ideas can be implemented. That is, not until about December 15, when time is again running out and there's all too often a frenetic scramble to save taxes by making quick decisions about the very appealing tax shelter investments that advertise $9 of write-off in the current year for every $1 of investment by the taxpayer. Such decisions are often poor because, too frequently, they are made about investments that capitalize on the taxpayer's emotional desire to avoid taxes, that lack economic substance, and that may be fraudulent schemes. No wonder a noted columnist observing the American scene has called such promotions "fleecing the lambs."

There's a better way, a much better way. It starts right after you have completed last year's return, with projections of your estimated total income, deductions, and taxable income for the current year. Next you must set yourself a taxable income target—in other words, what you would like your taxable income to be. Your target should not be zero but some realistic level that can be achieved through implementing legitimate tax-saving ideas without undue risk on your part.

By starting with an estimate of your current year's taxable income and targeting a desired taxable income, you will be active in your tax-saving research and have the time to seek out good tax-saving investments. You will be managing your taxes rather than reacting emotionally to flaky promoters at the end of the year. Again, it's your choice. Do you want to control your tax expenditures, or do you prefer to watch your taxes increase year after year, always constituting one of your largest annual expenditures?

FORM 11—TAX-PLANNING WORKSHEET

Before or while you complete this form, it might be helpful to look at Figure 5-1, which is an example of the completed form.

LAST YEAR The starting points will be Form 1040 and Schedule A of your last federal tax return. Use the information to complete the *Last Year* column of this form. You will notice that this form follows the format of your tax return pretty closely, though it combines some of the items and gives some of them different captions in order to help you with your analysis and estimates.

When you have transferred all the relevant figures to the *Last Year* column and have entered last year's taxable income on line 6a, look that amount up in the appropriate tax schedule in Appendix II and find out the percentage at which your top dollars were taxed. Then list that percentage on line 6b.

ESTIMATE FOR CURRENT YEAR The next step in analyzing your tax situation is to estimate your taxable income for the current year by performing the following steps.

1. Estimate gross income:

- On line 1a, estimate taxable wages and salaries from employment for this year. In our example, we assumed an increase of 7.5 percent over last year in estimating taxable wages and salaries. You may have a different assumption on which to base an estimate of your employment income.
- On line 1b, estimate your taxable dividends and interest for this year. Refer to your net worth statement (Form 4) for your present dividend- and interest-paying investments and make some assumptions about the amount they will produce. In our example, we have assumed a decrease in dividends and interest based on the assumption that interest rates will decline during the next year.
- On line 1c, estimate your net business income. Many people who work for a company do not have business income. In our example, we have shown no business income.

- On lines 1d and 1e, estimate taxable long-term and short-term capital gains and losses. These estimates should be based on your assumptions about sales of capital assets during the next year.

  List only 40 percent of your net long-term gain, since only 40 percent of such gains count as gross income. List only 50 percent of your net long-term loss, since you can only deduct 50 percent of such losses from your gross income. The maximum loss that can be deducted in one year is $3,000.
- On line 1f, estimate your net rent income or loss. Such income or loss will come from rental assets you presently own or plan to own during the next year. Remember, the net amount is your total rental income less cash expenses paid on the properties and depreciation. We have included such income in our example. Our assumption is that net rental income will increase by approximately 10 percent during the next year.
- On line 1g, estimate any partnership income or loss. Such income or loss comes from partnership investments you presently own or plan to own during the next year. Many partnership investments are tax-sheltered investments that generate substantial losses in early years, declining losses in subsequent years, and, hopefully, income after the loss years. In our example, we have shown a smaller loss during the next year as compared to last year.
- On line 1h, estimate other income or loss. We have shown such income in our example—income from a trust established by the taxpayer's recently deceased father.
- On line 1i, total the estimated gross income for the next year. In our example, the estimated gross income is $94,300.

2. Estimate adjusted gross income:

- On lines 2a through 2g, estimate any adjustments to gross income and record the total adjustments on line 2h.
- On line 3, enter the result of subtracting your total estimated adjustments for next year (line 2h) from your estimated gross income (line 1i). This is your adjusted gross income. In our example, the adjusted gross income estimate is $89,300.

3. Estimate itemized deductions:

- On lines 4a through 4f, enter your estimated itemized deductions.
  - You can only deduct medical expenses in excess of 5 percent of adjusted gross income.
  - Taxes include state income taxes, real estate taxes, sales taxes, and personal property taxes. For most people, they will increase during the next year.
  - The big item of interest for most Americans is home mortgage interest and generally it will decrease as your mortgage balance decreases.
  - Unreimbursed casualty and theft losses can be deducted only if the total losses exceed 10 percent of adjusted gross income after each casualty loss is reduced by $100.
- On line 4g, add up your itemized deductions for the year and enter the total.

- On line 4h, enter the estimate of your standard deduction—$2,300 for a single taxpayer; $3,400 if married.

4. Estimate total deductions and exemptions

- On line 5a, enter the result of subtracting the estimated amount on line 4h from the amount on line 4g.
- On line 5b, enter your estimate of personal exemptions ($1,000 for each exemption). Some taxpayers will have more exemptions because of age or because of new family members; some will have fewer exemptions because their older children will no longer qualify as dependents.
- On line 5c, add the amounts on lines 5a and 5b and enter the total for each year.

5. Estimate taxable income

- On line 6a, enter the result of subtracting line 5c from line 3.
- Determine the top tax bracket for your estimated taxable income from the appropriate tax rate schedule in Appendix II. In our example, the estimated taxable income is $69,700; the tax bracket is 42 percent.

TARGET TAXABLE INCOME

You have now estimated your taxable income for the next year. For those of you still in your working years, your estimated taxable income is probably higher than it was last year. This is because your employment earnings probably will increase.

Now you are ready to start tax planning. It begins with your setting a *target* taxable income. If you have never set a target for taxable income, don't fret. It is like setting any other target. The target should be realistic. You should feel good when you achieve the target (remember, you are saving taxes and that's a good feeling). You should keep the following points in mind as you set the target.

- Feasibility. Set a target that you are able to reach. To reduce one's taxable income to a substantially lower target level will require one to find good tax-saving products and *cash* to buy the products.
- Risk. Substantial reductions of taxable income usually require tax-shelter investments, and such investments are usually risky.
- Tax bracket. To target one's taxable income at a level substantially below a 30 percent tax bracket is often self-defeating, since many tax-saving strategies are tax-deferral programs. Your reducing taxable income now in order to be taxed at lower rates usually results in your being taxed at higher rates in later years. Substantial reduction of taxable income involves risk. It is not a good idea to deal in risky investments in order to save taxes at marginal rates much below 30 percent.
- Fluctuating income. Try to keep your taxable income from fluctuating widely from year to year. For example, if you had taxable income of $24,600, $60,000, and $45,800 over a three-year period, your total would be $130,400 and the total federal income taxes for those three years (using 1983 rates) would be about $30,000. If you divided $130,400 by three, your taxable income would be $43,500 each year and your

FIGURE 5-1

File under TAX PLANNING Date: April 19

FORM 11 TAX-PLANNING WORKSHEET

	LAST YR.	CURRENT YR.
1 Gross Income		
a. Taxable Wages/Salaries	$83,000	$89,200
b. Taxable Dividends and Interest	6,200	6,000
c. Net Business Income (Loss)		
d. Net Taxable Long-Term Capital Gain (Loss)	1,600	2,000
e. Net Taxable Short-Term Capital Gain (Loss)		
f. Net Rent Income (Loss)	4,500	5,000
g. Net Partnership Income (Loss)	(12,000)	(9,500)
h. Other Income (Loss)	—	1,600
i. TOTAL Gross Income	$83,300	$94,300
2 Adjustments to Gross Income		
a. Alimony Paid		
b. IRA Payments	4,000	4,000
c. Keogh Plan Payments		
d. Unreimbursed Business Expenses		
e. Unreimbursed Moving Expenses		
f. Deduction for Married Couple When Both Work	500	1,000
g. Other Adjustments		
h. TOTAL Adjustments	$4,500	$5,000
3 Adjusted Gross Income	$78,800	$89,300

FIGURE 5-1, cont'd.

4	Itemized Deductions		
a.	Medical	—	—
b.	Taxes	2,000	2,500
c.	Interest Paid	12,000	11,500
d.	Charitable Contributions	2,000	2,500
e.	Casualty and Theft Losses	500	—
f.	Miscellaneous Deductions	1,000	1,500
g.	TOTAL Itemized Deductions	$17,500	$18,000
h.	Standard (zero bracket) Deduction	(3,400)	(3,400)
5a.	Excess Deductions	14,100	14,600
b.	Exemptions	5,000	5,000
c.	TOTAL Deductions and Exemptions	$19,100	$19,600
6a.	Taxable Income	$59,700	$69,700
b.	Tax Bracket	40%	42%
7a.	Targeted Taxable Income		$50,000
b.	Targeted Tax Bracket		38%

federal income taxes would be approximately $28,500. If you cannot keep your income from fluctuating widely, you might consider income averaging, which we will discuss in the next chapter.

- Defer income to years when your tax bracket may be low. You may be planning to take a sabbatical, for example, that would mean a substantial decrease of your employment income for that year. By deferring income, such as sale of property, to a year when your taxable income will be low, you may not only defer taxes but actually reduce them.
- Don't "shelter" long-term capital gains. Long-term capital gains are taxed at a maximum rate of 20 percent, which is pretty low, so leave well enough alone.

With these various observations in mind, enter your targeted taxable income and tax bracket on lines 7a and 7b of Form 11. You will, of course, need to take action if you are to reduce your taxable income to the targeted amount. The means you can use to achieve this will be discussed in the next chapters.

6

WHERE AND HOW TAXES ARE SAVED

The question that people ask us most frequently is, "How can I save on my income taxes?" The answer to that is, "You can save on your taxes by knowing how various types of income are taxed and what tax-planning techniques you can use to reduce your taxes, and then by taking the appropriate action."

Governments provide certain economic incentives by taxing different types of income at different rates. Some income is tax-free; some income is given tax-favored treatment; some income gets tax-deferred treatment, meaning that it is not taxed until several years later. Some investments, called tax shelters, enable investors to take deductions that require no additional cash outlay, such as depreciation on real estate. If you want to lower your taxes, you should know which types of income are taxed at low rates or not taxed at all.

This chapter will give you a lot of tax ideas in a general sense, but bear in mind that the tax laws are complex. The Internal Revenue Code and Income Tax Regulations consist of thousands of closely printed pages. A good tax practice has knowledgeable professionals and a library of case law books and loose-leaf tax services to support their research. In this one chapter, the best thing we can do is to sketch an outline of tax-saving ideas for you, with some brief explanations of these ideas. Applied to your own situation, with some additional research on your part or on the part of a tax professional, these ideas should help you to cut your taxes. Needless to say, the ideas by themselves will not do it. When you have found an idea that fits your situation, you'll have to put it into practice. All too often, taxes are not saved because people procrastinate and don't follow through on their tax-saving ideas.

TAX-SAVING IDEAS

Generally speaking, the following six means can be used to effect long-term tax savings:

1. Tax-free income
2. Tax-favored income

3. Tax-deferred income
4. Shifting income to a family member whose tax bracket is lower than yours in order to achieve such family goals as education
5. Expenditures that result in tax deductions or in credits against your tax liability
6. Tax-sheltered investments, which combine some tax-saving aspects of the means mentioned above with certain noncash deductions

TAX-FREE INCOME

For tax purposes, your tax-free income is entirely excluded from your income. Tax-free income falls into one or more of the following categories:

- Taxable dividends received on stock you own—$200 for married couples, $100 for an unmarried person.
- Interest on the obligations of a state, city, or other political subdivision. Such obligations are commonly called tax-free bonds or municipal bonds.
- Interest on All Savers Certificates purchased between October 1, 1981, and December 31, 1982—up to $2,000 for married couples filing jointly, up to $1,000 for an unmarried person.
- Up to $125,000 of the gain on the sale of your personal residence if you are 55 years or older prior to the sale and you have owned this residence for at least three of the five years preceding the sale. This is a once-in-a-lifetime exclusion.
- Any amount you receive through gifts or inheritances. That's why it is said that the simplest way to become financially independent is to choose your parents wisely.
- Any proceeds you receive from a life insurance policy of which you are the designated beneficiary.
- Some or all of the Social Security benefits you receive after you retire.

TAX-FAVORED INCOME

Any investment income that qualifies for long-term capital gain treatment is tax-favored. Long-term capital gain treatment will normally be given to any gain realized from the sale of capital assets like stocks, bonds, and real estate that you held for more than one year. For tax purposes, only 40 percent of any realized capital gain will be included in your income. The other 60 percent of the gain is excluded.

Gain is realized to the extent that the price at which you sold an asset exceeded your so-called basis. Your basis is your cost of acquiring the asset, plus or minus any tax adjustment made during the period you held the asset. Let's say you bought a house for rental and you paid $50,000 for it, and over the ten years you have owned the house you have spent $15,000 on it for capital improvements and deducted $2,000 per year for depreciation. Let's further assume that five years ago a tree fell on the house, and you therefore deducted $2,000 for unreimbursed casualty losses on your tax return. If you were now to sell your house for $100,000, your gain would be $57,000, since your basis is $43,000, as computed below:

Original Cost		$50,000
plus Improvements		15,000
minus Depreciation	(20,000)	$65,000
Casualty Loss	(2,000)	(22,000)
Basis		$43,000

One of the provisions of the Economic Recovery Tax Act of 1981 enables investors to convert dividends on utility stocks from ordinary income to tax-favored capital gain income. Starting in 1982 and ending in 1985, up to $1,500 per year ($750 for a single taxpayer) of otherwise taxable dividends on certain public utility shares are excluded if you can and do elect to take the dividend in stock rather than cash. The stock dividends received under such a plan will have a tax basis of zero, since you did not pay anything for the stock. If you hold the stock dividend shares more than one year, the proceeds are taxed as long-term capital gains, whereas the cash dividend would have been taxed as ordinary income. But if you sell *any* shares of your public utility stock within one year of receiving the stock dividend, those shares will be deemed to be the zero-basis shares and the income will be classed as ordinary income, not tax-favored income.

TAX-DEFERRED INCOME

The income from some investments is tax-free for a specified period and is therefore known as tax-deferred income. Since there is a protracted period in which the compound interest is not diminished by taxation, tax-deferred income can increase at a relatively fast rate.

EMPLOYEE PENSION AND PROFIT-SHARING PLANS

Many taxpayers take advantage of the opportunities offered by tax deferment. One of these opportunities is often provided by their employers through a qualified pension or profit-sharing plan. The employer makes a contribution to the plan and deducts the contribution as a business expense. The contributed funds are invested, and the income builds up tax-free. The employee receives the benefits at a later date—at retirement or upon termination of employment. Only then do the benefits become taxable as ordinary income.

INDIVIDUAL RETIREMENT ACCOUNTS

The most advertised and perhaps the best-known type of tax-deferred investment is the Individual Retirement Account (IRA). Since 1982, everyone with earned income has had the option to establish an IRA, even while participating in an employee retirement plan. An IRA offers two great advantages:

- What you contribute to your IRA in a given year can be deducted from your income for that year. It becomes taxable only as you withdraw it.
- Your IRA fund accumulates and compounds tax-free, and becomes taxable only as you withdraw some or all of it.

TABLE 6-1
INVESTMENT GROWTH IN IRAs WITH ANNUAL COMPOUNDING

Annual Contributions of $2,000

Years in Plan	Your Deposits	Principal With Interest		
		8%	10%	12%
10	$20,000	$ 28,970	$ 31,870	$ 35,100
20	$40,000	$ 91,520	$114,550	$144,100
30	$60,000	$226,570	$328,990	$482,670

Annual Contributions of $2,250

Years in Plan	Your Deposits	Principal With Interest		
		8%	10%	12%
10	$22,500	$ 32,590	$ 35,860	$ 39,480
20	$45,000	$102,960	$128,870	$162,120
30	$67,500	$254,890	$370,110	$543,000

To take full advantage of these provisions, the money must remain in your IRA until you reach the age of 59 years and 6 months (or until you become disabled), though you may roll it over into another IRA at any time without incurring any penalty. A premature withdrawal for any other purpose will saddle you with a 10 percent penalty tax (plus a regular income tax) on the amount withdrawn.

For one person, the maximum annual contribution to an IRA is $2,000 or 100 percent of earned income, whichever is less. For spousal IRAs, where a nonearning spouse as well as the earning spouse is a beneficiary of the plan, the maximum is $2,250.

To appreciate how much investments of pretax dollars can grow while the interest on them goes untaxed, take a look at Table 6-1. Also note the great differences that result from different rates of return. Investing $2,000 for 30 years at 8 percent will give you $226,570, while at 12 percent it will give you $482,670. That is a difference of $256,100, or about 210 percent, though the difference in rates of return is only 50 percent.

KEOGH PLANS

Keogh plans are similar to Individual Retirement Accounts, but the contributor has to be self-employed, either full-time or part-time, and must have self-employment income. The maximum annual contribution that can be made in 1984 to a Keogh plan is 15 percent of net self-employment income or $30,000 ($15,000 in 1983), whichever is less. If you have some self-employment income, you can have both an IRA and a Keogh plan. For example, if an executive employed by one corporation is also a board member of another corporation and receives board fees, the board fees are deemed to be self-employment income, and so this executive could contribute to a Keogh plan.

ANNUITIES

To many Americans, a tax-deferred annuity has been an attractive investment in recent years. Such an annuity is based on a contract between you and an insurance company. You purchase the annuity from the insurance company with one or more payments. The earnings on the annuity accumulate tax-deferred until some future date when you start to receive guaranteed regular payments from the insurance company. The tax-deferred earning rate is guaranteed by the issuing insurance company.

SALE AND PURCHASE OF PERSONAL RESIDENCE

Another good example of a tax-deferred investment is your personal residence. Any time you sell a residence and reinvest the proceeds in another personal residence within 24 months before or after the sale of the old residence, you can defer the gain on the sale. The following paragraphs will explain how such deferrals work in practice.

Suppose you bought your first house in 1950 for $20,000 and made improvements to it of $5,000 during the ten years you owned it. If you sold it in 1960 for $35,000, your gain—called a *realized gain* for tax purposes—would be $10,000. A realized gain is the amount by which your sales price ($35,000) exceeds your basis ($20,000 plus $5,000). Now watch where the deferral comes in.

If you bought another house within the prescribed period before or after selling your first house, and its purchase price was greater than $35,000 (the proceeds from your first home), then you could defer all of the $10,000 gain on the sale of your first house. In tax terms, you would not have to *recognize* your *realized gain* of $10,000. Recognized gain is the amount of realized gain you have to report on your tax return in the year you realized the gain. So far, great—no gain to recognize. But it's not all cake and ice cream; you do have to reduce the basis of your second house by the amount of the deferred gain. To illustrate, let's assume that your second home, purchased in 1960, cost $50,000. Normally, your basis for that would be the price that you paid for it. But since you could and did defer the gain on the first house, that gain must be deducted from the basis of your next house. Hence the basis of your second house must be reduced to $40,000.

So far you're doing very well, but you may wonder whether this deferral scheme will not catch up with you. Not necessarily, so let's proceed further with the American dream—home ownership and trading up.

You live in your second house for another ten years and then decide to get a bigger house with a better view in a quiet neighborhood. Bigger and better and quiet cost you $125,000 in 1970. You promptly sell your second house for $90,000. Since you have reinvested all the proceeds from House #2 in House #3, you can defer any realized gain on the sale of House #2. What is the realized gain on House #2? It is $50,000 ($90,000 minus its basis of $40,000).

So the basis of House #3 is $75,000 ($125,000 minus your deferred gain of $50,000).

Finally, as you blow out the candles on your 58th birthday, you realize that bigger and better and quiet has served its purpose, but from now on you want to live in a condominium and leave the maintenance to someone else. After a few weeks of hunting, you find one for $150,000 that is to your and your spouse's liking. The price you can get for House #3 is $300,000. You remember deferral and the tax reprieves that you got when the gain from selling one home was used for the purchase of your next home. This time, however, you are not trading up but trading down, so you will not be reinvesting your gain in your next home. Does that mean that the whole tax-deferral scheme will come to an end and you will be taxed on the whole gain? Not in your case. Being 55 years or older, you can now avail yourself of the once-in-a-lifetime tax-free gain of up to $125,000 on the sale of your residence.

The realized gain on the sale of House #3 would be $225,000 ($300,000 minus its basis of $75,000, assuming you made no capital improvements).

How much of the gain do you have to recognize? Well, you could elect to take $125,000 of the gain tax-free. Then the maximum recognized gain would be $100,000 ($225,000 of realized gain on the sale of House #3 minus the tax-free $125,000). However, you could even defer some of the $100,000 realized gain. For purposes of determining how much you have to reinvest in the condominium to get additional deferral, the amount of the proceeds from House #3 is reduced by the tax-free amount ($300,000, the sale price of House #3, minus $125,000, the tax-free gain, which amounts to $175,000). You reinvested only $150,000 in the condo, so the amount of the recognized gain is only $25,000; $75,000 is deferred, and so the basis of the condo is $75,000. To recap the sale of House #3 and the purchase of the condo:

Realized Gain

Sale of House #3		$300,000
Basis: Cost	$125,000	
Deferred gain	(50,000)	(75,000)
Gain		225,000
Less: Tax-free amount of gain up to $125,000		(125,000)
Realized gain		$100,000

Recognized Gain

Sales proceeds of House #3	$300,000
Less: Tax-free gain	(125,000)
Amount needed to be reinvested to defer all of realized gain	175,000
Amount reinvested in condo	(150,000)
Amount of recognized gain	$ 25,000

Deferred Gain

Realized gain	$100,000
Recognized gain	(25,000)
Deferred gain	$ 75,000

Basis of Condo

Purchase price	$150,000
Deferred gain	(75,000)
Basis	$ 75,000

INSTALLMENT SALES

An installment sale, primarily used in the sale of real estate, presents another way of deferring taxes on capital asset transactions. By this method, the proceeds of the sale will automatically be reported in installments unless the buyer pays the total purchase price at closing or the seller elects not to report on this installment basis. The installment method allows the seller to defer recognition of the gain until payments are received from the purchaser.

In some cases, a sale in installments can result in an actual tax reduction. Take a person with a recognized gain of $40,000 from real estate sold in 1983, and assume that this person is in a top tax bracket of 50 percent in 1983, but only 42 percent in 1984. If the full proceeds of the sale were received in 1983, the tax on them would be $20,000. If only 20 percent were received in 1983 and 80 percent in 1984, the tax payable would be $4,000 in 1983 (50 percent of $8,000) and $13,440 in 1984 (42 percent of $32,000), producing a tax total of $17,440 instead of $20,000 and a tax saving of $2,560.

LIKE-KIND EXCHANGES Other, less frequently used tax-deferral methods include like-kind exchanges and involuntary conversions. In a like-kind exchange, property held for productive use in trade or business, or investment property other than stocks and bonds, is exchanged for property of the same kind. Such an exchange will not be taxable, and any recognition of gain on it will be deferred until the exchanged property is sold.

INVOLUNTARY CONVERSIONS An involuntary conversion results from the loss or destruction of property through theft, casualty, or condemnation. Any gain realized on an involuntary conversion can, at the taxpayer's election, be deferred, provided the owner reinvests the proceeds in similar property within a prescribed period.

SHIFTING INCOME TO SOMEONE IN A LOWER TAX BRACKET

The basis of several tax-planning techniques is the fact that the tax bracket of children or parents to whom you provide funds may be lower than your own tax bracket. Therefore, any given source of income will yield them more spendable after-tax dollars than it would yield to you.

There are three primary techniques for shifting income to family members in a lower tax bracket: gifts, short-term trusts, and interest-free loans. Each of these techniques is explained below. The examples will use income transfers from parents to children, but the same methods will work for shifting income to elderly parents.

GIFTS An individual taxpayer can make any number of gifts to any number of people, but when the gift to any one particular recipient exceeds $10,000 in one calendar year, the donor may have to pay gift tax on the excess. A husband and wife are liable for gift tax only when their joint gift to one recipient exceeds $20,000 in one calendar year. The taxable portion of a $100,000 gift made by a husband and wife to one child would be $80,000—$40,000 for each spouse—and the gift tax would be $8,200 each. This gift tax may not have to be rendered, though. Each taxpayer is entitled to a combined gift and estate tax credit. Up to a limited total, the federal gift taxes you incur and/or the federal estate tax on the estate you leave can be set off against this credit. Due to congressional action, the maximum in gift and/or estate taxes to be set off against the so-called unified credit will increase each year, as follows:

Year	Unified Credit
1983	$ 79,300
1984	96,300
1985	121,800
1986	155,000
1987 and thereafter	192,800

Unless the parents in our example above who gave their child $100,000 in one year had less than $8,200 left of their unified credit, they would pay no gift tax; but the child would have unconditional use of the $100,000 without being liable for any gift or income tax on it. Any income that results from investing the $100,000 is taxed at the child's lower tax rate. This transfer will also have an estate tax advantage, in that any future appreciation in the asset has already been transferred to the child.

Any assets of value can be used to make such gifts—cash, securities, income-producing real estate, rare books, even a high-demand, short-supply bubblegum card collection.

The disadvantage to the donor is that the transferred asset is gone forever, unconditionally, and if the amount is large enough, there is also the gift tax to consider.

SHORT-TERM TRUSTS

Another technique used to shift income is for parents to transfer capital to a short-term trust (at least ten years and one day) for the benefit of a child. The income from the trust must be distributed to the child each year during the life of the trust.

Using our previous example of $100,000, and assuming the trustee can invest the capital to yield 12 percent each year, the child would receive $12,000 per year before taxes or $120,000 in ten years, thus reducing the family's overall tax burden by $36,000. See the illustration in Table 6-2.

The child, however, is not allowed to use income from the trust to satisfy the parents' support obligations for the child's housing, food, clothing, and medical care; but the child's tuition can be paid for by income from the trust.

As an income-shifting technique, the short-term trust has the following advantages over outright gifts:

- You have more control over the use of the assets, since the assets would be controlled by a trustee who might be a trusted friend, or by a corporate trustee such as a bank.
- Your assets are not given away forever, but only for the term of the trust. You get your assets back when the trust expires.

TABLE 6-2
SHIFTING INCOME TO SOMEONE IN A LOWER TAX BRACKET

Assumptions

Your tax bracket—50 percent
Child's (or elderly parent's) tax bracket—20 percent
Capital shifted—$100,000
Yield on capital invested—$12,000

	You in 50% Tax Bracket Invest	Family Member in 20% Tax Bracket Invests
Amount invested	$100,000	$100,000
Yield at 12 percent	12,000	12,000
Taxes	(6,000)	(2,400)
After-tax income	$ 6,000	$ 9,600
Annual tax savings to family unit		$ 3,600

Note: If the lower-tax-bracket family member is in a tax bracket lower than 20 percent, the tax savings are even greater.

- The trustee can change the nature of the assets during the life of the trust—for instance, sell stocks you initially put into the trust and buy bonds.

As with most things, there are some disadvantages as well. There is a fee to the attorney who sets up the trust. There are annual trustee fees. Furthermore, if the trustee sells any assets and a capital gain is realized, it passes directly to the grantor of the trust—the parents, in our example—and is includable in the grantor's tax return for the year in which it is realized.

If the grantor dies before the property reverts to the grantor, the trust's remaining value at the time of death will be includable in the grantor's estate.

Depending on the present value of the interest that the child (or other beneficiary) has in the trust, the transfer of property to a short-term trust may result in gift taxes for the grantor. If the trust income is to be distributed to the beneficiary every year, rather than accumulated and distributed later on, the annual $10,000 gift-tax exclusion ($20,000 if both spouses are grantors) will be available in computing any taxable gift. Also, of course, there is the unified gift and estate tax credit ($96,300 in 1984) to offset each grantor's gift tax.

Before you decide on a short-term trust, get some professional counsel as to how it should be used and set up by someone in your situation. A short-term trust requires someone to keep the appropriate records, to account for assets and distributions to beneficiaries, and to prepare the trust's tax returns.

INTEREST-FREE LOANS

An interest-free loan has two distinct advantages over a gift or short-term trust. The first is that there may be no gift tax on it, since in most situations it is not a gift. Its second advantage is that you can relate the length of the loan period to the length of time that your offspring will need the income produced by the loaned amount. Assume you have a college sophomore, for example, and you want to create more after-tax dollars to pay your offspring's educational costs in the next three years. You make an interest-free cash loan to your sophomore. The sophomore invests this cash in liquid assets, such as a money market fund, and uses the income from the fund for college expenses. The result in dollars available for college costs is now much greater, because the investment income is taxable to your sophomore, and your sophomore's tax bracket is much lower than your own.

Income shifting by means of an interest-free loan must be carefully structured if the results are to withstand the scrutiny of the Internal Revenue Service. Care must also be taken to avoid imposition of gift tax. To ensure the desired tax savings, the following requirements must be met:

- The parents must retain neither explicit nor implicit control over the funds loaned to their children or over the investments the children make with these funds. If the Internal Revenue Service finds evidence of control, it will argue that the transaction was an "assignment of income," and if that argument is upheld, the income earned by investing the loan will be taxed to the parents, not to the children. In such a case, all tax advantages from the transaction would be lost.
- The transaction must constitute a true loan that creates a genuine indebtedness. To establish a true loan, the following three conditions must be fulfilled:

  1. There must be a written loan agreement signed by both parties.

2. The agreement must contain adequate provisions for repayment.
3. Repayment should be strictly enforced.

If these safeguards are not observed, the Internal Revenue Service can argue that the transaction constitutes a gift, not a loan. If that argument proves successful, the desired shifting of income does not occur, and the transaction will be subject to the gift tax provisions.

- The note evidencing the loan should state specifically that the lender has no intention of charging any interest and that the children have no obligation to pay any interest. If this interest-free aspect of the loan is not clearly documented, the Internal Revenue Service may attribute some of the interest income to the parents and treat it as a gift from the parents to the children.
- The loan must be a demand note—that is, it must be repaid when the party making the loan wants it repaid. There should be no indication of any maturity date on the note. We strongly recommend that you demand the repayment of the loan at least once a year. In the case of the college sophomore, you would issue a demand note at the end of the sophomore year, reissue a note for the junior year and demand payment at the end of the junior year, and reissue another for the senior year. If the loan needs to be extended, then you should issue a new demand note.

In 1973, the Internal Revenue Service ruled that an interest-free demand loan to a child constitutes a taxable gift by the parent-lender. Until recently, courts have rejected this ruling. Check with your tax advisor on the current status of interest-free loans and the best way to structure them.

DEDUCTIONS, EXEMPTIONS, CREDITS, AND PREPAYMENTS

So far, we have discussed how you can minimize your taxable income by making use of all available exclusions from income, by shifting income, and by making tax-favored and tax-deferred investments. These are the methods used to pare down the amount of income that must be classified as gross income in the first place. Another means by which you can reduce your taxable income is to incur expenditures that result in tax deductions. There are numerous opportunities for reducing taxable income, and thus reducing your taxes, if you know what types of deductions the Internal Revenue Service will accept and what you must do to obtain them. Such deductions fall into two categories: deductions from gross income and deductions from adjusted gross income.

DEDUCTIONS FROM GROSS INCOME These include trade or business deductions, expenses incurred as an employee, contributions to retirement plans, alimony, and job-related moving expenses.

TRADE OR BUSINESS DEDUCTIONS These are generally available to someone who is self-employed on either a full-time or a part-time basis. They are reported on Schedule C of the income tax return and include the following: advertising, depreciation, dues paid to professional societies or business associations, employee salaries and benefits, entertainment, insurance, interest on borrowings for business purposes, legal and professional services, rents and repairs paid for business property, taxes, travel and transportation costs, and utilities.

DEDUCTIBLE EXPENSES INCURRED AS AN EMPLOYEE

- All expenses for away-from-home travel that the taxpayer has incurred and paid while performing services as an employee, such as meals and lodging
- Transportation expenses, excepting those for commuting between home and work, incurred and paid while performing services as an employee
- Any other reimbursed expenses, but only to the extent of the reimbursement
- All expenses associated with activities conducted as an "outside salesperson"

DEDUCTIBLE CONTRIBUTIONS TO RETIREMENT PLANS

- Contributions by taxpayers to their own self-employment retirement plans
- Contributions by employees to their own individual retirement accounts

OTHER DEDUCTIBLE ITEMS

- Alimony
- Losses from sales or exchanges of property
- Moving expenses
- Penalties forfeited because of premature withdrawal of funds from time savings accounts

DEDUCTIONS FROM ADJUSTED GROSS INCOME

All deductions of this type fall into one of two categories. The first comprises the standard deduction (or zero-bracket amount) and any itemized deductions that exceed the zero amount. The second comprises the personal and dependent exemptions.

ZERO-BRACKET AMOUNTS AND ITEMIZED DEDUCTIONS

The tax law gives each individual taxpayer a standard deduction, which is called the zero-bracket amount. The actual amount is determined by the taxpayer's filing status. The amounts for 1983 and 1984 are shown below.

Married taxpayers filing joint return, or surviving spouse	$3,400
Married taxpayer filing separate return	1,700
Single taxpayer and head of household	2,300

These zero-bracket amounts are not computed by the taxpayer on his or her income tax return. They have already been incorporated into the tax rate schedules. Since each individual taxpayer receives the benefit of a zero-bracket amount in the rate schedules or tax tables, taxpayers who itemize deductions must subtract the applicable zero-bracket amount from the total itemized deductions on their tax returns. In other words, taxpayers who itemize are entitled to deduct only the amount by which their itemized deductions exceed the relevant zero-bracket amount.

Following are the major types of itemized deductions.

MEDICAL COSTS

You can deduct all medical costs, including medical insurance premiums and prescription drugs, in excess of 5 percent of adjusted gross income.

STATE AND LOCAL TAXES

Taxes on income, real estate, personal property, stock transfers, and sales are deductible. In general, almost any state or local tax that is imposed on the individual can be deducted.

INTEREST PAID Interest on debts incurred for personal purposes, such as home mortgages, credit cards, and small loans, is fully deductible. Interest paid to purchase or carry tax-exempt bonds is not deductible. Also, there is a limit on the deductibility of interest paid for the purchase or carrying of other investment property when the interest, after subtracting investment income, exceeds $10,000.

CHARITABLE CONTRIBUTIONS Cash contributions to qualified charitable organizations can be deducted up to a maximum of 50 percent of adjusted gross income. For the typical non-cash contributions to charities of books, clothing, and "rummage," the amount deductible is the amount that would have to be paid to replace the goods in their used condition.

CASUALTY AND THEFT LOSSES OF NONBUSINESS PROPERTY To calculate the deduction for such losses, begin by computing the following two amounts:

- The decline in the value of the property—the difference between the value of the property before and after the casualty
- The cost of the property lost

Now take the lower of the two amounts you have just computed. Reduce it by any insurance recovery, and then reduce it further by $100 to get a "total casualty loss" for each occurrence. Next, add up all the total casualty losses during the year to get a "grand total casualty loss" for the year. If the grand total casualty loss exceeds 10 percent of your adjusted gross income (AGI), you can deduct the excess.

To illustrate, let's say you have two casualty losses during the year: the theft of a stereo and damage to the top of your ski boat when a tree branch fell on it in a windstorm. The unreimbursed stereo loss is $600, and the unreimbursed loss for the hole in the boat is $800. Each loss is first reduced by $100, making the total casualty loss $500 for the stereo and $700 for the boat. Your grand total casualty loss will thus be $1200. For any of the $1200 to be tax deductible, your AGI would have to be $12,000 or less. If your adjusted gross income was $13,000, you could not deduct any of the casualty loss of $1200.

EDUCATION EXPENSES Any unreimbursed educational expenses incurred to maintain or improve the skills necessary for your present job are deductible.

MISCELLANEOUS EXPENSES The most common items of this kind relate to employment or to costs associated with holding investment assets. The following are typical examples:

- Union dues
- Membership dues of trade and professional organizations
- Rental of a safe deposit box for securities
- Subscriptions to investment advisory services
- Professional tax advice
- Professional preparation of tax returns

Table 6-3 shows the average itemized deductions claimed in 1981 (the latest year for which data is available) for various levels of taxable income.

TABLE 6-3
AVERAGE ITEMIZED DEDUCTIONS CLAIMED

The figures in this table are based on Internal Revenue Service statistics and indicate the average amounts deducted on 1981 returns. The figures are for reference purposes only and should not be relied upon in claiming your own deductions.

Adjusted Gross Income (thousands)	Deductions			
	Interest	Medical	Taxes	Donations
$ 16-18	$ 2,720	$ 995	$ 1,329	$ 667
18-20	2,654	887	1,488	651
20-25	2,887	756	1,718	670
25-30	3,122	672	1,983	697
30-40	3,483	605	2,496	834
40-50	4,282	553	3,211	1,079
50-75	5,586	676	4,400	1,567
75-100	8,312	859	6,637	2,512
100 or more	16,414	1,387	14,166	9,522

EXEMPTIONS Every exemption enables the taxpayer to take a deduction from adjusted gross income. For 1983 and 1984, the amount allowed for each exemption is $1,000. There are two types of exemptions: personal exemptions and exemptions for dependents.

Personal exemptions fit into four categories:

- Exemption for the taxpayer
- Exemption for the taxpayer's spouse on a joint return
- Extra exemption for self or spouse aged 65 or more
- Extra exemption for self or spouse who is blind

The rules governing exemptions for dependents are a little more complicated. Basically, there are five tests to be met before a dependent exemption is allowed.

1. The claimed dependent must have less than $1,000 of gross income for the calendar year in which the taxable year of the taxpayer begins, unless the dependent is a child of the taxpayer and is either under 19 at the close of such calendar year or else a full-time student at least five months of the year.
2. More than one-half of the dependent's support for the calendar year must have been furnished by the taxpayer. Support includes all expenditures for food, clothing, shelter, medical care, and education.
3. The dependent must have one of the following relationships to the taxpayer or the taxpayer's spouse:
   - Son or daughter, or descendent of either, or stepchild
   - Brother or sister
   - Brother or sister by the half blood
   - Stepbrother or stepsister
   - Parent, or ancestor of such parent
   - Stepfather or stepmother

- Son or daughter of taxpayer's brother or sister
- Son-in-law, or daughter-in-law, or father-in-law, or mother-in-law, or brother-in-law, or sister-in-law
- A person (other than the taxpayer's spouse) who lived in the taxpayer's home and was a member of the taxpayer's household throughout the taxpayer's taxable year (unless that person's relationship to the taxpayer was in violation of local law)

4. The dependent must not have filed a joint return with his or her spouse.
5. The dependent must be: a citizen or resident of the United States; or a resident of Canada or Mexico at some time during the calendar year in which the taxpayer's taxable year begins; or an alien child adopted by and living with a U.S. citizen in a foreign country as a member of this citizen's household for the entire taxable year.

Because the conditions of dependent exemptions are subject to many exceptions and special interpretations, it may be worth your while to seek professional advice when dealing with some of the more complex tests.

TAX CREDITS

By subtracting personal exemptions, dependent exemptions, and itemized deductions exceeding the zero-bracket amount from adjusted gross income, you establish the amount of your taxable income. Then you use the appropriate tax schedule to establish the gross tax payable on your taxable income. Once the gross tax payable has been computed, tax credits and tax prepayments are subtracted from the gross tax payable before you arrive at the net tax payable.

Through the economic incentive that tax credits offer the individual, Congress encourages various social and economic developments that it regards as desirable. Thus, while deductions merely reduce the income on which you pay taxes, credits are deductible from the taxes themselves. However, only a percentage of the qualifying expenditures are deductible from your gross tax. Tax credits are available for the following expenditures:

POLITICAL CONTRIBUTIONS

You can take credit for one-half of your contributions to candidates, candidates' committees, or the committees of national political parties, up to a maximum credit of $50. The $50 maximum applies to each taxpayer; so on a joint return, the maximum credit is $100.

CHILD OR DEPENDENT CARE

Credit can be taken for a percentage of the expenses paid for the care of a qualifying child or dependent when such care allows the taxpayer to be gainfully employed. The maximum credit for one qualifying child or dependent is $720; for two or more, the maximum is $1,440.

The highest percentage that can be claimed as credit for such expenditures is 30 percent, and this rate applies to people with an adjusted gross income (AGI) of up to $10,000. Above that, the rate decreases by 1 percent for every additional $2,000 of AGI or fraction thereof until it decreases to 20% for taxpayers with AGI over $28,000.

INVESTMENT CREDIT

For investment in depreciable personal property, credit can be taken for up to 10 percent of the investment. If you spent $5,000 on a personal computer to be used for business purposes, you could take an investment credit of $500. However, you could not depreciate the full cost of the $5,000 over five years if you claim the investment credit. To claim the credit, you would have to either

- reduce the basis ($5,000 in our example) by 50 percent of the credit ($250 in our example), or
- reduce the investment credit by 2 percent (down to 8 percent in our example, so that the credit would be $400 instead of $500).

RESIDENTIAL ENERGY CREDIT

A 15 percent credit is allowed on the first $2,000 of expenditures for energy conservation measures such as insulation, storm windows, caulking and weatherstripping, and replacement burners. The credit is based on cumulative expenditures and has a maximum of $300. If you spent $1,000 on energy conservation measures in 1982, you could take a credit of $150. If you then spent another $2,000 in 1983, you would exceed the cumulative total of $2,000, and would be limited to a credit of $150 in 1983.

Separate credit is allowed for the cost of purchasing and installing a renewable energy source—solar, wind, and geothermal energy devices—in your principal U.S. residence. This equipment must be new when installed and must be expected to remain in operation for five years. The credit is 40 percent for cumulative expenditures up to $10,000, so the maximum credit is $4,000. Any unused energy credit may be carried over, but cannot be used after 1987.

FOREIGN TAX CREDIT

You can claim a credit for income taxes paid to foreign countries. The credit is limited to U.S. taxes due on income from foreign sources and does not apply to income from sources within the U.S.

CREDIT FOR THE ELDERLY

A person aged 65 or older who has a low income and does not receive substantial tax-free Social Security benefits may receive a tax credit, not to exceed his or her tax liability. The maximum credit is $375 for a single individual and $562.50 for a married couple, both over 65.

EARNED INCOME CREDIT

Low-income workers who maintain a household with dependent children can claim credit equal to 10 percent of their earned income up to $5,000.

PREPAYMENT OF TAXES

Prepayment is the method by which an individual's income taxes are paid in advance of the filing date, which is April 15 for most people. The most common type of prepayment is the obligatory withholding of income tax from the salary of an employee. This withholding, based on the employee's marital status, exemptions claimed, and earnings, is designed to put the employee on a pay-as-you-earn basis as far as income tax is concerned.

This does not mean that everyone who is self-employed escapes prepayment. The Internal Revenue Service, ever eager to receive our taxes as soon as possible, if not sooner, demands estimated tax returns and periodic payments of the "estimated tax" from those whose income tax is not withheld.

The amount of the quarterly payment must be for at least 80 percent of the gross tax liability for the quarter. If the payment is not made or if the

TABLE 6-4
INCOME AVERAGING

Taxable income for current year	$70,000*
Less: 120 percent of the average taxable income of the previous four years (called "average base period income") $45,000 × 120 percent	(54,000)
Averageable income	$16,000
Tax, determined in the regular way, on a taxable income equal to (1) 120 percent of the taxpayer's average base period income plus (2) 20 percent of the averageable income	$14,894
Less: tax, determined in the regular way, on a taxable income equal to 120 percent of average base period income	(13,614)
	$ 1,280
Multiply the difference by 5	5
Tax on averageable income	$ 6,400
Add the tax, determined in the regular way, on a taxable income equal to 120 percent of the averageable base period income	13,614
Tax using income averaging	$20,014
Tax on taxable income using regular method	$20,414
Tax savings	$ 400

* This example assumes a married taxpayer using 1983 rates.

payment is less than 80 percent of the quarterly gross tax liability, a penalty will be charged.

There is no penalty, however, if any one of several conditions is met. The simplest one to comply with is that of making quarterly payments—April 15, June 15, September 15, and January 15—each in an amount equal to one-fourth of the tax shown on last year's tax return.

The nondeductible penalty is charged on any underpayment of tax from the original due date of the payment to the date on which payment is received. The penalty rate is determined semiannually and is based on the average prime interest rate for a previous period.

TAX CALCULATION

To save taxes, the management of taxable income is the most important task. However, most people are interested in knowing the federal income tax that will be paid on a taxable income amount. This section of the chapter briefly discusses methods of tax calculation.

REGULAR CALCULATION AND USE OF RATE SCHEDULES

Most readers of this book will compute their taxes using tax rate schedules such as those set forth in Appendix II. These rate schedules must be used if taxable income is $50,000 or more (tax tables may be used by people with taxable income of less than $50,000) and if income averaging is used.

INCOME AVERAGING

If your income fluctuates widely from year to year, you will pay a larger amount than other taxpayers earning the same total taxable income in somewhat equal amounts over several years. This is due to the progressive rate schedules used by individual taxpayers. To minimize the extra tax incurred due to an unusually large income in any single year, income averaging has been provided by the Internal Revenue Code. With income averaging, a percentage of your income, called "averageable income," is taxed as though you had received it in equal slices over a five-year period instead of in one year. When thus spread over five years, some of your income may be taxed at a lower rate. The general formula for income averaging is shown in the example in Table 6-4.

7

WHERE AND HOW TAXES ARE SAVED: TAX-SHELTERED INVESTMENTS

Another very important tax-saving technique involves investing in tax-sheltered investments. Simply put, a good tax shelter enables you to use dollars that you would otherwise pay in taxes (along with some of your own investment dollars) to acquire investments that will increase your net worth.

Most tax shelters are a means of deferring taxes and not of eliminating taxes. Most, if not all, tax shelters are characterized by leverage and the availability of deductions that require no investor cash to obtain.

LEVERAGE

Leverage is a term used to describe a situation in which you control a large investment with a relatively small amount of your own money. The rest is financed with somebody else's money, and this will give you interest deductions. But leverage increases risk.

To illustrate, assume you invest in a $100,000 two-bedroom condominium for rental purposes. You make a $20,000 down payment and get a five-year contract from the seller at 13.5 percent a year for the remaining $80,000. The seller allows you to make payments on the loan using an amortization schedule of 30 years, but expects you to pay off the remaining balance on the loan at the end of five years. After three years, you resell this condo for $133,000 (net of selling expenses). Your annual payments on the $80,000 loan are about $11,000. After three years, you've paid off about $700 on the loan. Assuming that the after-tax rental income you received on the condo has covered your interest payments on the loan, then your total outlay has been $20,700 (the down payment plus the principal payments), but your long-term gain before taxes would be about $33,000. That's a profit of almost 160 percent in only three years. If you had paid $100,000 cash down, your gain would still have been $33,000, or 33 percent. Note, however, that instead of using your rental income for interest payments, you would have received significant cash amounts each year, and these would increase your rate of return.

However, leverage also increases risk, as some real estate speculators found out when real estate prices softened in recent years. Using the same condo example, let's assume that you can't sell your condo after three years for as much as you paid for it, so to pay off the loan balance of $79,150, you have to sell it for $90,000. Now you have lost $10,000. Since you invested $20,850, that is a loss of about 50 percent. If you had paid the $100,000 in cash, your loss would have been a mere 10 percent.

DEDUCTIONS

One attractive feature of tax shelters is that they provide you with deductions without requiring any cash contributions on your part. Tax shelters normally provide one of the following deductions:

DEPRECIATION This is the recovery of the capital cost of equipment or a building over a period shorter than its estimated useful life. In the case of equipment, the recovery period is three or five years; for real property, the recovery period is fifteen years in most cases.

DEPLETION This is similar to depreciation but applies to recovering the cost of such assets as oil, gas, coal, and other minerals extracted from the ground.

INTANGIBLE DRILLING AND DEVELOPMENT COSTS In oil and gas exploration programs, deductions are available for labor, fuel, hauling, supplies, and other items that have no salvage value but are necessary for drilling wells and preparing wells for production. Such deductions may range from 50 to 90 percent of the investment in the first year, with smaller deductions in subsequent years.

INVESTMENT TAX CREDIT

This is a dollar-for-dollar reduction of taxes due. The investment tax credit can amount to as much as 10 percent of the cost of equipment or other tangible personal property used to produce income. Tax credits are more valuable than tax deductions. A deductible dollar reduces your taxable income by one dollar. A dollar of tax credit reduces your taxes by one dollar. Say you have taxable income of $65,000 and are considering a tax-sheltered investment. You are considering one investment that provides current year deductions of $5,000 and another investment that provides current year deductions of $3,000 and tax credits of $2,000. Which investment is best from a tax standpoint in the current year? The analysis below will help answer the question.

	Investment #1	Investment #2
Taxable income before tax-sheltered investment	$65,000	$65,000
Deductions	(5,000)	(3,000)
Taxable income after investment	60,000	62,000
Tax on taxable income (using 1983 rates)	16,014	16,894
Credit against tax	—	(2,000)
Net Tax Due	$16,014	$14,894

DEFERRAL OF TAXES

Most tax shelters do not eliminate taxes; they simply defer them to a later period. The tax deferral created by claiming tax losses in earlier years and recognizing the income in later years may have varying results:

- It may be a simple deferral of tax that gives the investor the benefit of using the tax dollars for a period of years before repaying them without interest.
- The deductions may be taken when your tax rate is high (or low), and when the income is recognized your tax rate may be low (or high). Depending on your circumstances, this might be to your advantage or disadvantage. You should therefore know what your tax bracket is at the time you invest in a tax shelter and what it will be at the time you plan to dispose of the investment.
- In some limited instances, the losses claimed by the investor may later have to be included in income, but at the favorable long-term capital gain rates.

UNFAVORABLE TAX CONSEQUENCES

Tax-sheltered investments have "tax goodies." They also have some "tax gotchas." The "tax gotchas" include at-risk rules, investment interest limitations, tax-preference items, and alternative minimum tax. All these will be discussed in the following paragraphs.

THE AT-RISK RULES In a typical tax shelter, a substantial portion of the activity is financed with funds for which the borrower has no personal liability (nonrecourse indebtedness). Before the at-risk rules were introduced in 1976, investors were allowed deductions not only for their cash investment but also for their borrowed funds. Thus, they could greatly increase their benefits from deferral by getting deductions that substantially exceeded their equity investment. The basic concept of the at-risk rules is that losses should only be deductible to the extent of the taxpayer's own economic investment, since, with nonrecourse indebtedness, that is all the taxpayer could possibly lose. The original at-risk rules applied only to certain investment categories; as amended by the 1978 Revenue Act, they extend the deduction limitation to all investments other than real estate.

INVESTMENT INTEREST LIMITATION If you leverage your investment in tax shelters with borrowed funds, you get an interest deduction that reduces your taxable income. This deduction, however, is limited to $10,000 plus your income from the investments. Assume, for example, that you borrowed $100,000 at 15 percent to buy various investments. Further assume that after deducting expenses other than interest you have investment income of $4,000. If the annual interest on your borrowings amounts to $15,000, you would be able to deduct only $14,000 ($10,000 plus $4,000 of net investment income). The additional $1,000 of investment interest would not be deductible this year, but could be carried forward to a year when it could be deducted.

Investment interest does not include interest on your home mortgages and installment purchases. Be sure to check the type of interest in any tax-sheltered investments you make.

TAX PREFERENCES AND MINIMUM TAX

Tax preferences and minimum tax were enacted because Congress became concerned about research that showed that some taxpayers with large incomes were able to avoid paying part or all of their income tax. The avoidance was being accomplished legally through tax-sheltered investments that received preferential treatment for tax purposes—hence the term "tax preferences." Congress felt that this was unfair and that no one should be permitted to avoid his or her fair share of the tax burden.

Thus the minimum tax on items of tax preference came about. It has gone through several changes over the years. At present, the tax law includes a comprehensive minimum tax—called an "alternative minimum tax"—that increases the likelihood that a taxpayer with tax-sheltered investments will pay such tax. The alternative minimum tax is a flat rate of 20 percent on the amount by which "alternative minimum taxable income" exceeds $30,000 ($40,000 on a joint return, $20,000 for married couples filing separately and for trusts and estates). If the tax is greater than the regular tax for the year, the greater amount is the tax liability for the year, reduced only by a limited foreign tax credit.

"I think I understand the why of the alternative minimum tax and the 20 percent flat rate, but how do I calculate alternative minimum taxable income?" Basically, the calculation begins with adjusted gross income (AGI), to which are added any tax-preference items minus specified deductions. Some tax preferences include accelerated depreciation on real and leased personal property and intangible drilling costs and the 60 percent exclusion on long-term capital gains. Be aware of an alternative minimum tax problem when you are involved in tax-sheltered investments such as real estate, equipment leasing, and oil and gas, and where you have significant capital gains. Obtain tax advice on these potential tax-preference items and how they may affect your tax situation. For example, at Touche Ross we provide our clients with analyses showing the impact the alternative minimum tax might have on tax-sheltered investments.

ECONOMIC SUBSTANCE

An investor needs to analyze any prospective tax shelter from an economic viewpoint. The potential profit should be commensurate with the risk involved. If an investment fails economically, you are probably going to lose money in real dollars, and consequently it does not make much sense to go into it only for tax reasons.

Unfortunately, many individuals are lured into "investments' by tax shelter promoters who promise large tax savings. Upon objective analysis, many shelters with promises of large tax savings turn out to have very little economic potential and a very aggressive interpretation of tax laws. The promised deductions are often challenged and disallowed by the Internal Revenue Service, or the tax shelter itself may be deemed to be a fraud, which will cause you more problems. Take care, therefore, to evaluate the economic substance of any tax shelter. Get a prospectus, read it, have your questions and concerns answered to your satisfaction. Check on the reliability, reputation, and track record of the promoter, and apply the following tests, adapted from an article in *Medical Economics*.*

---

*"Tax Shelters—Seven Tests Any Deal Should Pass."*Medical Economics*, March 31, 1980.

1. Why is the tax shelter promoter contacting you? Is it based on a long-standing business relationship, or is it an unknown phone-call promotion from an out-of-state orange-growing project? Perhaps the promoter has run out of close contacts who trust his projects.
2. What's the track record of the tax shelter manager? Has he or she compiled a successful track record in substantially similar projects? Tax shelters have some common characteristics, but they are worlds apart in most business aspects. A specialist in cable TV may know very little about oil-drilling ventures.
3. Can you read the prospectus without raising your eyebrows? See what the general partner in the deal is taking out. How much of your money will actually go to the proposed project rather than into the promoter's pocket through commissions and management and acquisition fees? If much less than eighty-five cents of every investment dollar is going to the project, be skeptical. The more money the promoters skim off the top in fees, commissions, and promotion costs, the smaller the part of your investment that will actually be working for you.
4. Is there a clear profit motive in the deal? The IRS policy toward tax shelters can be summed up in two words: economic reality. This means that a shelter should be structured as Congress intended—to encourage investment in a risky but potentially profitable business venture. If a venture has little chance of making a profit, the IRS is likely to say that the true purpose is only to avoid taxes.
5. What do tax advisors think? After you have done the initial research on a tax-sheltered investment possibility, get backup advice from a lawyer or tax expert whose advice you trust—and one whose specialty is the field you're interested in. Get advice on the economic substance of the investment and the credibility of the tax benefits. This advice may cost you several hundred tax-deductible dollars in fees paid to the expert, but may save you a bundle later on.
6. Is there a better way? After you have checked out the risks and rewards, and if the tax shelter still looks like a good bet, ask yourself whether there isn't some other way to shave your tax bill just as much without the risk of a tax shelter—with an IRA, with a tax-free municipal bond, or by making a voluntary contribution to your employee retirement plan.

TYPES OF TAX SHELTERS

As you study the tax shelters described below, keep in mind that each type of investment has its own range of economic risk. The following comments relate solely to the tax issues and do not deal with investment potential or provide a risk analysis.

REAL ESTATE The at-risk rules, which limit loss deductions for other leverage investments to the amount an investor has at risk, do not apply to real estate investments. Interest, property taxes, and other expenses are currently deductible for tax purposes. The appreciation in the property is not taxed until you dispose of the property, and when the property is traded for other similar property the gain can be deferred.

DEPRECIATION

Depreciation can be taken on real estate investments based on a 15-year life, using either a straight-line method or an accelerated method. With straight-line depreciation you deduct the same amount of depreciation in each year of the asset's cost-recovery period. With accelerated depreciation, you deduct a greater proportion of the depreciation in the early years of the asset's cost-recovery period and thereby recover costs faster than under the straight-line method.

Let's say you buy a residential building (other than low-income housing) for $900,000, excluding the cost of the land, at the beginning of a taxable year. Using straight-line depreciation, you would deduct $60,000 a year for 15 years. Using accelerated depreciation—175% declining balance method—you would deduct $108,000 of depreciation the first year, $90,000 the second year, $81,000 the third year, $72,000 the fourth year, and $63,000 the fifth year. You would thus recover $414,000 by the end of the fifth year, compared to $300,000 by straight-line depreciation. From now on, however, you will be deducting less than the annual straight-line $60,000 if you have chosen accelerated depreciation. From the sixth through the ninth year you would deduct $54,000, and from the tenth through the fifteenth year you would deduct $45,000.

By either method you would, of course, have deducted the full $900,000 if you held the asset for the full 15 years. You may have made up your mind by this time that it is smarter to use accelerated depreciation because you get faster deductions, could reinvest the tax savings of the earlier years, and would therefore be better off than by using straight-line depreciation. Good economic thinking, but the tax laws get back at users of accelerated depreciation in two ways.

TAXATION OF ACCELERATED DEPRECIATION

One of the tax consequences of accelerated depreciation is that the amount by which it exceeds the straight-line depreciation for the year becomes an item of tax preference. This may sound advantageous, but in reality a tax preference is an item that can make you liable for the alternative minimum tax, if that would extract more tax from you than your regular income tax.

The other unwelcome surprise you could have with accelerated depreciation may arrive after you sell your residential building. Whatever profit you make on this sale would normally be treated as a capital gain, taxed at a maximum rate of 20 percent. Now, since you used accelerated depreciation, some of this gain may have to be treated as ordinary income and taxed accordingly. The amount that would be taxable as ordinary income is the amount by which your accelerated depreciation since 1975 exceeded the comparable straight-line depreciation over the same period.

Returning to our previous example, if you had used accelerated depreciation and sold this residential property after owning it for three years, then $99,000 (the excess of accelerated depreciation over the straight-line amount) of your profit could be taxable as ordinary income, for which the top rate is 50 percent. By the same token, though, if the sale of this property were to result in a loss, the loss ranks as ordinary in nature and can be offset against ordinary income.

With nonresidential property purchased after 1980, the tax treatment when you use accelerated depreciation is different. All depreciation, to the extent of the gain on the sale of the property, is deemed to be ordinary income.

REAL ESTATE FOR RENTAL TO FAMILY MEMBERS

Recent tax law changes have made it possible to take all deductions related to homes you own and rent to other family members at a fair market rental.

If you are interested in real estate investments and your parents or your children need a principal place to live, consider purchasing a single family house or a condominium for their use. Rent it to them at a monthly rent you would normally charge a third party and then deduct all the expenses of the residence, including depreciation.

OIL AND GAS There are advantages as well as disadvantages to tax-sheltered investments in oil and gas. The principal ones are listed here below.

Advantages

- You can deduct the intangible costs of well drilling and development on a current basis.
- You can claim the statutory depletion allowance (about 15 percent) when income is received, so that only 85 percent of this income is taxed.
- You can deduct business expenses, interest, and depreciation and have investment tax credits.

Disadvantages

- It creates a tax-preference item to the extent that the current deduction for intangible drilling costs exceeds the net income from the property plus the amortization of such costs (if they were originally capitalized).
- Another tax preference is created if you deduct statutory (percentage) depletion against future oil and gas revenues.
- Any gain on the ultimate sale or other disposition of the property will be part capital gain and part ordinary income.

LEASING THE INVESTOR'S PERSONAL PROPERTY This shelter takes advantage of accelerated depreciation coupled with investment tax credits, but the following caveats should be observed.

- The excess of accelerated depreciation over straight-line depreciation is a tax-preference item.
- To qualify for an investment tax credit, the lease must be an *operating lease*. With an operating lease, the lessee acquires the use of the asset for less than half of the useful life of the asset, and the rental payments must not by themselves be sufficient to let the owner recover the full cost of the asset. Also, the owner must retain the financial responsibility for the asset's maintenance, insurance, and taxes.
- Unless such rules are met, the lease will be deemed a net lease, and would then not qualify for investment tax credits.
- Near the end of the lease, the early deductions obtained through accelerated depreciation will reverse and create large amounts of ordinary income. Generally, this type of investment does not provide a capital gain.

AGRICULTURE Agricultural investments can offer a substantial tax shelter through rapid depreciation, investment tax credits, and the use of the cash basis of accounting, although the latter is becoming more restricted every year. Investments in farming, fruit or nut trees, and wine grapes are among the many possible types of agricultural investments. Then there is also the expectation that agricultural land will ultimately turn into more valuable property through urbanization, and this has increased investor interest in agricultural land.

FORM 12—YOUR TAX-SAVING IDEAS

Now that you know how taxes can be saved and you have a targeted taxable income on Form 11, which you completed before, fill in Form 12. Then take *action*. You may want to discuss your tax-saving ideas with a tax advisor before you take action. You will probably make best use of your advisor's time by first doing your homework on Forms 11 and 12. Figure 7-1 shows you a sample of a filled-in form related to the sample shown in Form 11 in Chapter 5.

- Many tax-saving ideas, once implemented, have a multi-year impact. For example, when you purchase real estate for rental purposes, depreciation and interest deductions are predictable for many years according to a depreciation schedule and a loan repayment schedule.
- You may need significant resources to implement some tax-saving ideas. For example, to purchase rental real estate you may need a substantial down payment. Other tax-saving ideas may require the sale of existing investment assets or borrowing against these assets.
- Prepayment of planned multi-year tax-deductible expenditures such as large charitable contributions is a very good idea when your top tax rate will decrease over the next few years.
- The earlier you implement your tax-saving ideas, the better. The later it is in the year, the harder it is to reduce your taxable income without making riskier investments.

FIGURE 7-1

File under TAX PLANNING Date: April 28

FORM 12 TAX-SAVING IDEAS

TAX-SAVING IDEA

Tax-Free Income: Shift $40,000 of investments into tax-free securities

Tax-Favored Income: Purchase utility stocks with stock dividends using $20,000 of existing assets

Tax-Deferred Income: Continue maximum contribution to I.R.A.

Tax-Sheltered Income: Buy real estate for rental to family members

Shifting Income to Dependents: Interest-free loan to children in college

Tax-Deductible Expenditures: Pay all three years of capital drive pledge in current year

Action	Action Date	Funds Needed	Reduction of Taxable Income
Tax-Free Income	6/30	None-use existing assets	$1,000
Tax-Favored Income	6/30	None-use existing assets	$ 500
Tax-Deferred Income	12/31	$4,000	Already in my plan
Tax-Sheltered Investments	5/31	$20,000 (down payment)	$ 9,000

FIGURE 7-1, cont'd.

Shift Income to Dependents	6/30	\$60,000 (hopefully borrow these funds)	\$4,500
Tax Deductible Expenditures	12/31	\$2,000 (\$1,000 already in current plan)	\$2,000
TOTALS			\$17,000

8

YEAR-END PLANNING

The last steps in the tax-planning process as the end of the year approaches are the computation of your current year's actual taxable income; the comparison of your actual taxable income with the targeted taxable income for the current year that you established some months ago; and the implementation of some year-end action steps to make sure you achieve your targeted taxable income.

Thus, year-end action is merely the last phase of a process that began with your formulation of your tax plan and the implementation of some tax-saving ideas some months or even years ago. Although these are the last steps in the process, they are very important, for after December 31 there is little you can do to save taxes. For those of you who have procrastinated, despite our discussions in Chapters 5, 6, and 7 about the importance of tax planning long before year-end, year-end is the only time you have to do any tax planning.

The best time to do year-end tax planning is the fall, no later than November. Fall is the proper time of year for finalizing your tax plan, for by then you have most of your financial data for the year, but there is still time to take action before the end of the financial year.

If you have capital gains or losses for the year, probably the best place to begin year-end planning is with Forms 13A and 13B. If you have no capital assets, skip Forms 13A and 13B, and begin your final tax-saving thrust by completing Form 14, *Your Year-End Tax Plan*.

FORMS 13A AND 13B—CAPITAL GAINS AND LOSSES

The Internal Revenue Service divides capital gains and losses into two categories: short-term and long-term. You derive a short-term gain or loss from the sale of a capital asset you have owned for one year or less. You derive a long-term gain or loss from selling a capital asset you have owned for at least one year and a day.

The rules regarding the tax treatment of capital gains and losses are easy to state:

- *Rule 1*. If you have a net short-term gain, the gain counts as part of your gross income and is taxed at the rates that apply to ordinary income.

- *Rule 2.* If you have a net long-term gain, you are entitled to a capital gain deduction equal to 60 percent of the net gain. The remaining 40 percent becomes part of your gross income.
- *Rule 3.* If you have a net short-term loss, it can be deducted from your gross income, but you cannot deduct more than $3,000 in any one year. What remains of the loss can be deducted in subsequent years.
- *Rule 4.* If you have a net long-term loss, you can partially deduct it from your gross income. For every $2 lost, you can deduct $1 from your gross income. You cannot deduct more than $3,000 of your net capital losses in any one year, but can deduct your remaining losses in subsequent years at the same two-to-one rate.

Based on these rules, you can see that, in terms of taxes, long-term gains are preferable to short-term gains, and that short-term losses are preferable to long-term losses. All this is fundamental and pretty easy to apply if you sell only one capital asset each year. But many people have more than one capital asset transaction each year, and the application of the rules is a bit more complicated.

To illustrate the process you go through when you have more than one capital asset transaction, let's assume you have the following capital gains and losses for the taxable year:

Long-term gains: $15,000

Long-term losses: $10,000

Short-term gains: $15,000

Short-term losses: $5,000

- The first step is to net your long-term gains and losses and net your short-term gains and losses. In our example, you would have a $5,000 net long-term gain and a $10,000 net short-term gain.
- The second step is to compute the net capital gain or loss. In our example, you would have a net overall capital gain of $15,000.
- The third step is to analyze the net capital gain or loss and apply one or more of the four fundamental tax rules outlined above.

In our example, $5,000 of the net gain is long-term, so we apply Rule 2 and take 60 percent or $3,000 as a capital gain deduction and include 40 percent or $2,000 as gross income. For the $10,000 of net short-term gain, we apply Rule 1 and include all $10,000 as gross income.

How about these additional examples?

- Assume you have a net long-term gain of $10,000 and a net short-term loss of $4,000. Your net capital gain is $6,000; it is all long-term, and you apply Rule 2.
- Assume you have a net long-term capital loss of $4,000 and a net short-term capital gain of $10,000. Your net capital gain is $6,000; it is all short-term, and you apply Rule 1.
- Assume you have a net long-term loss of $1,800 and a net short-term gain of $500. Your net capital loss is $1,300; it is all long-term, and you apply Rule 4.
- Assume you have a net short-term loss of $1,800 and a net long-term

gain of $500. Your net capital loss is $1,300; all of it is short-term, and you apply Rule 3.

- Assume you have a net long-term loss of $11,000 and a net short-term loss of $1,000. You first apply Rule 3 and deduct $1,000 from your gross income. You still have $2,000 of capital loss deduction left since the maximum is $3,000 in any one year. Since the $11,000 loss is long-term, you apply Rule 4. In applying Rule 4, remember that it takes $2 of long-term loss to deduct $1. Therefore, to take the remaining $2,000 of capital loss deduction, you have to use $4,000 of long-term loss in this taxable year. You can carry over to subsequent taxable years the $7,000 of long-term loss. If you have no capital transactions in the next year, you would use up $6,000 of the long-term loss to deduct the maximum of $3,000. You would then carry over $1,000 of the long-term loss to the next year.

Before you try to complete Forms 13A and 13B for your own situation, let's review an example of Forms 13A and 13B. Figure 8-1 shows a completed Form 13A for an individual's capital transactions actually completed for the year to date.

- The total short-term gains are $1,700; the total short-term losses are $1,800.
- Since there were short-term losses of $2,300 carried over from the prior year, the net short-term losses are $2,400 for the year to date.
- The total long-term gains to date are $2,700; the total long-term losses are $800.
- Since there were long-term losses of $1,700 carried over from the prior year, the net long-term gains are $200 for the year to date.

Figure 8-2 shows a completed Form 13B for this individual's capital assets where gains or losses have not been realized.

- The net unrealized short-term losses are $800.
- The net unrealized long-term gains are $2,500.

In analyzing our example situation, we might recommend selling the 100 shares of the Hotshot stock before year-end for tax purposes (assuming the stock will not be a hotshot one!). Such a sale would result in a short-term loss of $800.

Together with the $2,400 of the net short-term losses already realized, this transaction would bring the net short-term losses to $3,200 and the net long-term gains to $200. The net capital loss would be $3,000, all of it short-term, and all $3,000 of it deductible this year.

In selecting year-end strategies, do not be guided solely by tax considerations. For example, do not sell a stock for which you have an unrealized loss if you really believe it is ready to take off.

YOUR COMPLETION OF FORMS 13A AND 13B

Now it's your turn to complete Forms 13A and 13B. First, complete Form 13A for your realized capital gains and losses during this year. Next, using Form 13B, analyze your *unrealized* capital gains and losses and determine what year-end moves you want to make, keeping strategies shown in Table 8-1 in mind.

FIGURE 8-1

File under TAX PLANNING Date: ___________

FORM 13A CAPITAL GAINS AND LOSSES REALIZED TO DATE

Number Units	Investment Type	Date Acquired	Cost or Basis	Date Sold	Net Proceeds
100	Acme Stock	5/30/x2	$ 2,400	4/10/x3	$ 4,000
10	Best Bonds	2/15/x3	8,800	4/3/x3	8,900
300	Chance Stock	6/30/x2	3,200	4/1/x3	1,400
200	Dandy Stock	2/28/x0	3,000	5/1/x3	5,000
5	Early Bonds	11/30/x0	4,000	7/1/x3	3,200
200	Grinch Stock	8/15/x0	1,200	8/16/x3	1,900

CAPITAL GAINS AND LOSSES REALIZED

Investment Type	Short Term Gain	Short Term Loss	Long Term Gain	Long Term Loss
Acme Stock	$ 1,600			
Best Bonds	100			
Chance Stock		$ 1,800		
Dandy Stock			$2, 00	
Early Bonds				$ 800
Grinch Stock			700	
Subtotals	$ 1,700	$ 1,800	$2,700	$ 800
Capital Gain Dividends			—	
Short Term Capital Loss Carryovers		2,300		
Long Term Capital Loss Carryovers				1,700
TOTAL	1,700	4,100	2,700	2,500
NET Short Term Capital Gain or Loss	—	2,400		
NET Long Term Capital Gain or Loss			200	

FIGURE 8-2

File under TAX PLANNING

Date: 11/5/x3

FORM 13B UNREALIZED GAINS OR LOSSES IN CURRENT INVESTMENTS

Number Units	Investment Type	Date Acquired	Cost or Basis	Date of Becoming Long Term	Current Market Value
200	Dandystock	2/28/x0	$3,000	3/1/x1	$6,000
5	Early Bonds	11/30/x0	4,000	12/1/x1	3,500
100	Hotshot Stock	1/30/x3	2,000	1/31/x4	1,200

CAPITAL GAINS AND LOSSES UNREALIZED

Investment Type	Short Term Gain	Short Term Loss	Long Term Gain	Long Term Loss
Dandy Stock			$3,000	
Early Bonds				$500
Hotshot Stock		$800		
TOTAL Unrealized Capital Gains and Losses		$800	$3,000	$500
NET Short Term Capital Gain or Loss		800		
NET Long Term Capital Gain or Loss			$2,500	—

TABLE 8-1
SECURITIES STRATEGIES

If you have already sold securities this year and have realized:	AND	You own securities with unrealized:	You should consider these year-end moves:
Short-term gains only		Gains and losses	Sell securities with long-term losses first to offset short-term gains; then sell short-term loss shares.
Short-term gains only		Gains only	Nothing for tax purposes; moves should only be made for other purposes.
Short-term losses only		Gains only	There is no tax advantage to selling securities at a gain; in fact, selling long-term securities could be disadvantageous since the gains would offset the realized losses.
Long-term gains only		Gains and losses	Take long-term losses to offset long-term gains; then take short-term losses to a maximum of $3,000.
Long-term gains only		Gains only	No tax advantage to selling securities; however, long-term gains will be taxed at a maximum of 20 percent.
Long-term losses only		Gains only	Consider taking short-term gains to offset long-term losses. Remember, long-term losses will offset ordinary income, but it requires $2 of long-term loss to get $1 of deduction.
Long-term losses only		Losses only	Consider taking short-term losses of up to $3,000 to offset $1 of ordinary income for every $1 of short-term loss, then carry over long-term losses to offset short-term gains next year.

FORM 14—YOUR YEAR-END TAX PLAN

To help you analyze your tax situation for the current year and determine what year-end action is required, we have provided Form 14. The listed items on the form are the same as those on Form 11 and follow the structure of your tax return. In the first column, *Actual to Date*, you record your actual taxable transactions for the current year up to the date you complete Form 14. In the second column, *Estimates for Rest of Year*, you record your estimates of taxable transactions from now until the end of the year. In the third column, *Estimates for Total Year*, you place the total of the amounts in the first two columns.

To complete the form, use the following instructions, which are similar to those you used for completing Form 11.

- Gross income: record actual gross income to date, your estimate for the rest of the year, and the total of all your taxable income, such as taxable wages and salaries, interest and dividends, capital gains and losses, and so forth.
- Adjustments to gross income: record in each of the three columns your relevant adjustments, such as IRA contributions, unreimbursed business expenses, and so forth.

- Record adjusted gross income on line 3 in all three columns.
- Itemized deductions: record deductible medical expenses, taxes, interest paid, charitable contributions, casualty and theft losses, and miscellaneous deductions.
- On line 4g, put the total itemized deductions in all three columns.
- On line 4h, in the "actual" column and "total" column, enter the standard deduction—$2,300 for one taxpayer, $3,400 for a married couple filing a joint return.
- On line 5a, enter the excess of itemized deductions over the standard deduction in all three columns.
- On line 5b, in the "actual" column and the "total" column, enter the amount of your exemptions; then add the amounts on lines 5a and 5b to get your total deductions and exemptions on line 5c in all three columns.
- Determine your taxable income by subtracting the amount on line 5a from the amount on line 3 and record the amount on line 6a in all three columns. Add the amount on line 6a in the "actual" column to see if the result agrees with the amount on line 6a in the "total" column. If these numbers do not agree, check your computations again.

Figure 8-3 shows you a filled-in Form 14 related to the example used in Forms 11 (Chapter 5) and 12 (Chapter 7). Here are some observations on the sample that may be of help to you in completing Form 14:

- The amounts shown under *Actual to Date* come from your records—pay records, information from financial institutions on dividends and interest and securities transactions, partnership information for gains and losses, checkbook information on deductible expenditures, etc. You need to summarize this information to record it on Form 14. To summarize the data, you probably should have a legal-sized, lined pad and a calculator or home computer handy.
- The amounts shown under *Estimates for Rest of Year* are your best estimates of transactions that are likely to occur, if you do not take any other action, between the time you prepare Form 14 and the end of the year. In our example, the form was completed as of October 31, and $15,300 is the estimate for additional gross income during the remaining two months of the year. These estimates should be based on what you believe is likely to happen for each line on the form. For example, based on what you have received to date in compensation, you probably have a good idea of what you are likely to receive in compensation for the rest of the year. You may not have made your IRA payments yet, but if you plan to, as our example family does, then put the estimated amount of the IRA contribution under the "estimates" column.
- The amount of targeted taxable income comes from Form 11—*Tax Planning Worksheet* on which you targeted your taxable income for the current year. In our example, the targeted taxable income is $50,000. This amount is compared to the estimated taxable income for the year on line 6a of Form 14—$58,000 in our example. If you have implemented all your tax-saving ideas on Form 12, your estimated taxable income for the year should be pretty close to your targeted taxable income. If you have procrastinated, you may be way off your target. Again, let us emphasize the need to start tax planning long

FIGURE 8-3

File under TAX PLANNING   Date: October 31

FORM 14 YEAR-END TAX PLAN

	ACTUAL TO DATE	ESTIMATES TO END YR.	ESTIMATES TOTAL YR.
1 Gross Income			
a. Taxable Wages/Salaries	$76,700	$15,300	$92,000
b. Taxable Dividends and Interest	4,000	400	4,400
c. Net Business Income (Loss)			
d. Net Taxable Long-Term Capital Gain (Loss)			
e. Net Taxable Short-Term Capital Gain (Loss)			
f. Net Rent Income (Loss)	3,000	750	3,750
g. Net Partnership Income (Loss)	(10,000)	(6,500)	(16,500)
h. Other Income (Loss)	600	200	800
i. TOTAL Gross Income	$74,300	$10,150	$84,450
2 Adjustments to Gross Income			
a. Alimony Paid			
b. IRA Payments			
c. Keogh Plan Payments	—	(4,000)	(4,000)
d. Unreimbursed Business Expenses			
e. Unreimbursed Moving Expenses			
f. Deduction for Married Couple When Both Work			
g. Other Adjustments			
h. TOTAL Adjustments	—	(4,000)	(4,000)
3 Adjusted Gross Income	$74,300	$6,150	$80,450

FIGURE 8-3, cont'd.

4 Itemized Deductions			
a. Medical	—		—
b. Taxes	$2,800		$2,800
c. Interest Paid	$9,600	$4,250	$13,850
d. Charitable Contributions	$1,500	$1,000	$2,500
e. Casualty and Theft Losses	—	—	—
f. Miscellaneous Deductions	$1,500	$200	$1,700
g. TOTAL Itemized Deductions	$(15,400)	$(5,450)	$(20,850)
h. Standard (zero bracket) Deduction	$3,400	—	$3,400
5a. Excess Deductions	$(12,000)	$(5,450)	$(17,450)
b. Exemptions	$(5,000)		$(5,000)
c. TOTAL Deductions and Exemptions	$(17,000)	$(5,450)	$(22,450)
6a. Taxable Income	$57,300	$700	$58,000
b. Tax Bracket			38%
7a. Targeted Taxable Income			$50,000
b. Targeted Tax Bracket			38%

before year-end, so that you are on or near your target by the time the end of the year rolls around. In our example, the difference between estimated and targeted taxable income is $8,000. If no action is taken in the remainder of the current year, the example taxpayer, who is in a 40 percent tax bracket, will have to pay an additional $3,200 in taxes over the targeted amount—$8,000 multiplied by 40 percent.

- This brings us to the point of this whole year-end exercise—to highlight year-end action required. If you want to get closer to your targeted taxable income, you have to take some additional tax-saving steps between the time you prepare *Your Year-End Tax Plan* and December 31. The rest of this chapter will focus on year-end action.

As you read the rest of the chapter, list your action steps on Form 15—*Year-End Tax Action*. It would be useful now to complete the top of Form 15 from data on Form 14.

- At the top of Form 15 fill in your estimated taxable income from line 6a of your Form 14.
- On the next line of Form 15 fill in your targeted taxable income from line 7a of your Form 14.
- Then determine the required year-end reduction in taxable income. At the end of this chapter, we shall see if you have listed enough year-end action steps to reach the required reduction.

SHIFTING INCOME AND DEDUCTIONS

Effective year-end tax planning will generally involve the following:

- The implementation of tax-saving ideas you listed in Form 12 but have not yet carried out
- The postponement of income to next year
- The acceleration of deductions and credits into the current year

Because of recent tax law changes that have lowered tax rates through 1984, you may be able to achieve a tax saving by postponing income and/or accelerating deductions and credits this year in the expectation that your tax rate next year will be lower. Even if your tax rate is the same next year a deferral of taxable income to next year is the equivalent of an interest-free loan because it enables you to use funds that you would otherwise pay out in taxes. With a significant rate of inflation, any tax deferred to a later year will most likely be paid with cheaper dollars.

Bear in mind that in some situations shifting taxable income into the *current year* may result in greater tax savings. For example, if you anticipate that your income next year will be substantially higher, or if you think you will have unusually large investment losses or other deductions this year, then you may want to accelerate income this year and defer deductions until next year to minimize your tax liability over this year and next.

The counsel of tax professionals employing computerized "what-if" analyses can be very helpful at year-end. For example, at Touche Ross we provide such year-end analyses for many clients.

DEFERRING INCOME

You may have several ways of deferring income to next year, even though there is little room for such maneuvers as far as your income from salaries is concerned. Under the "constructive receipt" rules, you are considered to have received your salary when you have control of it or when it is set aside for you. Thus, you cannot defer your salary to next year by not cashing year-end paychecks or by arranging with your employer to be paid after December 31.

DEFERRED COMPENSATION PLANS

Some employers have *deferred compensation* plans under which an employee may opt to defer some part of a bonus or similar compensation in advance of the time it is earned. Such deferred compensation is usually paid in some future year or may be spread over several years.

SELF-EMPLOYMENT INCOME

In addition to their regular salaries, some taxpayers also have earned income from freelance jobs, from their own businesses, or from directors' fees. You can shift this type of income to next year simply by billing your clients after December 31, or by billing them so late in December that payment this year is unlikely.

INVESTMENT INCOME

A person has more flexibility when it comes to investment income such as interest income and rents. On some notes receivable, interest income can be deferred if in advance of the due date you and the debtor enter into a formal agreement by which the debtor's due date is extended. Interest can also be deferred by taking money out of a money market fund that pays interest daily and using it to acquire Treasury bills or bankers' acceptance notes. Both of these are short-term investments issued at a discount in the amount of the interest income, but this discount is not taxed until the investment matures.

On the rental property you own, you could defer collecting rent in the later months of this year and accelerate expenses such as repairs in order to reduce this year's net rental income.

On investments in limited partnerships, you may not be able to defer income or accelerate losses; nonetheless, get some information about the estimated taxable income or loss before year-end, so you can calculate your estimated taxable income for the year.

DISTRIBUTIONS FROM PENSION OR PROFIT-SHARING PLANS

If you are about to retire and expect to receive a lump-sum distribution from a qualified pension or profit-sharing plan in the near future, you may wish to defer the distribution to a lower-income year. Part or all of the distribution can generally be rolled over into an Individual Retirement Account.

YEAR-END CAPITAL ASSET TRANSACTIONS

We previously discussed year-end strategies related to capital asset transactions using Forms 13A and 13B. We summarized these strategies in Table 8-1. In addition to the strategies previously discussed, there are some other year-end securities transactions you may wish to consider.

SELLING SHORT

If you want to realize a long-term gain on a stock but you don't want to increase this year's tax liability, you can take the gain near year-end but defer taxes on it until next year by "going short against the box." This simply means that you sell short (sell stock you borrow from your broker) the same number of shares you own of the same stock. The gain is not taxed until you cover your short position by delivering the stock you own early next year. For example, let's say you own 100 shares of XYZ stock, with a market price of $40 per share, for which you paid $20 per share more than 12 months ago. Your long-term capital gain upon sale would be $20 per share or $2,000. If you believed that the stock had reached its peak and you wanted to defer the $2,000 gain until next year, you could arrange to sell 100 shares of XYZ at $40 per share by borrowing 100 XYZ shares from your broker's inventory. Selling borrowed shares is the selling-short side of the transaction. When you sell short, you have locked in your $2,000 gain because you have sold shares of $40 to be covered by shares you purchased at $20. But you pay no taxes until you close your short position by delivering the 100 shares you purchased at $20 sometime early next year.

WASH SALES If you want to realize a loss in securities you own but would also like to hold on to them because you expect them to do well, keep the "wash sales" rules in mind. If you sell your shares at a loss and buy similar shares within thirty days before or after the date you sold them, your loss, for tax purposes, will be deferred until you sell the new securities, and that is not what you want. That result can be avoided by "doubling up"—buying the same or similar shares at least thirty-one days before you sell your original holding and thereby recognizing the loss. The disadvantage of doubling up is that for thirty-one days you tie up and risk additional capital.

INSTALLMENT SALES You can defer gain on a capital asset by selling the appreciated asset in an installment sale. An installment sale does not require a down payment, and there is no requirement for two or more immediate payments. The gain is recognized only when you receive the payments. In this way, you could sell a capital asset in the latter part of this year and defer all or some portion of the gain until next year or even later.

Now that you have ideas as to how to defer income to next year, note them on Form 15—*Year-End Tax Action*.

USING DEDUCTIONS

Deferring income is one of the chief strategies of year-end tax planning, and the other one is to increase or accelerate your deductions and credits. Having already discussed the former, we will now investigate possible deductions, which largely relate to the following areas: business expenses, retirement plans, itemized deductions, exemptions, and tax credits. As you read of deductions you may want to take but have not yet included in your tax plan, note them down on Form 15—*Year-End Tax Action*.

We will discuss tax-planning ideas for these major areas of deductions or credits:

- Business expenses
- Retirement plans
- Itemized deductions
- Tax credits

BUSINESS USE OF HOME

Most taxpayers cannot deduct expenditures for the business use of space in their residences. Deductions (other than itemized deductions for interest, taxes, and casualty losses) are not allowed for the cost of maintaining a home office unless it is used as such on a regular and exclusive basis, which is defined as follows:

- It must be your principal place of business for a particular trade or business in which you engage. Accordingly, you could be an employee, but if you are also in business for yourself and use your home as your principal place of business, you can deduct that part of your home that is exclusively and regularly used to conduct that business.
- It must be the place of business that your patients, clients, or customers use for dealing or meeting with you in the normal course of that business.
- If you are using your home for business in your capacity as an employee, you must be able to prove that such business use of your home is for the convenience of your employer.

If you have any business activity in which you are generating *revenue* and are using a portion of your home exclusively as your principal place of business, add up all of the costs of maintaining your residence and deduct the portion of these expenses related to your business.

For example, let's say you live in a home with 2,500 square feet of space and you devote 250 square feet to a home office for a part-time consulting operation. Ten percent (250 of a total of 2,500 square feet) of the costs (other than interest, taxes, and casualty losses) of maintaining your home—that is, utilities, gardening, and depreciation—could be deducted against your consulting fees.

VACATION HOMES RENTED TO OTHERS

If you have a second home, such as a ski cabin or summer place, that you rent to other people, you may be able to take some deductions. If you have such a home and rented it out for fewer than fifteen days this year, the rental income is not taxable, but then you cannot deduct expenses on the property other than the always-allowable interest and taxes. If you have not rented it out so far this year, from a year-end tax-planning standpoint you may want to rent it out now for fourteen days and so gain the maximum amount of nonreportable rental income.

Where the actual rental period exceeds fifteen days, the rental income is taxable, but you can deduct all expenses related to the rental of the property, provided your personal use of the property did not exceed the longer of these two periods: fourteen days or 10 percent of the time the home was rented at a fair rental.

"Personal use" includes use by your or your spouse's brothers, sisters, parents, or children, unless they paid you a fair rental. Your use would not be considered personal for any day on which your principal purpose for being on the property was its repair or maintenance.

In the context of year-end tax planning, look at your actual number of personal-use days this year. If it is less than fifteen days or 10 percent of the period it has been rented this year, try to stay within the maximum of fourteen days' personal use for this year, so that you can deduct your entire rental expenses for the property. When you exceed this limited period for personal use, a portion of your expenses will still be deductible. This portion is determined by multiplying your total expenses by the number of days the property was rented, and dividing that by the total number of days the property was in use. However, you may not be able to deduct the whole of this amount.

Where the actual rental is fifteen days or more and personal use exceeds fourteen days or 10 percent of the rental days, your deduction for rental expense is limited to what is left of your rental income after subtracting interest, taxes, and casualty losses.

Since 1982, the law has allowed you to deduct all expenses on a second home that you rented to a family member for use as a principal residence, provided your tenant paid you a fair rental.

JOB-HUNTING AND MOVING EXPENSES

If you changed jobs or plan to do so this year, the cost of finding new employment and moving to a new job location must not be overlooked in your tax planning.

The costs of actually obtaining a new job in your present field, such as employment agency fees, are deductible. You may also be able to deduct the expenses of an unsuccessful job hunt. Unrefunded travel expenses incurred in a job hunt are deductible if the trip was undertaken for the primary purpose of seeking employment. The standard mileage rate to use in computing expenses is 9 cents per mile.

You may be able to deduct the expenses of moving to another location if the move is related to your beginning full-time employment in a new location. This move can be to a new employer or to a new place of work for the same employer. To qualify for the deduction, the distance between your new place of employment and your former residence must be at least 35 miles farther than the distance between your former residence and your previous place of work. You must also be a full-time employee in the general area of your new place of employment for at least 39 weeks of the twelve-month period immediately following arrival in the new location.

A self-employed person may claim a deduction if, in addition to meeting the mileage limitation test,

- the person performs service as a self-employed person or as an employee on a full-time basis during at least 78 weeks, and
- not less than 39 weeks of the 78 fall within the twelve-month period immediately following his or her arrival at the new place of work.

Moving expenses can be deducted even if the eligible taxpayer has not satisfied the 39- or 78-week residence requirement by the time prescribed for filing returns for the taxable year in which the moving expenses were incurred and paid.

OTHER BUSINESS EXPENSES

Taking some action now in order to avoid trouble later should be part of your tax planning. So be sure to document all your travel and entertainment expenses carefully. Court decisions have continually supported the Internal Revenue Service in disallowing numerous types of expenses because they were not adequately substantiated. All these cases showed the importance of maintaining a current record of expenses. Spending a little time now could save a lot of dollars later.

In the case of automobile expenses, the record-keeping problem can be reduced by using the standard mileage allowance, but you should still compare your actual operating expenses for the business use of your car with the standard mileage allowance. The standard rate for the first 15,000 miles of business use of an automobile is 20 cents a mile. For business use in excess of 15,000 miles a year, and for cars that have been fully depreciated, the standard rate is 11 cents a mile. Keep records to support the business mileage you claim. In addition to the standard mileage rate, you can deduct your interest payments on the car, state and local automobile taxes (other than gasoline tax), parking fees, and tolls.

It may be wise also to keep a record of your actual expenses for depreciation, insurance, gasoline, repairs, and oil, since your actual costs may give you a higher deduction than the standard allowance. Automobiles placed in service in 1981 or thereafter must be depreciated under the new Accelerated Cost Recovery System. Thus, you can depreciate an automobile over three years, using 25 percent in the first year (multiplied by the percent of business use), 38 percent in the second year, and 37 percent in the third year. For example, if you purchased for $10,000 an automobile that you used 60 percent of the time for business in each of three successive years, you could deduct $1,500 in the first year, $2,220 in the second year, and $2,280 in the third year—a total of $6,000, or 60 percent of the purchase price.

The law disallows most expenses related to facilities used for entertainment, amusement, or recreation. Expenses related to club dues, however, are still permitted if the taxpayer can show that the facility was used primarily for business. Club dues include all social, athletic, and sporting club dues or fees.

Retirement Plans

Following the 1981 tax act, all individuals—employees and the self-employed—can annually contribute to an Individual Retirement Account either $2,000 or their entire earned income, whichever is less. Married couples with only one earning spouse can contribute $2,250 a year to a spousal IRA; with both spouses working, each can contribute up to $2,000. Consider contributing to your IRA in the early part of each year, so that you maximize the deferral on the income earned by the IRA. You have until April 15 of next year to establish an IRA for the current year; you also have until April 15 of next year to make your current year's contribution. Remember, you cannot withdraw your IRA funds until age 59½ (or until disabled) without a withdrawal penalty, which we discuss in Chapter 12, Retirement Planning. Self-employed individuals can establish Keogh plans, and so can the owners of businesses, both as proprietors and as partners, but their plans must also cover their employees and must not discriminate in favor of the owners. Up to 15 percent of your net self-employment income can be set aside in a Keogh plan and deducted from your gross income, with a ceiling of $15,000 in 1983 for each individual ($30,000 starting in 1984). Thus, a self-employed individual who earns $100,000 or more in 1983 can annually defer tax on a principal of $17,000 and the interest thereon by contributing $15,000 to a Keogh plan and $2,000 to an IRA.

Employees with an outside income from self-employment can also avail themselves of such tax deferment by contributing up to 15 percent of their year's self-employment income to a Keogh plan. Corporate directors' fees are considered to be self-employment income. If you are eligible for a Keogh plan this year, you have to set it up by December 31 of this year. However, once you have set it up, you have until April 15 of next year to make the Keogh contribution for this year. It's somewhat complicated—but that's the law.

DIVIDEND EXCLUSION

You are entitled to exclude from your gross income the first $100 ($200 on joint returns) of dividends you receive from domestic sources.

INTEREST EXPENSES In general, there are no limitations on the deduction of personal interest unless it is prepaid; however, large interest deductions may affect you unfavorably through the alternative minimum tax. No deduction is permitted for interest paid by investors for amounts borrowed specifically to invest in tax-exempt investments.

Prepaid interest must be allocated over the period of the loan. For example, let's assume you borrowed $2,000 at 12 percent on January 1 of this year and agreed to repay the $2,000 on December 31 of next year. Let's further assume you have paid the $240 of interest payable in quarterly installments this year and want to prepay next year's $240 of interest before December 31 of this year. If you do, the $240 of interest related to next year is not deductible this year.

Thus, you cannot deduct interest prepaid for the use of money beyond the current year. As an exception, "points" paid to obtain a mortgage on your principal residence are fully deductible when paid, if it is general practice in your geographical area to charge that number of points and if the points are charged for the use of money rather than for other services of the lender.

Deductible interest on investment indebtedness is limited to an annual total of $10,000 plus your net investment income other than long-term capital gains. If the debt was incurred before September 11, 1975, the limit is an annual total of $25,000 plus net investment income (including long-term capital gains) plus half of the remainder. The unallowable interest deduction can be carried over indefinitely and deducted in future years to the extent of the aforementioned limitations.

To be deductible, interest charged on margin accounts with brokers must be paid before the end of the year or offset by dividends and interest credited to your margin account.

TAXES State and local taxes are deductible if you itemize. However, you have a choice concerning what year you wish to pay them. For example, if you want to accelerate taxes in the current year, prepay next year's real estate taxes if local law permits. Paying, this year, the final installments of next year's state and local income taxes can yield additional deductions that will reduce your current federal tax liability.

You can also increase your withholding of state and local income taxes to obtain additional deductions this year. Your refund next year for overpaying state and local taxes this year will be taxable then.

State and local gasoline taxes are not deductible unless you used the gasoline for business but do not claim the standard mileage.

MEDICAL EXPENSES In general, medical expenses are deductible only to the extent to which they exceed 5 percent of your adjusted gross income. Medical expenses include health insurance premiums, prescription drugs and insulin, and travel expenses for medical visits to doctors or clinics. The standard mileage allowance is 9 cents a mile.

Your medical expenses are generally deductible in the year in which they are paid, but no deduction is allowed for prepaid future expenses.

If one of your dependent relatives is in a retirement home, you can deduct the part of a lump-sum life care fee that the home charges for its obligation to provide medical care. You can also take a current deduction for a nonrefundable payment to an institution that agrees to provide care for your child—for example, a school for mentally handicapped children.

If your adjusted medical expenses this year do not exceed 5 percent of your adjusted gross income, you should try to delay what payments you can until next year because you may be able to deduct them next year. Conversely, if this year's medical expenses, including medical insurance premiums, exceed 5 percent of your adjusted gross income, try to pay every dental and medical expense incurred this year. This year they are deductible, but next year they may not be; next year your adjusted medical cost may not exceed 5 percent of your adjusted gross income.

The expenses you claim must never include those that your insurance company has refunded. There can, however, be a lag between your payment of bills and your reimbursement by the insurer; in such cases, you can claim a current deduction even though you expect reimbursement. The eventual reimbursement will constitute income in accordance with the tax-benefit rules.

DISASTER LOSSES

Let's assume you have disaster losses in the current year sufficient to qualify for deduction (greater than 10 percent of adjusted gross income after deducting $100 from the loss). If you have suffered losses attributable to a disaster in an area that the President has declared a disaster area under the Disaster Relief Act of 1974, you may deduct the losses you suffered this year on your tax return for last year. This legislation enables taxpayers who have been struck by a disaster to get a deduction when they need it the most.

This "throwback" of disaster losses is elective. If you have losses this year, you can claim them either on your return for last year or on your return for the current year. Obviously, you want to deduct it in the year in which it will benefit you the most.

CHARITABLE CONTRIBUTIONS

Generally, charitable contributions are deductible when paid or donated. Therefore, such contributions afford great possibilities for acceleration or deferral. For example, let's say you have decided to make an extraordinary contribution of $5,000 to your favorite charity, to be paid in annual installments of $1,000 over the next five years. As you approach year-end, you may decide to reduce your taxable income by $3,000 instead of $1,000 by paying three installments this year. Your charity would love it, and perhaps you can reduce this year's taxes by as much as $1,000 if you are in a 50 percent top tax bracket. In fact, it might even be a good idea to borrow the money to make the accelerated contribution.

Apart from acceleration or deferral possibilities, keep these points in mind when making charitable contributions:

- Cash contributions to qualified charitable organizations can be deducted, with a maximum deduction in any one year of 50 percent of your adjusted gross income.
- Noncash charitable contributions have some special rules:
  - If you contribute property that has increased in value and that would have produced long-term capital gain if sold, the amount of the deduction is the fair market value of the property at the date of donation. However, when such property is contributed, the maximum deduction changes to 30 percent of adjusted gross income. But, the 50 percent limit will remain if the donor is willing to reduce contribution deduction to the fair market value of the property less 40 percent of the increase in value of the property since owned by the donor.
  - Donations of property that would not produce long-term gain if sold

will give a deduction only for its value or its cost basis, whichever is smaller.

- Donations of property to private foundations are limited to 20 percent of adjusted gross income.
- To the extent to which contributions exceed the percentage of adjusted gross income limitations, the excess may be carried over for up to five years, except those contributions made to private foundations.
- Donations of depreciated property should not be made. Sell the property, take the loss, and deduct the gift of the cash proceeds *and* the loss.
- When you donate small items to charities—books, clothing, old furniture—keep accurate records of them and claim reasonable amounts for the deduction. The amount claimed is what would have to be paid to replace them in their used condition.

- Personal services provided to charitable organizations cannot be deducted, but the out-of-pocket expenses required to provide such services can be. This includes a 9-cents-per-mile deduction for use of a personal car.
- Those taxpayers not otherwise itemizing deductions can take 25 percent of the first $100 of charitable contributions as a deduction in 1983. This deduction will increase to 100 percent of contributions in 1986.

BUNCHING DEDUCTIONS

Many people in the United States itemize their deductions because they exceed the standard deduction (zero-bracket amount) of $3,400 for married persons filing jointly ($1,700 if filing separately) and $2,300 for single persons and heads of household. But if your itemized deductions are close to the zero-bracket amount in any one year, you should consider "bunching' deductions in either this year or next year to obtain the maximum benefit of itemizing deductions in one year and using the zero-bracket amount in the other.

You do this by timing your expenditures at year-end and by keeping good records. In the years in which the taxpayer elects to take the itemized deductions, he or she should accelerate into this year all tax-deductible expenditures to the greatest extent possible by

- Making the maximum charitable contributions
- Prepaying property tax payments
- Accelerating major purchases on which sales taxes may be significant
- Arranging to pay all doctor and dentist bills this year

To illustrate this method of maximizing deductions, let's assume a single taxpayer who has no mortgage balance on his home normally has the following itemized deductions in a year:

Real estate taxes on home	$1,500
Sales tax	350
Contributions	400
Medical expenses (generally limited since only expenses in excess of 5 percent of adjusted gross income are deductible)	0
Total Itemized Deductions	$2,250

TABLE 8-2
MAXIMIZING ITEMIZED DEDUCTIONS

	This Year	Next Year
Real estate taxes	$3,000	$ 0
Sales tax	350	350
Contributions	800	0
	$4,150	$350

A single taxpayer's standard deduction is $2,300 and therefore it looks like the itemized deductions are too small to do the taxpayer any good. But wait. How about doing some planning and shifting some of the itemized deductions for next year into this year? The taxpayer can probably prepay payments on the real estate taxes and accelerate contributions. By doing so every other year, the taxpayer would achieve an itemized deduction pattern as shown in Table 8-2.

By taking itemized deductions this year and the standard deduction next year, the taxpayer's total deductions every two years will be $6,450 instead of $4,600. If the taxpayer has a tax bracket of 25 percent, he or she will be saving about $460 ($6,450 − $4,600 × 25 percent) over two years.

EXEMPTIONS AND CREDITS

In addition to deductions, there are exemptions and credits that you should evaluate as part of your year-end tax planning.

POLITICAL CONTRIBUTIONS

Political contributions are not treated as itemized deductions but as tax credits. The maximum credit is whichever is less: half of your annual contribution or $50 ($100 on a joint return). You should have receipts for the contributions you claim.

DEPENDENT EXEMPTIONS

As Chapter 6 explains in some detail, you can claim an exemption for each person who qualifies as a dependent. Such a person must receive more than half of his or her annual support from you. For a child under 19, or older if your child is a full-time student, you can claim the exemption regardless of the child's income level if you provide more than 50 percent of the child's support. For dependents other than your children, you cannot claim exemption if they have a gross income of $1,000 or more.

From the standpoint of year-end tax planning, you might consider the following:

- If those who must earn less than $1,000 to qualify as your dependents have received close to $1,000 in other income as the end of the year approaches, ask if they can defer all additional outside income to next year.
- If any of your dependents have supplied almost 50 percent of their own support as you get close to year's end, consider whether they should save or invest all further outside income this year instead of using it for their own support.

- If a child for whom you have provided more than half of his or her support has married this year, you can claim a dependent exemption unless the child files a joint return. Compute how much additional tax the newlyweds would pay by filing separately. If the tax you would save by claiming the $1,000 exemption (or $2,000 if you support both of them) exceeds the additional tax they would owe if they filed separately, you might be better off if you give them the money for the additional tax and get the exemption.

DIVORCE SETTLEMENTS

Alimony payments are deductible from the paying spouse's gross income whether deductions are itemized or not, and must be included in the receiving spouse's gross income. Payments for child support can neither be deducted by the supporting spouse nor included in the custodial spouse's income.

Child support payments can determine who claims the dependency exemption for the child, though the IRS does not care which of the former spouses claims it. You may be entitled to a dependency exemption for your child even if the child was in the custody of your ex-spouse. If you contributed $600 or more for your child's support and your ex-spouse agrees in writing that you will take the exemption, or if the divorce decree so provides, you can claim the exemption on your tax return. Such a written agreement can be made before, during, or after the year in question, but its retroactive effect extends only to "open" tax return years—three years or less.

Even if your ex-spouse refuses to consent, you may still be able to claim the exemption. Showing that you contributed at least $1,200 for your child's support will entitle you to the exemption unless your ex-spouse can prove that he or she provided more support than you did.

HOUSEHOLD AND DEPENDENT CARE CREDIT

You can claim for employment-related child or dependent care expenses. The maximum claim for the care of one dependent is $2,400; for the care of two or more, thc maximum is $4,800. You can claim 30 percent of actual employment-related child or dependent care expenses if you have an adjusted gross income of $10,000 or less. This percentage diminishes as your income rises. With an adjusted gross income of $28,000 or more, you can only claim 20 percent of your child-care expenditures.

You can achieve some very welcome tax savings here, provided the care you have paid for enabled you or your spouse to follow some gainful employment. Credit can be claimed for such paid care even when it is given by relatives, as long as these relatives are not your dependents, and provided their pay is subject to Social Security tax.

INDIVIDUAL ENERGY CREDITS

Homeowners and renters can claim tax credits for qualified expenditures on energy conservation and renewable energy sources made between April 20, 1977, and January 1, 1986. For insulation, storm windows, improved furnace burners, clock thermostats, and similar energy-conserving devices that have an expected operational life of at least three years and were installed by you for your own use, there is a 15 percent tax credit on the first $2,000 of cumulative energy conservation expenditures.

For providing your principal residence with a source of renewable energy, such as a wind or solar energy device, you can claim an additional tax credit for 40 percent of the first $10,000 you spent on acquiring and installing such a device. This credit will be available through 1985.

ESTIMATED TAXES

Toward the end of the year, check whether you are exposed to a penalty for underpayment of estimated tax. The penalty rate is adjusted semiannually and is based on the average prime rate for a previous period.

If you are an employee, the simple way to avoid an underpayment penalty is to have additional tax withheld at the end of the year. The Internal Revenue Service will treat the entire amount withheld during the tax year as if it had been paid in equal quarterly installments.

If you find that the success of your recent transactions has materially raised your tax liability above your previously filed estimate, you can amend your estimate until January 15. Another way of avoiding an underpayment penalty on your fourth installment is to file your tax return and pay your tax by February 1.

ESTATE AND GIFT TAXES

As we shall discuss fully in Chapter 14—*Estate Planning*, estate and gift taxes are independent of income taxes, with their own tax laws and rates and planning techniques. We mention them as part of year-end tax planning primarily to have you consider yearly gifts.

You can make any number of tax-free gifts to any number of people, provided your gifts to any one person in any one year do not exceed $10,000 or its equivalent. If you were interested in making gifts to each of your three children each year, you could transfer up to $30,000 of your net worth to them—up to $10,000 each—without incurring any estate or gift tax. If you split gifts with your spouse, $60,000 could be transferred to the three children without any estate or gift tax.

Gifts to one donee totaling more than $10,000 in one year are taxable gifts and may be subject to a gift tax (as we shall see in the chapter on estate planning). Taking advantage of the annual exclusion of $10,000 per donee is an excellent way to make transfers of substantial property over a lifetime to family members without incurring any estate or gift taxes. So, as part of your year-end planning, evaluate the use of your annual exclusion of up to $10,000 in a gifting program. The value of any such gift, no matter what the amount, is not deductible for income tax purposes. On the other hand, the recipient of the gift, no matter what the amount, does not have to include the value of the gift on his or her return. Now you can see that one easy way of becoming financially secure is to choose your parents wisely.

FORM 15—YEAR-END TAX ACTION

Year-end is the last time you have available to do anything about this year's tax situation. Hopefully, you have already completed the top of Form 15 to determine the required reduction of taxable income by year-end. Also, we hope you have listed action steps on Form 15 as you read this chapter. If not, spend some time now listing those steps you want to take between now and year-end to reduce your taxable income.

Some of the action steps you listed or will list on this form may require no cash expenditures on your part, but others will. Work out and list how much cash is required for each of the tax-reducing steps you have proposed. Eliminate the steps for which the necessary funds are not available either from your capital or from borrowing. Then work out and list by how much each of the remaining steps will reduce your taxable income. Total the reductions. Compare that figure with the required reduction you computed at the top of the form to see whether your year-end action steps result in the reduction in taxable income you require. Then put the feasible, desirable tax-saving steps into action as soon as you can. After all the work and thought involved in analyzing your tax situation and targeting the taxable income you desire, you don't want to end up with a lot of splendid ideas but no results.

9

SETTING FINANCIAL OBJECTIVES

The setting of objectives may be the single most important part of financial planning. We tend to live from day to day, with only the haziest notion of where we are going or what we really want out of life. Some social observers have called this "muddling through" or "operating in mediocrity." A TV show calls it "One Day at a Time." Living in that way, we may never have the sense of fulfillment or the variety of experiences we vaguely hoped for, and we may never be in control of our lives or achieve financial security. Through making the effort to focus on what we really want to achieve and do with our lives, we are not only propelled toward those goals, we also gain a sense of purpose and direction.

As you set your financial objectives, you will find and evaluate what trade-offs there are between your short-term and your long-term goals, you will investigate the various alternatives you have for using your financial resources, and then you will decide which ones are the best for you.

Keep in mind that researchers who have studied peak performance in individuals—executives, professionals, athletes, teachers—have observed that the successful ones have one common characteristic: They set goals for themselves. So give these next four forms on your objectives—Forms 16, 17, 18, and 19—some careful thought and set goals you can live by, goals you can achieve with knowledge, effort, commitment, and persistence.

FORM 16—FINANCIAL SECURITY

Item 1 asks you to define financial security, which has different meanings to different people. Some might say, "It is not having to depend on a salary," or "Financial security is $60,000 a year before taxes." Some express it in terms of debt: "I'll feel financially secure when I have no more debts." To others, financial security is a way of life: "Being able to do what I want when I want," or "Not having to think or worry about meeting income needs."

First, write your own definition of financial security. Then try to express it in quantitative, measurable terms that will give you specific targets to reach for.

- What specific annual income would give you financial security? Maybe you would feel financially secure with *earned income* of $50,000, or $75,000, or more than $100,000. Maybe you would rather express financial security in terms of annual *investment income*—having your money work for you so you would be free to pursue your avocational interests more frequently or for longer periods of time.

- What specific net worth are you seeking in order to gain financial security? If you are concerned about having $60,000 of annual investment income, then you will need a certain level of investment assets. For example, if $60,000 will do it and you believe you can realize an 8 percent before-tax return on your investments, you will need investment assets of $750,000 to achieve financial security.

- What specific debt level do you want to accept in order to achieve financial security? Most people we counsel still believe in having relatively little debt when discussing financial security. They may have relatively high debt levels at some stages of their lives in order to finance investments and personal assets, but when they get around to financial security, they are really worried about keeping debt at high levels. For most people, high debt levels mean anxiety and stress that they would rather do without at some point.

Item 2 on Form 16 asks you to determine when you want to achieve financial security, based on your present financial position, earning power, expenditure patterns, and investment strategy. This question may be less difficult to answer than most people initially believe if you use the information you prepared in the first part of this book. For example, if you believe you need $750,000 of investment assets to achieve financial security and your net worth statement, Form 4, currently shows investments of $500,000, you may be able to achieve that goal in the next few years. If, on the other hand, you currently have investment assets of $1.23 and a pack of chewing gum, you may take a long time to achieve your goal without marrying for money or becoming the favorite niece or nephew of that aging, rich uncle.

Item 3, asking what you perceive as the chief obstacles to your financial security, commonly receives one of the following answers: *taxes, inflation, my boss, lack of knowledge, lack of time.* Most of the obstacles people perceive, though, are self-imposed, and therefore can usually be removed by self-management. There is something you can do about your taxes, your inflation rate, your lack of knowledge. You can choose to spend time on financial planning instead of some other activity.

To determine whether your timetable for achieving financial security is realistic or a pipe dream, it is important to do some overall analysis.

- Use the Rule of 72 to determine how many years it will take to double your money. Merely divide 72 by the expected annual after-tax rate of return on your investments. For example, if your expected annual after-tax rate of return is 6 percent, your investments will double in twelve years ($72 \div 6 = 12$). For your investments to double in five years, you will need an annual after-tax rate of return of 14.4 percent ($72 \div 5 = 14.4$).

- Use compound tables such as Tables 9-1, 9-2, 9-3, and 9-4, and the more complete tables in Appendix I.

Table 9-1 allows you to see what a lump sum investment will grow to in various years at varying rates of return. Merely multiply the amount listed for the rate of return and number of years involved by a factor equal to your investment assets divided by 10,000. For example, if you have $100,000 to invest and you want to know what such a lump sum will grow to in fifteen years at 12 percent, you find the amount $54,735 in Table 9-1 and multiply it by 10 ($100,000 ÷ $10,000) to get your answer—$547,350.

Table 9-2 lets you determine what lump-sum investment you need in order to accumulate a targeted investment amount by the end of a specified period. Let's say you want to have $500,000 of investment assets in ten years and believe you could invest your present assets to return 15 percent per year. You would need to invest $123,590 today ($24,718 × $500,000/100,000).

Tables 9-3 and 9-4 show you what an invested amount will grow to at varying rates for varying periods. For example, if you have $1,200 per year to invest (approximately $100 per month), such an investment program will produce $160,000 in 25 years if your investment funds return 12 percent per year. If you were able to invest $2,400 per year ($200 per month) at 15 percent, your investments would grow to $245,864 at the end of 20 years, according to Table 9-3.

Table 9-4 shows how much you have to invest each year for how many years and at what rate in order to get $100,000. For example, if you wanted $100,000 in five years and thought you could get a 10 percent return each year, you would need to invest $14,890 per year.

Obviously, these tables can also be used to see what your investments might be at the end of an expected number of years with an expected rate of return, assuming you invested a lump sum (your present investment assets) and/or an annual amount. For example, if you have $50,000 of investment assets today and can invest another $5,000 per year, your investment assets would be $842,600 at the end of twenty years at a rate of 12 percent. The computation is shown below:

- From Table 9-1:
  $50,000/10,000 × 96,462 = $482,310
- From Table 9-3:
  $5,000/1,200 × 86,463 = $360,290
  $482,310 + $360,290 = $842,600

TABLE 9-1
$10,000 LUMP-SUM INVESTMENT COMPOUNDED ANNUALLY END OF YEAR VALUES

End of Year	6%	8%	10%	12%	15%
5	13,382	14,693	16,105	17,623	20,113
6	14,185	15,868	17,715	19,738	23,130
7	15,036	17,138	19,478	22,016	26,600
8	15,938	18,509	21,435	24,759	30,590
9	16,894	19,990	23,579	27,730	35,178
10	17,908	21,589	25,937	31,058	40,455
15	23,965	31,721	41,772	54,735	81,370
20	32,071	46,609	67,274	96,462	163,665
25	42,918	68,484	108,347	170,000	329,189

TABLE 9-2
RATES OF RETURN AND THE INVESTMENT AMOUNTS REQUIRED TO HAVE $100,000 AVAILABLE AT END OF SPECIFIED PERIOD

Rate of Return	End of Year				
	5	10	15	20	25
6%	74,726	55,839	41,727	31,180	23,300
8%	68,058	46,319	31,524	21,455	14,602
10%	62,092	38,554	23,940	14,864	9,230
12%	56,743	32,197	18,270	10,367	5,882
15%	49,718	24,718	12,289	6,110	3,040

Other than using the Rule of 72 and compound tables, use an inexpensive financial analysis calculator to do the calculations. For less than $40, you can buy some makes of hand-held calculators programmed to do financial analysis. Such calculators have keys for each of the five financial variables we have used in the calculations with the compound tables. These five keys are:

1. PV, or the present value or amount of your investment assets
2. PMT, or the annual amount or payment you can make in your investment program
3. N, or the number of periods (years, months) you expect to invest your money
4. i, or the rate of interest or return you expect to get on your investments
5. FV, or the future value or amount of your investment assets

Using a calculator with these five function keys, you can determine, in a matter of seconds, the answer to investment questions such as:

- If I have $20,000 (PV) in my present investment fund and can put aside $2,400 (PMT) per year to invest, what rate of return (i) do I need to have $500,000 (FV) in 10 years (N)? Answer: 32.88%.
- If financial security for me is $1,000,000 (FV), how long will it take to reach that objective if my present assets are $300,000 and I can set

TABLE 9-3
FUTURE WORTH OF $1,200 INVESTED EACH YEAR AT VARYING RATES COMPOUNDED EACH YEAR

Rate of Return	End of Year				
	5	10	15	20	25
6%	6,764	15,817	27,931	44,143	65,837
8%	7,040	17,384	32,583	54,914	87,727
10%	7,326	19,125	38,127	68,730	118,016
12%	7,623	21,058	44,736	86,463	160,001
15%	8,091	24,364	57,096	122,932	255,352

TABLE 9-4
APPROXIMATE ANNUAL INVESTMENT REQUIRED TO EQUAL $100,000 AT VARYING RATES

Rate of Return	End of Year				
	5	10	15	20	25
6%	16,736	7,157	4,053	2,565	1,720
8%	15,783	6,392	3,410	2,024	1,267
10%	14,890	5,704	2,861	1,587	924
12%	14,055	5,088	2,395	1,239	670
15%	12,898	4,283	1,828	849	409

aside $15,000 a year for investment and can get a 15 percent return on my investment? Answer: a little more than seven years.

FORM 17—INCOME AND EXPENDITURE OBJECTIVES

For most people, what is left of their employment income after paying current expenses is the primary means of accumulating net worth and achieving financial security. Therefore, any increase in employment income without a similar increase in expenditures, or any reduction in expenditures without a similar reduction in employment income, will provide you with that much more money to invest—money that could be working for you to help you reach future goals.

When answering the questions in this form, refer to Form 10—*Analysis of Earned Income and Expenditures* for your current total employment income and expenditures.

To answer item 2, refer to Form 7—*Basic Lifestyle Expenditures.*

To answer item 3, refer to Form 8—*Discretionary Expenditures.*

- When estimating your and your spouse's employment income for the next three years, start with an estimate of an annual percentage increase. For example, maybe you think employment income will increase by 10 percent per year for each of the next three years. Maybe you think next year your income will be the same as last year, but will increase by 10 percent per year for years 2 and 3. Once you have estimated a rate of increase, estimate the amount of employment income for each of the next three years.
- Questions 2 and 3 ask you to evaluate how much you could reduce your present expenditure levels. Such evaluation is important in order to do the following:
  - Determine whether your expenditures are resulting in the quality of life you expect
  - Determine whether your present lifestyle expenditures are using up dollars that are important for future goals
  - Remind you that the best way, from a tax standpoint, to increase amounts available for investment is to reduce your expenditures.

    Every expenditure dollar saved means one whole dollar available for investment. Every additional dollar of employment earnings produces only fifty cents for investing if you are in a 50 percent top tax bracket, or 67 cents if you are in a 33 percent top tax bracket.

- Question 4 gets at your "wish" list. Everybody has one. The items on the list are your dreams—the sleek sports car, the sailboat cutting sharply through the dashing waves, the cobblestone streets of a European village, the entertainment room in your home. If you are married, sit down with your family and discuss a family wish list. Determine what you would like. If you are single, talk to a close friend or advisor about your dreams and get some feedback on your list.

  In developing your list, determine not only what you want but by when. Keep in mind that some goals to be achieved must be done in the near-future. For example, our family wanted to live abroad when our children were aged 14, 13, and 4. If we had waited four or five more years, it would have been very difficult to have such an experience together as a family, considering the demands of college, athletic activities, and peer-group relationships on the older children. We went abroad and it was one of the finest family experiences we have had. So focus on your passion and go for it.

You will use your estimates of income and expenditures in building a summary financial plan in Chapter 15.

FORM 18—EDUCATION AND OTHER SUPPORT OF CHILDREN

Inflation has had a noticeable impact on family expenditures, particularly with regard to the education costs and living expenses of young adults after leaving high school. As a result, most of them now require assistance from their parents to pay for their college tuition and living expenses. Some families also incur, or plan to incur, considerable expenses for sending their children to private elementary or secondary schools.

- If you are planning to send your children to private elementary and secondary schools, be aware that it is expensive and that financial plans should be made well in advance. Good private elementary day schools may cost anywhere from $1,000 to $4,000 per year. Secondary schools run higher. Of course, boarding schools are even more expensive because they also cover room and board.

  Question 1 asks you to estimate for each child the total cost of private education in today's dollars. For example, if your children are ages 9 and 7 and you plan to send them to private secondary schools in six and eight years, respectively, and you estimate the cost for each year to be $5,000 (in today's dollars), the total estimated cost for each child will be $20,000; the total for both children will be $40,000.
- If you are planning to send your children to a college or university, you should begin well in advance to evaluate the potential costs. College education may cost anywhere between $4,000 and $12,000 per year, including room and board, books, and incidentals. Question 2 asks you to estimate the total costs you will provide for each child in today's dollars. For example, if you have two children and plan to help each of them with 80 percent of their college costs for each of

six years (including graduate study), you will have to pay $38,400 for each child if each year of college costs $8,000 in today's dollars ($8,000 × 80% × 6 years); a total of $76,800.

- Obviously, with many U.S. families facing the possibility of significant educational expenditures, plans should be made to set aside funds before the schooling begins. It may be a good idea to start an educational fund for your children when they are very young. Let the power of compounding work over a period of years so that significant funds are available when your children go off to college.

  Question 3 asks you to indicate what funds have been set aside for your children's education. Some families start a savings program for their children; some make annual money gifts to the children and invest the money in high-yielding securities; others set up a trust with a lump-sum fund and let the earnings on the fund accumulate in the trust until the children's education begins. In Chapter 11 we will discuss educational financing techniques and how to get the most after-tax dollars for your children's education.
- Question 4 asks you to estimate what support your children may need apart from education. Some families have a disabled child who needs support. Others are supporting unemployed children or helping their children finance a purchase of a house or condominium.

Again, you will use the information on your objectives for the education and support of your children to build your summary plan in Chapter 15.

FORM 19—RETIREMENT PLANNING

The retirement years are generally referred to as "the golden years"—a time for leisure activities and relaxation after many years of work. They are not likely to be golden, however, unless you have planned how you will use your time, where you will live, and how you will finance your expenses.

U.S. Department of Commerce statistics indicate that few people prepare adequately for retirement, particularly from the financial point of view. Its data indicate that only 5 percent of the population is financially independent at age 65. Of the 95 percent who cannot afford to retire comfortably, 22 percent must continue working; 28 percent depend on public charity, welfare, or Social Security; and 45 percent are dependent on relatives for all or some portion of their retirement support.

We strongly believe a retirement program should be started early in your life—at least ten to fifteen years before you plan to retire. This form asks you some questions about the financial aspects of retirement, such as the age at which you plan to retire, your financial requirements at retirement, and the financial sources available to meet your needs.

You will use the information on Form 19 in Chapter 12, when we ask you to analyze the feasibility of your retirement objectives.

SUMMARY

In this chapter, we have discussed the import of financial objectives and have asked you to determine your objectives for financial security, income and expenditures, education and support of your children, and retirement.

In setting objectives, you have to weigh the trade-offs between short-term and long-term goals (do I take an expensive vacation this year or set aside some funds for my child's college education five years from now?) and identify the issues involved in reaching your goals (to reach my financial security goal, I need to set aside more each year for investment and get a higher return on my assets. I should probably reduce my tax expenditures, get more knowledge about investment alternatives, and monitor my investments more closely).

Once your objectives have been established and your issues identified, you need to take some action. In the chapters that follow, we will discuss investments, educational financing, and retirement, and you will identify what action steps you can take.

10

INVESTMENTS

As you must surely realize by now, the road to financial independence is paved with good investments. You, too, should be able to obtain investment results that are above the average, once you know your investment objectives and take the time to evaluate and monitor your investments.

Broadly speaking, your investments consist of all the means by which you store up assets for the future. These would include your home and your retirement program, which should form a part of your overall investment program and should relate to such other investments as your stocks, bonds, and income-producing real estate.

This chapter will guide you to formulate an investment program of your own that is specifically geared to your age, responsibilities, and objectives, as well as your expendable income and your taxes.

INVESTMENT OBJECTIVES

What are the important factors in making an investment decision? Most people answer this very quickly by saying, "I want my investments to give me a good return." Then we say, "Okay, but what kind of return are you looking for?" Some reply, "A steady return." Some say, "The kind I don't have to watch and worry about." Others say, "The highest return I can get for the risk I am willing to take."

When you analyze these and other answers, you find the following concerns:

- Safety of principal
- Hedge against inflation
- Future income
- Current income
- Liquidity of the investment
- Marketability of the investment
- Ease of management

We will now investigate these objectives and, inasmuch as some are antithetical to others, we will consider them in pairs.

SAFETY OF PRINCIPAL VERSUS HEDGE AGAINST INFLATION

If your overriding concern is to keep a sum of money intact for a specific purpose, such as a down payment on a house, you might invest in a regular savings account, a savings certificate, or a money market fund, since these will pretty much guarantee that you can get your principal back when you need it. Liquidity and safety of principal are usually the main considerations when you invest in such funds. You should be aware, however, that in inflationary periods the longer you hold an investment that provides the safety of principal you get with something like a savings account, the more you will lose in purchasing power. As the inflation rate goes up, so the purchasing power of your funds goes down. Thus, investments that are safe with regard to return of principal are not a good hedge against inflation.

For those who want a return that will keep up with inflation, the primary objective should be safety of purchasing power, not safety of principal. In years of high inflation, safety of purchasing power has usually been achieved by investment alternatives that are not commonly chosen by Americans. Traditionally, Americans have invested in five areas: savings accounts, money market instruments, common stocks, bonds, and real estate. In the ten-year period from 1972 to 1982, real estate was the only traditional type of investment that brought a rate of return greater than the rate of inflation as measured by the Consumer Price Index. In Table 10-1, you can see how stocks, bonds, and real estate (farmland, housing) performed in relation to the Consumer Price Index and to some other, less traditional investment categories.

TABLE 10-1
INVESTMENT PERFORMANCE

The following data show the *annual* returns for investment categories for the ten years ended June 1, 1983, as well as the rise in the Consumer Price Index. For example, the Consumer Price Index (the inflation rate) increased by an average of 8.5 percent *per year* during this ten-year period. Gold increased in value 15.5 percent per year during the ten-year period. Therefore, an investor in gold during the ten-year period stayed well ahead of inflation.

Investment Category	Annual Return
U.S. Coins	25.7%
Oil	25.4
U.S. Stamps	19.2
Silver	17.3
Gold	15.5
Farmland	11.7
Diamonds	10.3
Treasury Bills	10.1
Housing	9.2
Consumer Price Index	8.5
Old Masters	8.4
Stocks	7.5
Bonds	6.6
Chinese Ceramics	4.0
Foreign Exchange	1.4

Source: Salomon Brothers Inc.

CURRENT INCOME VERSUS FUTURE APPRECIATION

Some people, particularly those who have retired or are widowed may regard current income as their primary investment objective. Such current income could take the form of interest on savings accounts or bonds, or dividends from common or preferred stock, or rent from income-producing real estate. In assessing current income from investments, the two terms commonly used are *current return* and *current yield*. Current return is usually expressed in dollars; yield is expressed as a percentage. Thus, the current return on a $1,000 savings account with a yield of 5 percent is $50. With common stock, the current return is the dollar amount of your dividend per share, while the current yield shows the dividend received as a percentage of the current price of the stock. So with a dividend of $1 per share and a stock price of $15, the current yield would be 1 divided by 15, or 6.67 percent.

Some investors have both safety of principal and current income as their investment objectives. They are the investors who need this investment income to cover their living expenses and cannot risk the loss of their principal. As a rule, this would apply to people who are unemployed or fear unemployment in the near future, those about to take a substantial reduction in employment income, and those in or near retirement.

For people whose employment income covers their lifestyle expenditures and people of substantial net worth, the *future return* or *appreciation* of their investments will be their main concern. Though they may not need further current income, they may want to add to their capital base through appreciation in order to meet future expenditures such as the costs of education or retirement. Known as *growth investments* or *capital gain investments*, these investments with a potential for appreciation will usually provide little or no current income.

Regarding your return on investment, there are three points to keep in mind. The first is *total return*. Investments—stocks and income-producing real estate, for instance—may result in appreciation as well as current income. Their total return is the sum you get from adding their current yield to their appreciation yield. Thus, a stock that had a 6 percent dividend yield and an appreciation of 5 percent in the last year had a total return of 11 percent for the year.

The second point to bear in mind is the investment's *after-tax return*. Current income (other than interest on municipal bonds) is taxed like ordinary earned income, whereas 60 percent of a long-term capital gain (the profit from selling capital assets held for more than one year) is exempt from taxation. Thus, total after-tax return is an important measure of investments.

The third point to consider is the *certainty of return* on your investment. With investments that solely or primarily provide current income, you can usually be quite certain of receiving this current income. Bonds, for instance, carry contractual agreements to pay their interest when due. Dividends are not contractually fixed, but are decided upon by the company's board of directors, who increase or decrease them according to the company's financial situation. The future capital appreciation of an investment is not a certainty. For that type of investment, the potential total return should therefore be much higher than for investments made to generate current income. Thus, the higher the potential of losing all or some portion of your invested capital, the higher should be the potential return.

LIQUIDITY

Liquidity refers to the ease and impunity with which you can convert an investment into cash. If you might need the money you invested to take care of emergencies or to avail yourself of some other investment opportunities, liquidity can be very important.

Regular savings accounts and money market investments provide great liquidity, and so do common stocks and the bonds of large companies. When you invest in smaller companies, you have less liquidity or marketability, because there are fewer shares of such stocks or bonds and fewer people interested in such investments.

Real estate is another example of a nonliquid investment. You may have to wait for months before you find a buyer who is willing to buy the property at your asking price, and then it will take additional time to close the transaction and get your cash out. Furthermore, your purchaser may not be able to give you the entire amount in a lump-sum payment, only in installments payable over several years.

Typically, a higher liquidity is yoked to a lower return. If you want high returns, be prepared to accept low liquidity.

EASE OF MANAGEMENT

There are a lot of people who say, "Investments and financial matters are not the most important things in my life, and I don't want to spend much time watching or worrying over them." For such people, ease of management is an important investment objective. If they don't want to spend much time managing their investments, they should either pay someone like an investment advisor, a bank, or a mutual fund to manage their investments, or they should choose the kind of investments that demand little involvement or judgment: savings accounts, savings certificates, and bonds held to maturity. What they need to avoid are investments that are subject to large and rapid price fluctuations.

Table 10-2 summarizes the investment characteristics we have been discussing.

RISK AND RETURN

Risk and *return* occur in tandem. Risk can be defined as the probability of loss in the future. Loss usually means partial loss of your invested capital, not total loss, although some investments may result in total loss. For example, if you are investing in an exploratory oil well deal and the drillers do not find oil, your investment is a total loss. A totally new company with unproven products has a much higher probability of going bankrupt in the near future than a company with a proven record of profitability in a stable industry.

With most investments, the probability of losing all of your investment capital in the foreseeable future is relatively low. However, the probability of losing some portion of your investment—say 20 percent—may be very high with such investments as common stock in a company in a volatile industry, or with real estate in a depressed market.

If you are prepared to accept greater risks, you have the chance of getting higher returns. The only way to attract investors to an enterprise with a high probability of loss is to offer them the possibility of a high return. Conversely, a low-risk enterprise attracts investors readily and therefore does not have to offer investors a chance of high return.

RISK OF PURCHASING POWER

As you know to your sorrow, high inflation results in reduced purchasing power of your dollar. In consequence, if you buy a four-year savings certificate and inflation increases significantly, the principal and interest that are returned to you will have less purchasing power than the dollars you paid for it four years ago. Even though such investments are good with regard to

TABLE 10-2
INVESTMENT OBJECTIVES

Type of Investment	Safety of Principal in Constant Dollars	Hedge Against Inflation	Current Income	Future Appreciation	Liquidity	Ease of Management
Regular savings accounts	Excellent	Not very good	Fixed; very steady but low rate	None	Excellent	Very easy
Money market investments (Treasury bills, money certificates, money market funds)	Good to excellent	Not very good	Fixed; very steady; rate near inflation rate	Generally none	Very good	Easy
Common stocks						
Income stocks	Fair	Fair	Relatively fixed; rate near inflation rate	Some	Good	Easy
Growth stocks	Moderate to poor	Generally good	Variable; low rate	Moderate to great	Good	Difficult
Bonds (high-quality corporate and government issues)	Good to excellent	Not very good	Fixed; very steady; rate near inflation rate	Generally none except discounted bonds	Good	Fairly easy
Mutual funds (common stocks)	Fair to poor	Variable but generally good	Variable	Moderate to great	Good	Easy
Real estate (income producing, other than residence)	Generally good	Generally good	Variable	Moderate to great	Relatively poor	Moderate to difficult
Precious metals (gold, silver)	Fair to poor	Generally good	None	Moderate to great	Good	Difficult

safety of principal, they are not good with regard to maintaining your purchasing power.

In recent years of high inflation, fixed-return investments in savings accounts, savings certificates, insurance policies, and bonds have conferred a substantial loss of purchasing power on those who invested in them.

Investments with a growth potential will usually offer better protection in periods of inflation. If you refer to Table 10-2 once again, you will see that real estate and growth stocks do relatively well in periods of inflation. During periods of declining prices and severe recession, fixed-return investments become profitable, while variable-return investments lose in value. During the 1930s, a period of economic depression, people who owned real estate and common stocks watched the value of their investments decline steeply as rents, corporate profits, and dividends declined.

FINANCIAL RISKS

Financial risk, also called business risk, is the possibility that unfavorable business conditions may reduce the expected returns from an investment. This might happen if the company you have invested in has a competitor who starts to produce a better product or finds a cheaper method of producing the same product, thereby reducing the earning potential of the company in which you have invested. It could happen if a tenants'-rights movement leads to the imposition of rent control in an apartment building that you own, and thereby makes it a less attractive proposition for potential buyers. It could also be brought about by environmental protection laws that increase the operating costs of a company whose shares you hold.

INTEREST RATE RISK

This risk is usually associated with fixed-return investments such as bonds. What you risk here is a decline in the market value of your investment due to a new and higher rate of return on comparable new investments.

As an example, take some bonds that AT&T issued in November 1972 and offered at 7⅛ percent annual interest, or $71.25 per $1,000 bond. In September 1983, these bonds, which mature in the year 2003, were selling for $630. AT&T is a financially sound company; so why did the price for these high-quality bonds go down by 37 percent? The reason is that between 1972 and 1983 the interest rates for bonds of similar quality and maturity had risen from 7⅛ percent to more than 11 percent.

If you had purchased those AT&T bonds in 1972 and sold them in September 1983, you would have suffered a capital loss of $370 for every $1,000 bond you held. You would have suffered the adverse effects of interest rate risk, because investors will not pay $1,000 for a bond that earns $71.25 a year when they can buy another bond of comparable quality and maturing date that pays them over $110 a year. By the same token, when interest rates have fallen, the bonds you bought before the fall will have risen in market value.

Real estate, too, is affected by interest levels. For example, when interest rates rose dramatically in the early 1980s, it became much more difficult for buyers to obtain financing at a rate they could afford. As a result, the housing market declined, and many a seller had to offer his house on contract at a lower interest rate or had to reduce the price of the house in order to make a sale.

MARKET RISK

Volatility in investment prices that is due to changes in "market psychology" or investors' attitudes is known as market risk. Such price fluctuations may affect the whole securities market—as was the case in the Depression and again in early 1975 when stock prices, as measured by widely used indexes, dropped by 50 percent. Price fluctuations may affect a particular industry or a particular security regardless of the financial ability of a particular company to pay the promised or expected investment returns. For example, in late 1982, one regional commercial bank was beset by substantial loan losses. Other regional banks in the area that were not experiencing unusual loan losses also experienced a drop in their stock prices. Their financial situation had not changed at all, but apparently investors decided to shy away from all regional banks in that area.

Price fluctuations give rise to buying and selling opportunities. For example, when the stock market in general is depressed because investors' attitudes are sour toward the market, buying opportunities in general for stocks may be very good. Also, when an individual stock is depressed but its fundamentals are still strong (our regional banks example), the buying opportunity may be very good. On the other hand, when the market in general has experienced a significant increase in prices and investor attitudes are favorable, look around, evaluate the price increases in the securities you hold, and contemplate selling.

LEVERAGE AND RISK

Leverage denotes the borrowed money you invest together with your own funds in order to get a higher return on your money. When leverage works in your favor, it is great; but when leverage works against you, it can be disastrous.

To illustrate how leverage works, let's use a common leverage investment like real estate. Assume you buy a condominium for $60,000 and finance it with a $15,000 down payment and a $45,000 mortgage. After three years, you decide to sell the condominium and get $65,000 for it. You now have a gain of roughly 33 percent—a $5,000 gain on your $15,000 investment. If the $60,000 you invested had all been your own money, your gain on the sale would only be about 8 percent—$5,000 on your investment of $60,000.

Conversely, with leverage you can lose money faster than without it when prices decline. Assume, for example, that after three years your leveraged $60,000 had dropped in price to $55,000. By selling it now, you would suffer a loss of 33 percent—a $5,000 loss on your $15,000 investment. Without leverage, your loss would be only 8 percent—a $5,000 loss on your $60,000 investment.

Using leverage in buying securities is called "buying on margin." When you buy on margin, you pay only a portion of the total cost, and your broker extends credit to you on the balance—and charges a monthly interest rate.

The reason for buying on margin is capital appreciation. If you choose a stock that you think will increase in price fairly rapidly, you may make more profit by buying a greater number of shares on margin than by buying a smaller number for cash—if the stock goes up in price. Table 10-3 shows the rate of return (or loss) you will reap, with and without using margin, when the stock price increases (or decreases). In our example, we assumed the stock was held for one year and we ignored brokerage commissions and the effect of taxes. The example shows that by trading on margin, an investor would realize 40 percent more return than would be realized through a cash transaction (without margin). But leverage works both ways. If the stock declined to $40 per share, as shown in the example, an investor would have incurred 160 percent more loss using margin.

The amount the investor has to put up when buying stock on the margin is determined by the board of governors of the Federal Reserve System and is binding on all brokers. The present margin requirement is 50 percent. The New York Stock Exchange requires that an investor must have at least $2,000

TABLE 10-3
INVESTMENT RETURNS (OR LOSSES) BUYING ON MARGIN

	With Margin	Without Margin
Dollars Invested		
Your funds	$ 5,000	$ 5,000
Broker's funds	5,000	0
Total purchases (per share price $50)	$10,000 (200 shares)	$ 5,000 (100 shares)
1. Sale of stock for $60 per share		
Gross proceeds	$12,000	$ 6,000
Less repayment of borrowed funds	(5,000)	0
Less interest on borrowed funds at 12%	(600)	0
Net proceeds after repayment of borrowed funds	$ 6,400	$ 6,000
Return of original dollars invested	5,000	5,000
Net profit (or loss)	$ 1,400	$ 1,000
Return on your investment	$ 1,400 ÷ $5,000 = 28%	$ 1,000 ÷ $5,000 = 20%
2. Sale of stock for $40 per share		
Gross proceeds	$ 8,000	$ 4,000
Less repayment of borrowed funds	(5,000)	0
Less interest on borrowed funds at 12%	(600)	0
Net proceeds after repayment of borrowed funds	$ 2,400	$ 4,000
Return of original dollars invested	5,000	5,000
Net profit (or loss)	$(2,600)	$(1,000)
Return on your investment	$(2,600) ÷ $5,000 = (52%)	$(1,000) ÷ $5,000 = (20%)

in his or her account to enter into a new margin trade. Once you have bought stock on the margin, the New York Stock Exchange requires that the equity in your account must always represent at least 25 percent of the market value of your stock. (Equity is determined by subtracting from the current market value of your stocks the amount you have borrowed from the broker.)

Using our example in Table 10-3, the account of an investor who buys 200 shares at $50 would show the following:

Market Value	$10,000
Debit Balance (amount owed the broker)	(5,000)
Equity	$ 5,000

The investor's equity of $5,000 in the foregoing example above is in excess of the New York Stock Exchange requirement of $2,500 (25 percent of current value of stocks, or $10,000). If the price of the stock declines, the investor's equity declines proportionately. If the decline continued, the investor's equity would be at or below the New York Stock Exchange minimum requirement, and the investor would have to deposit additional funds in the margin account.

MINIMIZING RISK

Eventually, you will have to choose between the various investment alternatives available to you and judge the risk inherent in each type of investment. You will have to decide what investment risks you are willing to take. If you are in your twenties, for example, and trying to save enough money for a down payment on a condominium, you will probably want to avoid investments with high financial and market risks. If, on the other hand, you have already bought your own house and are earning more than your current expenditures, and you have money put away for emergencies, then you may be quite willing to accept high financial and market risks in hopes of getting a high return.

As your needs and economic status change, so will your investment objectives and the risks you are ready to take. Regardless of such changes, however, good investment strategy will dictate that you minimize overall risks through knowledge and diversification.

As a rule, the people who are successful investors know more than the average person about specific investments, about particular types of industries, about economic cycles, and about diverse factors of the economy. If you understand an investment opportunity and study its future potential, you should be able to reduce your risks substantially.

You will minimize risk by diversifying your investments so that they will not all be open to the same risks. Then, for example, if rising inflation and high interest rates decrease the value of your bonds, they will also increase the returns on your money market funds. You spread your risk by having various types of investments.

FORM 20—INVESTMENT OBJECTIVES

Now that you have an overview of the various types of investment objectives and risks, you can evaluate the relative importance that each of the listed investment objectives has for you. Once you have forced yourself to become clear about your priorities, you will have a sound basis for your investment decisions. On Form 20 are listed the objectives we discussed earlier in the chapter.

Figure 10-1 is an example for a couple in their mid-forties with significant employment income. They are primarily concerned about investments with growth potential and tax advantages that do not require a lot of time and effort to manage. They are also interested in using leverage and having diversification in their investment program. They are not very concerned about safety, liquidity, and current income.

FORM 21—REVIEW OF YOUR PRESENT INVESTMENTS

The next step in your investment analysis is to review your present investments using Form 21. Before you complete this form, it might be helpful to look at the example in Figure 10-2 for the couple whose investment objectives are shown in Figure 10-1. Once you have completed Form 21, you can evaluate your present investments in terms of your objectives and see what changes should be considered.

FIGURE 10-1

File under INVESTMENT STRATEGY   Date: May 5

FORM 20 INVESTMENT OBJECTIVES

Indicate the relative importance you attribute to the following considerations by placing the appropriate number after each statement.

NOT IMPORTANT -- 1
MARGINALLY IMPORTANT -- 2
REASONABLY IMPORTANT -- 3
DEFINITELY IMPORTANT -- 4
MOST IMPORTANT -- 5

Diversification	How important is it for you to hedge against big losses by spreading your risks?	3
Liquidity	How important is it that you have cash available for emergencies or investment opportunities?	2
Safety	If we went into a deep economic depression, how important would it be for you to sell your investments at about the price you paid for them?	2
Current Income	How important is it that you get maximum income from your investments this year and next?	1
Future Appreciation	How important is it that your investment dollars keep pace with inflation or do better than inflation?	5
Tax Advantage	How important is it that you get all the tax relief that may be available to you?	4
Leverage	How important is it for you to use borrowed money in hopes of reaping a higher return on your investment?	3
Ease of Management	How important is it for you to have investments you do not have to watch or worry about?	4

FIGURE 10-2

File under INVESTMENT STRATEGY Date: May 6

FORM 21 REVIEW OF YOUR PRESENT INVESTMENTS

TYPE OF ASSET	CURRENT VALUE	% OF TOTAL	INVESTMENT OBJECTIVES	CURRENT INCOME	APPR'N (LOSS)	ANNUAL RATE OF RETURN
Savings	$9,100	3%	Liquidity & Safety	5%	—	5%
Money Market Funds	24,400	10%	Liquidity & Safety	10%	—	10%
Stocks	67,200	27%	Growth	5%	10%	15%
Bonds	33,200	13%	Tax-free income	7%	8.4%	15.4%
Real Estate	90,000	36%	Tax-savings, growth	5%	10.3%	15.3%
Limited partnership in oil	20,000	8%	Tax-savings, growth	–	Too early to tell	–
IRA	8,500	3%	Tax-deferred growth	12%	—	12%
TOTAL	$252,400	100%				

- In the first column, list all the types of investment that make up the total of your liquid and investment assets on your net worth statement (Form 4).
- In the second column, enter the current value of each investment. The totals should agree with the amounts shown on your net worth statement (Form 4). In our example, total liquid assets are $33,500; other investments are $218,900; total investments are $252,400.
- In the third column, determine how diversified your present investment program is by dividing the amount of each investment by the total amount of your investments. In our example, real estate of $90,000 is 36 percent of the total investments of $252,400.
- In the fourth column, list the investment objectives shown on Form 20 that each of your investments is designed to accomplish.
- Next, compute each investment's current yield before taxes as a percentage by dividing the income you received from it in the last year by the current value as listed in column 2.
- For those investments that had growth in value or a loss in value, enter the estimated annual percentage of gain or loss in column 6 using the following simple formula: [Current value (in column 2) minus purchase price] ÷ [the number of years you have owned the asset]. This formula is a simple way to approximate annual gain or loss. There are other, more sophisticated ways to compute the annual gain or loss in value, and if you know one, use it, by all means.
- To compute the total annual return for each investment, add the percentages in columns 5 and 6.

Now that you have completed Form 21, you are in a position to evaluate your present investments in light of your objectives. The data on your form should tell you a lot about your present investment behavior and is the starting point for making any changes in your investments.

1. How important is diversification? Look at the percentages in column 3. If a particular investment is more than 30 percent of the total, you might want to consider further diversification. In our example in Figure 10-2, one of the seven investment categories is more than 30 percent of the total.
2. How important is liquidity? Look at the total of your liquid assets and compare it to your employment income. If it is more than 50 percent of your employment income, you probably have too much liquidity. In our example, the liquid assets of $33,500 represent about 40 percent of employment income.
3. How important are safety and current income? These two objectives are closely related. Add up the current values of those investments for which you listed safety and current income as objectives under column 4. If these objectives are very important, the current values of investments providing safety and current income should exceed 70 percent of the total investment assets.
4. How important is growth? Add up the current values of those investments for which you listed future appreciation (inflation hedge)

as an objective. If appreciation is very important to you, the current values of investments providing appreciation should exceed 70 percent of the total investment assets. In our example in Figure 10-2, those investments for which appreciation is listed as one of the objectives comprise 74 percent of the total.

5. What about tax shelter? Often an investor interested in appreciation is also interested in tax-saving investments. If tax shelter is important, evaluate those investments in which tax advantage is a factor—real estate, oil and gas, equipment leasing, and retirement funds. If saving taxes is important to you, probably at least 40 to 50 percent of your investment funds should be invested in tax-advantaged investments. In our example in Figure 10-2, those investments for which tax advantage is an objective comprise 60 percent of the total.
6. What about leverage? Are you interested in using borrowed money to make money? If so, analyze your investments to see to what extent you are using borrowed funds. Leverage is frequently used in investing in real estate, stocks, and bonds, where growth is a primary objective.
7. What about ease of management? If you believe it is important for professionals to assist you in selecting and managing your investments, then many of your investments should be made with the advice of investment counselors, or purchased through mutual funds or limited partnerships. If you want to spend your time managing your own investments or if you are interested primarily in safety and current income and can easily find investments providing such objectives, then select and manage your investments yourself.

RATE OF RETURN ANALYSIS

In column 7 of Form 21, you should have entered the total annual rate of return before taxes that you achieved on each of your investments. How have you done? One measure of performance is inflation. Did you stay ahead of last year's increase in the Consumer Price Index (a widely used measure of inflation) in each of your investments? If not, which ones lagged behind inflation? Does it concern you to have some investments not keeping up with inflation?

Another measure of performance is the Salomon Brothers index in Table 10-1. How well did your stocks, bonds, real estate, and other investments compare with the average rate of return for similar investments listed in Table 10-1?

You should evaluate your total rate of return against some commonly used measures of performance to see how your present investment program stacks up.

After you have completed the analysis of your present investments, you are ready to evaluate investment alternatives and consider changes in your present investment strategy.

ALLOCATION OF INVESTMENT DOLLARS

There are many investments to which you can allocate your investment funds, but the best way is to allocate your funds according to investment objectives appropriate for you. What is appropriate is related to stages in your lifetime. Normally, safety, liquidity, and current income are important when you are young and interested in acquiring a car, furnishings, a home. As your employment income increases and you have additional funds for investment, growth and tax savings become of primary importance. As you approach retirement, safety and current income along with some inflation hedge usually become the important investment objectives.

Because of the large number of variables involved, such as health, employment stability, divorce, and inheritances, it is important to individualize an investment strategy, usually with the help of someone who can take an informed, unbiased view of your financial situation and objectives. With the information on Form 21, the independent advisor can review your present program and help you allocate your investment funds to meet your objectives.

The following guidelines can help you develop an investment plan that is appropriate for your particular stage in life.

BEFORE MARRIAGE

As a financial stage in your life, this period begins with the first paycheck you receive in your first full-time job, and it lasts until you acquire family responsibilities. You may have a student loan to repay, but apart from that, you can probably do as you please with what is left after you've paid for your living expenses.

One of the best investments at this stage is in additional education or self-improvement programs that will raise your professional prospects and your earning potential. This calls for some extra effort, of course, and takes up some of your precious spare time; but it pays off very handsomely, as a rule.

It is also sensible at this stage to establish a cash reserve in a savings account. This should be primarily for emergencies; but it can also help one over the common discomfort of being high and dry on Thursday and standing in a huge line at the bank on Friday.

Do not let anyone persuade you to buy life insurance at this stage in your life. You do not need it unless you are supporting someone other than yourself.

If, like many young people nowadays, you are making quite a lot of money, and if you can keep your expenditures fairly low, you may be able to save substantial amounts that you can put into long-term investments. Given a reasonable housing market, you might use them to start acquiring a house or condominium of your own. Such an investment has great tax advantages, and in recent years has also been an excellent hedge against inflation.

In addition to this, or as an alternative, you could look for investments with a potential for growth. A growth-oriented mutual fund might be your best investment of this type, since it allows you to diversify even when you do not have a lot of capital to invest. It is, moreover, managed for you, which is important to you at this stage in your life, when you should be spending your time and energy promoting your career prospects.

BEFORE YOU HAVE CHILDREN

In our current social environment, it has become quite common for young couples to wait several years before they have children, or to decide not to have any children at all. With both spouses working, you have the income and opportunity to build up your net worth before you start to assume financial responsibility for children. Insurance is not a big factor yet, since there is little need for such protection when both spouses are working and the survivor can continue to work after the death of his or her spouse.

If the couple can keep their committed expenses at a reasonable level, then significant sums may be available for an investment program. Of course, in the early years of marriage, there may be tremendous pressure to spend money on furnishings for a house or apartment, to have two cars if both spouses are working, and to buy labor-saving appliances because both spouses go out to work. Nonetheless, one should start on some careful budgeting during this period in order to ensure that funds are set aside for investment.

BEFORE YOUR CHILDREN ARE IN COLLEGE

From the time that your first child arrives to the time that your youngest child has become self-supporting, financial considerations will have a high order of importance. The first and most compelling aspect of financial planning then will be the protection of the spouse and children in case the primary wage earner should die, and this protection will have to be increased as the size of the family increases. Your need for life insurance should be analyzed carefully during this period, to determine the length of time for which insurance will be needed and how to obtain that coverage in the most economical way.

Aside from that, this is a time for living—a time when spending money may be the best way of using it. There are the obvious needs for additional clothing, housing, and food, which raise your basic committed expenses. There is also a need for vacations and travel, and maybe for private school fees as well.

Fortunately, your income, too, is likely to go up quite a lot in this period, and therefore tax planning will become a critical aspect of your overall financial planning. And if your spouse is also working, tax planning will be much more critical. If your spouse has been primarily a homemaker, he or she may decide to enter or return to the job market when the children begin school. But before you become a two-income family, there may be some education expenditures if the non-working spouse needs to prepare for a career change.

The financing of children's college costs is something that parents should start to consider a great many years ahead of time. No matter how you finance these costs (the options that have some tax advantages will be discussed in Chapter 11), you will need to have fairly substantial funds available as your children reach college age.

WHEN YOUR CHILDREN NO LONGER REQUIRE SUPPORT

The time when your earning power is at its highest will usually start when your children's education has been completed and you and your spouse are in your late forties or early fifties (maybe even the sixties for couples who delayed childbearing). That time should be used to establish your retirement income. Once your children need little or no financial support, your committed expenses decline, and you will have funds to invest in income-producing assets. You may also be able to spend more time managing your investments, which usually means that you can accept higher risks.

At this stage, you should review your life insurance. Taking your total resources into consideration, you may find that your need for insurance has become minimal. If so, the money you save by reducing or even eliminating insurance premiums can be used to build up your retirement fund.

As you get close to retirement, your investment strategy can still be aimed at building capital, but risk should be viewed as a more negative factor than it was in the earlier stages of your life. You may now want to start shifting your capital to investments that will provide income during retirement and will also provide a hedge against inflation. At this point, it will probably be advisable to get financial counseling to help you develop an effective investment strategy and assess the tax aspects of the various ways you might be paid your retirement funds.

RETIREMENT A comfortable income during retirement is one of the primary goals of financial planning and investment decisions. Financial independence during retirement is the result of planning and self-discipline in the earlier stages in one's life. For most people, it requires an early start, investments suitable to the various stages in one's life, an intelligent compromise between too much and too little insurance, and a great deal of determination.

It would be correct to conclude from the foregoing discussion that your investment objectives will and should change as your life situation changes. One thing that will not change is the need to keep your objectives clearly in mind as you formulate your investment strategies and make your investment decisions.

INVESTMENT MIX

An investment program has to be related to the major periods of a planner's lifetime. In Table 10-4 we have provided some guidance as to how one might allocate investment funds in different periods of a lifetime to reflect changing investment objectives. As the table indicates, the need for safety and current income is usually greater in one's twenties and sixties than in one's thirties and forties. Also, the table reflects only selected investments—four traditional ones, and precious metals, which have become more important as the country has experienced high levels of inflation.

ASSESSING YOUR INVESTMENT STRATEGY

Just as the different stages in your life should be reflected in your investment strategies, so there are some specific events—a new child, a higher-paying job, a large bonus, an inheritance, a large capital gain, a higher tax bracket, a change in the tax laws—that may call for modification of your investment strategy. Given such specific events as well as the overall changes, it is im-

TABLE 10-4
SUGGESTED INVESTMENT MIX AMONG SELECTED INVESTMENTS

	ALLOCATION IN PERCENTAGES			
Age	**Liquidity (Savings and Money Market Investments)**	**Current Income (Bonds, Low-Leverage Real Estate)**	**Growth (Common Stocks, Leveraged Real Estate)**	**Purchasing Power Hedge (Precious Metals)**
20s	40-50%	20-30%	20-35%	5-10%
30s	10-20	10-20	60-80	10-15
40s	5-10	10-15	70-90	10-15
50s	5-10	15-20	55-70	10-15
60s	20-30	20-30	25-40	5-10

perative that once, or better twice, a year you reassess your status, your investment objectives, and your investment strategy. We also recommend a minor review monthly or quarterly, or whenever there has been some change that will have financial consequences.

FORM 22—YOUR INVESTMENT STRATEGY

We strongly believe that you will achieve the best investment results by setting specific investment goals and then following an investment program that is designed to accomplish your goals.

On Form 20, you assessed your current investment objectives. You then completed Form 21—*Review of Your Present Investments*. Now it is time for you to select from among your objectives those that will be the most important to you over the next three years. When that is clear to you, determine what changes you want to make in your present investment position.

- The first step in formulating your investment strategy is to review Form 20—*Investment Objectives* and enter those objectives most important for you during the next three years under question 1 on Form 22.
- Next, enter your assumption for the inflation rate during the next three years. One of the measures of performance you should consider in targeting an overall return on your investments is the inflation rate.
- In light of your assumption for inflation and your past investment performance, enter your target overall annual return for the next three years under question 3 on Form 22. Be realistic in setting this target return; take into consideration your objectives and the time and effort you will devote to your investments.
- Under question 4, list the specific changes, if any, you want to make in your present investments. If you desire a higher return than you are presently achieving, you may have to reallocate some investment funds presently in safe, liquid investments to investments with greater growth potential.
- Another important factor in your investment program is to determine what annual amount you can set aside from your current employment income during each of the next three years. For example, you and your spouse may plan to set aside $4,000 a year for investment in an IRA. Or you may be planning to set aside $5,000 a year for an investment in a limited real estate partnership. Try to set a goal for investing some amount of your employment income each year and enter that amount under question 5.
- Under question 6, list those investments you will make with the funds you have identified under question 5. These investments should be related to your objectives as well.

Figure 10-3 illustrates a completed Form 22 for the mid-life couple we used as an example in Figures 10-1 and 10-2.

FIGURE 10-3

File under INVESTMENT STRATEGY Date: May 7

FORM 22 YOUR INVESTMENT STRATEGY

1 What investment objectives (see Form 20) will be most important for you during the next three years?

Growth, tax shelter

2 What is your assumption for the inflation rate during the next three years? 6-8%

3 What overall annual pre-tax return on your investments do you want to achieve in the next three years? 15%

4 What specific changes do you have to make in your present investments to achieve your objectives and overall rate of return in the next three years?

Decrease real estate investments to about 30% of total investments

5 What annual amount do you believe you can set aside for investment during the next three years? Very little except through tax savings and investment income of approximately $10,000

6 What investments will you make with your additional investment dollars?

Growth stocks, precious metals

11

EDUCATIONAL FINANCING

Education is a very special investment. It can introduce one to an entirely new way of looking at things. It can open up new directions and options in life. It can be a rare period of unencumbered time to pursue ideas for their own sake, to reflect, and to philosophize; and like many other special investments, it requires significant financial resources.

Although the most important considerations in choosing a school program are educational, there are financial considerations also, and these have become a matter of concern for a great many families. Educational expenditures are no longer confined to four years of college. Many families have children attending private preschools, elementary schools, and secondary schools, where tuition and fees may approach or exceed $5,000 a year per child. On the other side of undergraduate school, there may also be masters' and doctoral programs that require additional years of funding.

In this chapter, we will discuss the costs of education and how to meet them. We will focus on college costs, but much of this discussion will also be applicable to graduate and private secondary schools. Part of this chapter is a summary of material contained in *The College Cost Book 1982-1983*, which is an excellent reference source. It is published by the College Entrance Examination Board, and can be ordered from your local bookstore or from College Board of Publication Orders, Box 2815, Princeton, New Jersey 08541.

HOW MUCH WILL COLLEGE COST?

Typically, college costs consist of the following major items:

- Tuition and fees
- Books and supplies
- Room and board
- Transportation
- Personal expenses

At private colleges, tuition and fees are usually the largest component of education costs. At state or city colleges that is usually not so, at least not for the students who qualify as residents of the state in which the college is located.

The costs of books and supplies do not vary much from one college to the next. However, certain fields of study, such as engineering and the physical sciences, will generally require more expensive books and supplies than other fields of study.

Room and board vary considerably. For students who live at home and commute to school, room and board will be considerably less than for students who live on or near campus. For students who do not live at home, the costs vary with the type of residence chosen, which might be a dormitory on campus, a fraternity or sorority house, or a privately owned apartment or rooming house.

Transportation expenses for students who attend school a great distance from home are often considerable at the beginning and end of an academic year or term, while students who commute will have small daily transportation expenses.

Personal expenses include such items as laundry, toiletries, recreation, health insurance, and furnishings for the student's "home away from home."

The most accurate information about the cost of a particular school can be found, of course, in the school's admissions office. You can, however, get a rough idea of the costs from Table 11-1, which comes from *The College*

TABLE 11-1
STUDENT'S MEAN EXPENSES
ACADEMIC YEAR 1982-1983

RESIDENT STUDENTS

	TWO-YEAR		FOUR-YEAR	
	Public	**Private**	**Public**	**Private**
Tuition and Fees	$ 595	$2,486	$ 979	$4,021
Books and Supplies	262	295	279	298
Room and Board	1,748	2,077	2,087	2,226
Personal Expenses	629	615	714	604
Transportation	328	278	329	326
Total Expenses	$3,562	$5,751	$4,388	$7,475

COMMUTER STUDENTS

	TWO-YEAR		FOUR-YEAR	
	Public	**Private**	**Public**	**Private**
Tuition and Fees	$ 595	$2,486	$ 979	$4,021
Books and Supplies	262	295	279	298
Room and Board	1,057	1,023	1,038	1,118
Personal Expenses	643	640	673	625
Transportation	619	498	570	519
Total Expenses	$3,176	$4,942	$3,539	$6,581

Source: The College Cost Book 1982-1983 (Princeton, N.J.: College Entrance Examination Board, 1982). Reprinted by permission.

Cost Book 1982-1983 and shows the estimated expenses for resident and commuter students at more than 3,200 American colleges and universities.

FORM 23—COLLEGE COSTS

College costs can be very high. It is therefore a good idea to do some planning ahead of time, and the first step in that process is to estimate what those costs are likely to be. Before or while you are filling in this form, it might be helpful to look at Figure 11-1, which shows you an example of the filled-in form.

- On line 1, list your children's first names.
- On line 2, list your children's present ages.
- On line 3, list in how many years from now each child will be starting college. If a child is already in college, put a zero on line 3.
- On line 4, enter the estimated number of years each child will attend college and graduate school. If a child is presently in college or graduate school, enter the number of years required to complete his or her education.
- On line 5, compute the number of years to be used in an inflation adjustment. This number is determined by adding the years on line 3 to 50 percent of the years on line 4.
- On line 6, estimate the average annual inflation rate between now and the end of the child's educational program.
- On line 7, enter the compound factor from Table 1 in Appendix I for the number of years on line 5 and for the estimated inflation rate on line 6.
- On line 8, enter for each of your children the present cost of one year's attendance at a suitable college. Obtain the approximate figures from Table 11-1 or from the relevant college catalogues.
- On line 9, estimate the inflation-adjusted annual college costs for each child by multiplying the amount on line 8 by the factor on line 7.
- On line 10, calculate the total estimated college costs for each child by multiplying the amount on line 9 by the number of years on line 4.
- On line 11, estimate the annual after-tax rate of return on educational funds invested.
- On line 12, enter the compound factor from Table 1 in Appendix 1 for the number of years on line 5 and for the estimated rate of return on line 11.
- On line 13, enter the amount of funds presently set aside for the education of each child.
- On line 14, calculate the estimated future value of the present educational funds by multiplying the amount on line 13 by the factor on line 12.
- On line 15, calculate the annual amount to be invested for each child's education.
    a. First subtract the amount on line 14 from the amount on line 10.
    b. Divide the result in 15a by the compound factor from Table

FIGURE 11-1

File under EDUCATIONAL FINANCING — Date: 6/11

FORM 23 COLLEGE AND GRADUATE SCHOOL COSTS

1	Children's Names	Paige	Thompson	Elizabeth
2	Ages of Children	20	19	10
3	Number of Years Until College	in college	in college	8
4	Est. Number of Years in College and Graduate School	4	5	6
5	Number of Years for Inflation Adjustment	2	2.5	11
6	Est. Annual Inflation Rate Between Now and End of Education	8	8	6
7	Inflation Factor	1.17	1.21	1.90
8	Est. Annual College Costs in Today's Dollars	$5,000	$5,000	$5,000
9	Est. Annual Costs Adjusted	5,850	6,050	9,500
10	Est. TOTAL Costs Adjusted	$23,400	$30,250	$57,000
11	Est. After-Tax Rate of Return on Educational Funds	8%	8%	9%
12	Compound Factor for Rate of Return on Line 11	1.17	1.21	2.58
13	Present Value of Funds Set Aside for Education	$10,000	$8,000	0
14	Future Value of Funds Set Aside	$11,700	$9,680	0
15	Annual Amount to Be Invested for Education	a) Total needed: $11,700	$20,570	$57,000
		b) Compound factor 2.08	2.68	17.56
		c) Annual amount required: $5,625	$7,675	$3,246

2 in Appendix 1 for the estimated rate of return on line 11 and the number of years on line 5. The result is the annual amount to be invested for each child, to be entered on line 15.

Now that you have picked yourself up off the floor after the fainting spell induced by the grand total of your children's estimated college costs and the annual amount to be expended, let us consider the various means of footing such costs.

WHO PAYS?

Most colleges and grantors of financial aid have developed guidelines for determining how much a student's family can pay for education and how much financial aid may be needed. They start with the premise that the responsibility for paying college costs falls on the student's parents and the student to the extent of their ability to pay them. The College Scholarship Service, which colleges and private secondary schools use to determine financial aid, prepares a need analysis to estimate how much a family can pay. This analysis takes the following factors into account:

- The parents' income from employment and investments.
- Parents' living expenses, including taxes.
- Parents' assets, including home equity, other real estate equity, and other investment assets. Their asset total is then reduced by an amount called the "asset protection allowance," which is based on the parents' other responsibilities and their age.
- The student's earnings from summer employment. The student is expected to contribute at least $700 from such earnings.
- The student's savings and other sources of income, such as Social Security and veteran's educational benefits.

If your various assets are judged sufficient for covering total college costs, you should investigate such other avenues of minimizing your costs as scholarships, grants, loans, and what we call the *tax scholarship*.

THE TAX SCHOLARSHIP

The concept of a tax scholarship is derived from one of the tax-planning techniques discussed in Chapter 6. It consists of shifting income from the parent who is in a high tax bracket to the student who is in a low tax bracket. Since this will reduce the taxes paid by the family as a whole, it provides the same kind of financial relief as a scholarship grant.

Now let us see how income shifting might work for you if your child has been admitted to a school that costs $10,000 a year. We will assume that your child has agreed to earn and pay $1,000 of that cost and you have agreed to pay the remaining $9,000. If you are in the 50 percent tax bracket, you would have to earn $18,000 to have $9,000 left after taxes, and that is a very expensive way to go.

Now let us look at the child's tax bracket. With an income of $1,000 for the year, the child's tax bracket is zero. Even if the child had income that would amount to $10,000 after taxes, the child's top tax rate would be less than 20 percent. Assuming the child had a top tax rate of 18 percent, how much would it take to net $10,000 after taxes? The formula for computing that is as follows:

$$\text{Amount of Income Required before Taxes} = \frac{\text{College Costs}}{\text{100\% minus the child's top tax rate}} =$$

$$\frac{\$10{,}000}{100\% - 18\%} = \frac{\$10{,}000 \times 100}{82} = \$12{,}195$$

Now deduct the $1,000 that the child will contribute, and that brings your obligation down to $11,195, which is a lot less than $18,000. The $6,805 difference is the tax you saved. Now you will understand why we call this a tax scholarship.

To shift income, you have to shift capital either through a gift, or a short-term trust (set up for at least ten years), or an interest-free loan. Before you make that choice, you may want to consult a tax advisor about the pros and cons and the legal requirements of each type of transfer. After that, your mode of operation would be as follows:

- Choose the investment opportunity that best combines safety of capital, liquidity, and current income. A money market instrument would be an example of such an investment.
- Determine the rate of return you can get on the capital you will shift to your child.
- Determine the amount of capital that has to be shifted to your child. To do so, divide the pretax income your child must receive from you by the rate of return on your proposed investment.

Using our example, your child needs $11,195 from you before taxes. Assuming that the rate of return your child can get on the capital you shift to him is 12 percent, you get the following equation:

$$\text{Capital Required} = \frac{\text{Pretax Income}}{\text{Rate of Return}} = \frac{\$11{,}195}{12\%} = \frac{\$11{,}195 \times 100}{12} = \$93{,}292$$

Where can you get $93,292 of capital to shift? You may be able to borrow it, if you don't have it in your current investment portfolio. The interest you pay on this loan will be tax deductible.

Suppose, then, you borrow $93,292 at 15 percent, your interest will be about $14,000; but since you can deduct the interest for tax purposes, your after-tax cost is only $7,000. To put it another way, you would only need to earn $14,000 before taxes to pay the interest on the borrowings to finance your child's education using the tax scholarship idea versus $18,000 before taxes you would have to earn to pay for the child's education if you did not use the tax scholarship. That's quite a nice savings, isn't it?

FINANCIAL AID

Financial aid programs come in all shapes and sizes. Some, like scholarships and grants, are gifts that impose no employment or repayment obligation on the student. Other types of financial aid require a payback—either part-time work while the student attends school, or the repayment of a loan after college.

Financial aid programs are provided by the federal government, state governments, colleges, and private organizations. If you are interested in such assistance, do one or all of the following:

- Get a copy of the *College Cost Book* we mentioned earlier in the chapter.
- Contact your high school college counseling office.
- Contact the financial aid office of the colleges in which you are interested.
- Contact a local representative of the federal or state department of education.

12

RETIREMENT PLANNING

Until they retire, people who have been working most of their adult years are usually unaware of how much their jobs and their work environments mean to them. Unprepared, many of them experience a tremendous sense of loss, emptiness, and uselessness. Some companies now hold preretirement clinics to help their employees make the transition from organizational life to private life. Essentially, such clinics tell the impending retirees to do the following:

- Evaluate your accomplishments; assess your strengths and weaknesses, your likes and dislikes; and envisage your activities during your retirement years.
- Widen your personal interests. Explore pursuits from which you would derive great satisfaction—a hobby, a service project, an autobiography.
- Analyze your financial requirements and the sources of your retirement income.

There are regrettably few retirees whose financial provisions for their retirement prove to be adequate. As mentioned before, only 5 percent of the population is financially independent at age 65. Of the 95 percent who cannot afford to retire comfortably, 22 percent must continue to work; 28 percent depend on either public charity, welfare, or Social Security; and 45 percent are dependent on relatives for some or all of their retirement needs.

Those figures should convince you that retirement planning is essential if you are to reach the goals you have set for that period of your life. To do this effectively, you should start to work on your retirement program ten to fifteen years before you expect to retire.

You will have to work out what your financial requirements will be at retirement and then plan to have the necessary financial resources available.

FORM 24—ESTIMATED BASIC LIFESTYLE EXPENDITURES AT RETIREMENT

Before you can estimate your financial needs and resources at retirement, you must set a time frame for your projections by deciding at what age you want to retire. Most people think of 65 as retirement age, but you may want to retire earlier or later than that, or maybe plan on partial retirement instead of complete retirement.

The simplest way of estimating your financial needs at retirement is to begin with your present pattern of expenditures, and then to visualize in what respects the pattern will be different once you have retired.

- Begin by completing the first column, *Current Year*, with the figures you listed on Form 7—*Basic Lifestyle Expenditures*, filed under *Financial Profile*.
- In the second column, *At Retirement*, complete lines 1 through 18 by putting your estimated expenditures in terms of today's dollars (present-day prices). In some categories, such as medical care, it may be wise to allow for greater expenses than those you have at present. In other categories, such as housing, clothing, and transportation, you are likely to have smaller expenses than at present. Your home mortgage, for example, may be completely paid off by the time you retire.
- On line 19, enter the total of your estimated annual expenditures in retirement. This will not be your final forecast, because so far it has not taken inflation into account.
- On line 20, list in how many years you plan to retire.
- On line 21, estimate the average annual rate of inflation for the years before you retire.
- For line 22, select the right figure from Table 1 in Appendix I. Choose the column with the same percentage as the one you listed on line 21. Then go down that column until you get to the number of years you listed on line 20, and there you have your compound factor.
- For line 23, multiply the total on line 19 by the inflation factor on line 21.

FORM 25—ESTIMATED DISCRETIONARY EXPENDITURES AT RETIREMENT

In completing this form, you will essentially do the same things you did to complete the previous form.

- Begin by completing the first column, *Current Year*, with the figures you listed on Form 8—*Discretionary Expenditures*, filed under *Financial Profile*.
- In the second column, *At Retirement*, use today's dollars (present-day prices) for your estimates on lines 1 through 12.

In some categories, such as vacations or hobbies, you may want to spend more in retirement than you do now; but in others, such as support of relatives or contributions to retirement plans, you might be spending much less or nothing at all.

- On line 13, add up the amounts on lines 1 through 12 in the second column.
- On line 14, list the same inflation factor you listed on line 22 of Form 24.
- For line 15, multiply the total on line 13 by the factor on line 14.

FORM 26—ESTIMATED RETIREMENT NEEDS INCLUDING TAXES

- On line 1, list your total from line 21 of Form 24—*Estimated Basic Lifestyle Expenditures at Retirement*.
- On line 2, list your total from line 15 of Form 25—*Estimated Discretionary Expenditures at Retirement*.
- On line 3, put the sum of lines 1 and 2.

THE IMPACT OF TAXES

So far, none of your estimates have taken income taxes into account. Therefore, the next and last step in estimating your financial needs at retirement will be to calculate the impact of income taxes on your retirement needs. It is likely that some, if not most, of the income you will receive during retirement will be taxable. The Internal Revenue Service expects its share of your retirement income. Due to inflation, you may actually find yourself in quite a high tax bracket after you retire. One simple but pretty accurate way to estimate your tax requirements during retirement is to assume that taxes will constitute 20 percent of your estimated needs. Although this may seem lower than the average tax rate you are currently paying, remember that not all of your income during retirement will be taxed.

- To estimate retirement expenditures including taxes using an estimated average tax rate of 20 percent, put a tax factor of 80 percent on line 4 of Form 26.
- Then, on line 5, compute your total estimated retirement needs including taxes by dividing the amount on line 3 by the tax factor of 80 percent.

RETIREMENT INCOME

To have sufficient income to meet one's retirement needs requires some long-term planning. Although most people have an employee retirement plan, these plans are not designed to provide all your needs at retirement; typically, they are designed to provide 35 to 40 percent. The remaining 60 to 65 percent of your needs will hardly come from Social Security. So it is up to you to have sufficient investment income to make up the difference.

We have counseled some people who did not realize the importance of investment income to their retirement dreams until they were just a few years away from retirement. They were then faced with the need either to continue working or else to scale back their retirement lifestyle. The need to start serious retirement planning ten to fifteen years before you wish to retire cannot be emphasized enough. Ten to fifteen years before retirement, you have probably completed the children's education, settled comfortably into your dream house, and stopped your "accumulating phase." You have completed phases of your life that require heavy expenditures, so you will probably have more funds available for investment and should concentrate on funding your retirement.

Allocate your funds to investments with a solid growth potential. You should now avoid investments with a high risk because you do not have much time to recover from substantial losses. As you near retirement, you should continue to invest primarily in quality, growth-oriented investments; but start to look for quality income-oriented investments as well. You should, however, also be concerned about the impact of inflation during retirement, so investments that provide a hedge against inflation should be a substantial part of your investment program.

Below is a brief description of the more common sources of retirement income.

COMPANY RETIREMENT PLANS

The retirement plans of private companies in the United States are about equally divided between two types: pension plans and profit-sharing plans. A pension plan can be either benefit-oriented or contribution-oriented.

With a *defined benefit plan*, the amount of the benefits you will be paid at retirement has been set in advance, and the company's contributions to the plan are actuarially determined to give the plan the assets necessary for paying these predetermined benefits.

With a *defined contribution plan*, the company's contribution on behalf of its employee is either a flat dollar amount or a percentage of the employee's compensation. Here, the amount of the employee's retirement benefits will depend on how much capital has been contributed on the employee's behalf and on how much this capital has earned.

Profit-sharing plans, which are contribution-oriented, are funded by the company according to a set formula—usually a percentage of the company's profits. The level of these contributions varies with the company's profits, and if there are no profits, there are no contributions.

TAX ADVANTAGES The money you have in a company profit-sharing or pension plan does not become taxable until you receive it upon retiring or leaving the company for some other reason. It can therefore accumulate and gather a compound rate of return untaxed, and this is a tremendous advantage. A given sum of money invested at 8 percent untaxed will double itself in nine years; but it will take about eighteen years for that sum to double itself if your 8 percent return is taxable every year and you are in the 50 percent tax bracket.

Let us look at these two tax situations further by comparing two people, Joe and Fred. Each sets aside $2,000 a year of his current compensation for a retirement plan. Let's say that Joe contributes his $2,000 to a qualified retirement plan in his company, and that by so doing he does not have to include the $2,000 as taxable compensation for the year. Fred, however, operates on a do-it-yourself basis; he has to include his $2,000 of compensation as gross income, then takes what is left of his $2,000 after taxes and invests it. If both Joe and Fred are in the 25 percent tax bracket, Joe can invest his entire $2,000 because he paid no taxes on that portion of his salary.

Fred has only $1,500 to invest, because 25 percent of his $2,000 is the tax he has to pay.

Further, the income on Joe's annual $2,000 investment is tax-deferred because it is in a qualified retirement plan; the income on Fred's investment may be taxable. Assume that the qualified plan to which Joe contributes gets 8 percent and that Fred finds a similar type of investment that yields 8 percent before taxes. Joe's funds compound tax-free; Fred's compound annual rate will only be 6 percent because of his 25 percent tax bracket. If we go to our hand-held calculator and punch in the data for annual amount invested ($2,000 versus $1,500) and rate of return (8 percent versus 6 percent), the results after thirty years of steady investing will be:

Joe: $226,600
Fred: $118,600

The difference between the retirement funds of Joe and Fred, about $108,000, is due to the tax-free compounding of $2,000 per year at 8 percent in Joe's account versus the after-tax compounding of $1,500 per year at 6 percent in Fred's account. Well, you say, that's not a fair comparison because Joe's funds will be taxed when he receives them during retirement. That's right—your employee retirement benefit becomes taxable when you receive it, after you retire. It will be taxed as ordinary income (income from employment, which may be taxed at a rate of up to 50 percent). Fred would not be taxed on any of his $118,600 at the end of 30 years, since he has already been taxed on the capital he invested and on the earnings of this invested capital. However, there are tax-favored ways of receiving your retirement payments that we will discuss in a few pages. Using one of those tax-advantaged methods of receiving his retirement benefits, Joe would net out, after taxes, a lump-sum payment of approximately $166,600—about $48,000 more than Fred.

RETIREMENT PLAN STANDARDS

Retirement plans are generally administered by a trustee or several trustees, such as a bank or a group of the company's executives. Most companies have a "qualified" retirement plan that meets the standards established by the federal government and thereby qualifies the company for some tax advantages. The more important standards set for such plans will be discussed below.

ELIGIBILITY REQUIREMENTS

Normally, there is a waiting period before a new employee is eligible for coverage under a plan. You should find out how long this waiting period is with your company.

CONTRIBUTIONS TO THE PLAN

Contributions to finance a pension plan can be made in several ways:

- The company contributes all the funds.
- The company and the employees share in the contributions on some predetermined basis.
- The employees can make voluntary contributions in addition to their regular contributions.

RETIREMENT DATE

Most pension plans specify a retirement age for their employees, such as the first day of the month after which the employee reaches the age of 65. An employee may be able to retire earlier, but that will usually reduce the employee's retirement benefit according to a formula outlined in the plan.

RESIGNATION OR DISMISSAL

Pension benefits for employees who leave the company for reasons other than retirement are computed according to the amount of the employee's own contributions to the plan and to the pension plan's *vesting rules*. Whatever amount the employee has contributed is returned with interest when the employee leaves. Sometimes such employees have the option of leaving their contributions and the interest on them in the plan so that they can continue to earn interest tax-free.

VESTING RULES

Whether an employee will receive some part of the company's contributions upon dismissal or resignation is determined by the vesting rules set forth in the company's benefit package. According to these rules, the percentage of the company's contributions to which the employee is entitled will increase with the number of years of employment. A company might have a vesting schedule that fully vests its employees after ten years with the company. In that case, upon retiring or leaving for other reasons after ten years, the employee is entitled to 100 percent of the contributions made on his or her behalf. Pension plans have a deliberate bias in favor of employees who stay with the company for a long time.

If you are covered by a company retirement plan, make sure you understand the details of the plan and know your rights and benefits. Obtain a yearly update on the details of your retirement accounts; in particular, find out what monthly benefit you will receive at retirement and what vested benefits you have.

RETIREMENT PAYMENTS

Most plans give you several choices of the form in which your retirement benefits are to be paid. These choices generally include payment in installments, payment as an annuity (either for life, for a specified period, with a survivorship feature, or with some combination of these features), or payment in a lump sum.

TAXATION OF RETIREMENT PAYMENTS

When retirement payments are paid in a form other than a lump sum, they are taxed as ordinary income along with any other ordinary income, such as investment income, that you may be receiving during retirement. If you received your retirement payments in installments, for example, the installments would be taxed as ordinary income at ordinary tax rates, up to a maximum of 50 percent.

LUMP-SUM DISTRIBUTIONS

Suppose you have $200,000 in your company retirement account when you retire in 1983, and you elect to receive the entire amount as a lump sum. The prospect of having $200,000 in hand is intriguing, but that choice should not be made before you know its tax consequences.

For tax purposes, there are several different ways of treating a lump-sum distribution. The contributions that you, the employee, made to the pension plan are not taxable upon distribution because you have paid taxes on them already. The remainder—after a number of adjustments too complex to dwell upon here—is taxable. Some part of this taxable remainder—the part attributable to your company's contributions after 1973—will be taxed as ordinary income. With the other part—the part attributable to your company's contributions before 1974 plus the interest on them earned before 1974—you have the option of treating it as long-term capital gain, in which case 60 percent of the capital gain is untaxed and 40 percent ranks as ordinary income.

Going back to the $200,000 example, let's assume you have contributed $40,000 of the total and the remaining $160,000 represents the company's contribution and the tax-deferred earnings on your and your company's contributed funds. Assume also you participated in the plan for ten years prior to 1974. The capital gain portion of your distribution would be computed as follows:

$$\text{Amount other than your contribution} \times \frac{\text{Number of years prior to 1974}}{\text{Total number of years in the plan}}$$

$$\$160{,}000 \times 10/20 = \underline{\underline{\$80{,}000}}$$

TEN-YEAR AVERAGING

Before you elect to treat part of your retirement distribution as a capital gain, you should evaluate the use of ten-year-forward averaging. The ten-year averaging provisions are designed to ease the bite on lump-sum distributions and may be used to determine the tax on the ordinary income portion of a lump-sum distribution or on the entire distribution, including the capital gain portion.

Ten-year averaging extends only to your tax rate, not to the time at which the tax on the lump sum is payable. It prevents you from being propelled into an astronomical tax bracket by your lump sum and puts you into the tax bracket you would be in if you only received one-tenth of your lump sum. The resulting figure is then multiplied by ten to determine the overall tax. This tax is determined separately from that tax on your other taxable income, without any deductions, without regard to community property laws, and at the rate used by single persons.

As mentioned before, you may elect to treat all of the distribution, including the capital gain portion, as ordinary income, subject to the ten-year averaging provision. In some instances, the averaging provision makes it more advantageous to treat the lump sum as ordinary income rather than as long-term capital gain. In general, the use of ten-year averaging gets more attractive the more the ordinary income portion of the distribution increases.

Before you make your final decision, which must take all the possible tax consequences into account, there is one further option for you to consider.

THE ROLL-OVER PROVISIONS

You can postpone the evil day of taxation for all or part of your lump-sum distribution if, within sixty days of receiving it, you "roll over" all or part of your lump-sum distribution into an Individual Retirement Account. Your own contributions to your company's retirement plan, however, cannot be rolled over. Whatever can be and is rolled over into an IRA is not subject to tax until it is withdrawn from the IRA. Any portion of it that you don't withdraw can continue to accumulate interest in your IRA until you reach the age of 70 years and 6 months.

This tax deferral through roll-over into an IRA comes at a price, of course. It eliminates your other tax-saving options. Whether the whole or only a part of your lump-sum distribution is rolled over into an IRA, the whole of your lump sum will sooner or later be taxable at ordinary income rates. No ten-year averaging or capital gain treatment can be applied to any part of it. Any portion of the lump sum that you do not roll over (other than your own contributions) is taxable as ordinary income for the year in which you receive it.

THE REAL POWER OF IRAs AND KEOGHS

As we mentioned above, income placed in IRAs and Keogh plans is not taxable until you start to receive payments—no later than age 70½. If at that age you have other resources to use for your retirement needs and can afford to take the money out slowly, what happens then is a prime illustration of the miracle of compounding.

Consider the following: Let's say you are now 45 years old, and your spouse is 40 and does not work. You deposit the maximum of $2,250 a year into your IRA until age 70. If the $2,250 can be invested for 25 years at 15 percent compounded interest, your IRA account will contain about $550,000 when you reach age 70½. At that age, the IRS says, you must start withdrawing funds from your IRA according to a life expectancy table for the combined life expectancies of you and your spouse. Let's say the combined life expectancy for you, then age 70, and your spouse, then age 65, is 20 years. With 20 years of life expectancy, the IRS says, you must draw out one-twentieth of your account balance in the first year, one-nineteenth in the second year, and so on. So you draw out 5 percent of your balance at the beginning of the first year or approximately $27,500. But at 15 percent interest, your IRA funds earn more than that in the first year—approximately $78,400—and your IRA grows to about $600,900 at the beginning of the second year. During the first ten years, the reinvested earnings in your IRA will be greater than the withdrawals and your IRA balance will increase to over $1,000,000. At the end of 20 years, you will have withdrawn over $3,000,000—and you paid in only $56,250 ($2,250 for 25 years). What a deal.*

RETIREMENT PLANS FOR THE SELF-EMPLOYED

If you operate a business as a proprietor or a partner, either full-time or part-time, and you have no employees, then you could establish a Keogh plan, as we discussed in Chapter 6. The maximum annual contribution that can be made is 15 percent of self-employment income or $15,000 in 1983 ($30,000 after 1983), whichever is less. For example, if you have a net self-employment income of $25,000, you could contribute $3,750 to a Keogh plan in 1983. The Keogh plan contributions can be invested in any number of ways, and the income is tax-deferred until you start to receive payments (after age 59½, and no later than 70½).

If you operate a business as a proprietor or a partner and have employees working for you, you can have the benefits of a pension or profit-sharing plan provided that you include your employees in the plan after one year of employment. You cannot discriminate in the percentage you contribute to each employee's retirement account, including your own. If you contribute 15 percent of your own net self-employment income to your Keogh account, you have to contribute an amount equal to 15 percent of your employees' compensation to their accounts.

If you are self-employed and have employees, another option you have is to incorporate your business and have the benefits of corporate pension and profit-sharing plans. Again, your employees have to be covered in the plan.

As mentioned in Chapter 6, anyone with income from employment—self-employment income or income from working for someone else—can contribute 100 percent of his or her earned income, up to an annual maximum of $2,000, to an IRA. In spousal IRAs, for couples in which only one spouse has an earned income, the annual limit is $2,250.

A self-employed individual could have both a Keogh plan and an IRA and could contribute an annual maximum of $15,000 (in 1983) to a Keogh

---

* Adapted from, "Cashing in Your IRA," *Forbes*, February 15, 1982, p. 147.

plan and another $2,000 to an IRA—a total of $17,000. This can provide additional funds for retirement; it may also give you a very sizable tax break.

PERSONAL RESIDENCE

When a taxpayer 55 years of age or older sells his or her personal residence, $125,000 of the gain on the sale is tax-free. To profit from this provision, you must have owned this residence and used it as your principal residence for at least three of the five years preceding the sale. This tax benefit can be claimed only once in a lifetime. Any recognized capital gain in excess of the tax-free $125,000 is taxable as a long-term capital gain (see the example in Chapter 6).

This $125,000 tax-free fund can be very important in providing additional retirement capital.

INVESTMENT ASSETS

As mentioned earlier, retirement planning should include the buildup of your investments during the ten to fifteen years before you retire. Investment assets can be used to provide income during your retirement. To build up your investment funds prior to retirement, you need to manage your present investment assets effectively (see Form 21—*Review of Present Investments*). Try to boost the return on your investments. That generally means sacrificing some safety in order to be more aggressive. But you can go from a yield of 8 percent to 11 or 12 percent without unreasonably endangering your capital.

Another way to increase your investment assets at retirement is to put more income aside each year for investment. Maximize your IRA contributions and other tax-deferred programs available to you.

As you approach retirement, you will probably have current income as your primary investment objective. Such an objective can be achieved through quality bonds, income stocks, and income-producing real estate. You should still keep up to 50 percent of your investments at retirement in something with growth potential, such as growth stocks or real estate.

Another way of getting retirement income is to sell those investments that have increased in value. Consider, for example, two retirement funds of $250,000 each. If one fund consisted of bonds yielding 10 percent and maturing in ten years, the annual income would be $25,000—all taxed as ordinary income—and the $250,000 capital amount would not increase in value if the bonds were bought at face value and held to maturity; thus, no inflation protection. If the other fund consisted of growth stocks paying no dividends but appreciating at an average rate of 12 percent per year over the ten years, you could sell $25,000 of the stocks the first year. The fund would have grown to $252,500 at the end of the first year and to $254,200 at the end of the second year, after you sold another $25,000. Thus, even though you were deriving current income from it, your retirement fund would be appreciating and providing some hedge against inflation, and on top of that your income from it would be taxed as long-term capital gain.

SOCIAL SECURITY

The fundamental concept of our contributory Social Security system is the obligation of people to provide a security program for themselves. Our Social

Security system provides a monthly sum to replace part of a person's or a family's earnings when a worker retires, dies, or becomes disabled. Thus, its general payments fall under one of the following headings: retirement benefits, survivor's benefits, disability benefits, and Medicare benefits.

The amount of the retirement benefits you will receive is based on your earnings record. Whether you are entitled to any such benefits depends on whether you are considered to be insured. The general rule is that you are fully insured if you have worked forty quarter-years since 1936. The size of your benefits is based on your average yearly earnings after 1950. You receive full benefits if you retire at 65 and reduced benefits if you retire at 62. In either case, a dependent spouse is entitled to an additional 50 percent of your benefits when he or she reaches age 65 or 37.5 percent at age 62.

In 1983, Congress approved significant amendments to the Social Security system. The most significant changes affecting individuals follow.

1. Beginning in 1984, a portion of Social Security benefits will be included in taxable income for anyone whose adjusted gross income (AGI) combined with 50 percent of his or her benefits exceeds a base amount. The base amount is $25,000 for individuals, $32,000 for married couples filing joint returns, and zero for married persons filing separate returns. The amount includible in taxable income is limited to the lesser of (1) one-half of the Social Security benefits received, or (2) one-half of the excess of the taxpayer's combined income (AGI plus tax-exempt interest plus one-half of the benefits received) over the base amount. Thus, the maximum proportion of Social Security benefits that will be included in the taxable income of any taxpayer will be one-half of the benefits. The following examples illustrate this change.

- Assume a married couple with $10,000 of Social Security retirement benefits and $35,000 of adjusted gross income. To determine if any Social Security benefits are taxable, you would make the following computations:

AGI ($35,000) plus one-half of Social Security benefits ($5,000)	$40,000
Base amount	32,000
Excess	$ 8,000
One-half of excess	4,000
One-half of benefits	5,000
Taxable amount of Social Security benefits	$ 4,000

- Assume the same benefits as above, except that adjusted gross income is $25,000.

AGI plus one-half of Social Security benefits	$30,000
Base amount	32,000
Excess	-0-

Since modified AGI is less than the base amount, none of the Social Security benefits are taxable.

- Assume the same figures as in example 2, except that the taxpayers have $5,000 of income from tax-free state and municipal bonds.

AGI ($25,000) plus tax-exempt interest ($5,000) plus one-half of benefits ($5,000)	$35,000
Base amount	32,000
Excess	$3,000
One-half of excess	1,500
One-half of benefits	5,000
Taxable amount of Social Security benefits	$ 1,500

2. The Social Security taxes will be raised to 6.7% for employees in 1984; to 7% for employers. In the following years the rates, for both employees and employers, will be:

Calendar Year	Rate
1985	7.05
1986 and 1987	7.15
1988 and 1989	7.51
1990	7.65

For self-employed individuals, the rates will be increased to the combined employer-employee rates (14% in 1984). However, a credit will be allowed against the tax payable as follows:

Year	Credit
1984	2.7%
1985	2.3
1986–1989	2.0
1990 and thereafter	0

3. The normal retirement age (the age at which full Social Security retirement benefits can be received) will be raised from the current age of 65 in 1984 to 66 in 2009, and to 67 in 2027. The age 62 reduced early retirement benefit, currently 80 percent of the full benefit, will be reduced to 70 percent of the full benefit beginning in 2027.

4. Effective in 1990, individuals under age 70 receiving Social Security benefits will be penalized by a one-dollar reduction for every three (currently two) dollars of earnings above the exempt amount.

Because Social Security regulations may change from time to time and because cost-of-living increases and indexing computations can make it difficult to calculate the exact amount of your Social Security benefits, you should contact the local Social Security office and ask for specific information on benefit payments, eligibility, and how to apply as you near retirement.

WILL YOUR RETIREMENT INCOME MATCH YOUR EXPENDITURES?

You began by setting the date at which you might like to retire. Then you estimated how much an enjoyable retirement and its less-enjoyable taxes might cost you. But none of this has yet been measured against the financial resources you expect to have at retirement.

Now the moment has come to probe the feasibility of your various retirement objectives. Will the annual income from your retirement plans and present investments cover your anticipated expenditures? If not, will your retirement plans, your present investments, and the investments you will make before retirement give you an annual income that will cover your retirement expenditures? If not, there are some more questions to ask yourself. Could you step up your investment schedule by earning more or spending less? Were you too extravagant when you forecast your retirement expenditures? Should you retire later than you intended?

FORM 27—RETIREMENT INCOME

On this form, you will relate your retirement needs to your retirement sources. We have provided an example of Form 27 in Figure 12-1. You might want to review it before you complete your own.

- On line 1, enter the annual amount you listed on line 5 of Form 26.
- On lines 2a, 2b, and 2c, enter the annual amounts you are likely to receive after retirement from sources that will distribute payments in forms other than a lump sum. You may have to get the required information from your company's personnel office, your local Social Security office, and other sources from which retirement funds will come. Do not include projected IRA and/or Keogh plan income in this section of Form 27. You will consider these sources of retirement income further down on the form.
- Total the estimated annual income from all your retirement plans on line 3.
- Subtract the total annual income from your retirement plans (line 3) from your estimated annual retirement needs (line 1) and enter the result on line 4 of the worksheet. If the estimated income from your retirement plan exceeds your requirements, you could consider retiring earlier or look forward to a more comfortable retirement period. If you still need additional sources of retirement income, go on to the next step.
- Convert the annual income still needed on line 4 into a capital amount that will yield the annual income required. Perform these steps:
  - On line 5a, enter the estimated pretax rate of return on your investment capital when you retire.
  - On line 5b, enter the estimated capital required at retirement by dividing the amount on line 4 by the rate on line 5a.
- The next step on Form 27 is probably more complicated because it involves making judgments about your present investment assets, lump sum retirement plans, and IRAs and Keogh plans. It also involves forecasting what the value of these assets might be at retirement.
  - Enter on line 6a the present value of your investment assets, IRAs, and Keogh plans. Most of this data will come from your net worth statement (Form 4).
  - Enter on line 6b the estimated pretax rate of return you think you will get on your investment assets and IRA/Keogh plans between

FIGURE 12-1

File under RETIREMENT PLANNING — Date: 11/1

FORM 27 RETIREMENT INCOME

Projected Retirement Age: 62 — Number of Years to Retirement: 7

1 Estimated Annual Retirement Needs — $91,200

2 Estimated Annual Income from Retirement Plans (other than lump-sum distributions)

- a. Social Security — $12,000
- b. Company Retirement Plan — 37,200
- c. Defered Compensation — –
- d. Other Retirement Plans — –

3 TOTAL Annual Income from Retirement Plans — $49,200

4 Annual Income Gap — $42,000

5 Retirement Capital Required to Fill Gap

- a. Estimated Pre-Tax Rate of Return — 8%
- b. Retirement Capital Required — $525,000

6 Sources of Retirement Capital

	INVESTMENT ASSETS	LUMP SUMS FROM RETIREMENT PLANS	IRA/ KEOGH	TOTAL
a. Value of Present Investment Assets and and Retirement Accounts	$215,000		$4,700	$219,700
b. Estimated Rate of Return from Now until Retirement	10%		12%	
c. Years until Retirement	7		7	
d. Compound Factor from Table 1 (in Appendix I)	1.95		2.21	
e. Estimated Value of Your Investment Assets and Retirement Accounts at Retirement	$419,000	$22,000	$10,400	$451,400

FIGURE 12-1, cont'd.

	INVESTMENT ASSETS	IRA/ KEOGH	OTHER	TOTAL
7 Additional Capital from Annual Investments You Are Planning to Make				
a. Annual Amount to Be Invested Between Now and Retirement	$4,000	$2,250		$6,250
b. Estimated Pre-Tax Rate of Return on Annual Investment	10%	12%		
c. Years until Retirement	7	7		
d. Compound Factor from Table 2 (in Appendix I)	9.49	10.09		
e. Estimated Value of Additional Capital from Your Annual Investments	$38,000	$22,700		$60,700
8 TOTAL Estimated Retirement Capital				$512,100
9 Additional Capital Needed, if Any, to Provide Retirement Income				$12,900
10 Additional Annual Investment Needed to Provide Capital on Line 9				
a. Estimated Rate of Return from Now until Retirement			10%	
b. Years until Retirement			7	
c. Compound Factor from Table 2 (in Appendix I)			9.49	
d. Annual Amount Required				$1,360

now and your retirement. Refer to Form 22—*Your Investment Strategy* for your estimates.

- Enter on line 6c the number of years from now to retirement. Next, enter the approximate factor from Table 1 in Appendix I on line 6d.
- On line 6e, estimate the value of your investment assets and retirement capital at retirement by multiplying the amount on line 6a by the factor on line 6d. You are getting really good at these calculations! Also enter on 6e, under the "Lump Sum" column, the amount to be paid in a lump sum at retirement from retirement plans.
- Finally, add the totals across on line 6e to get the total estimated value of your capital at retirement.

- Compute the additional capital you will obtain by making annual additions to your investment funds and annual contributions to your IRA/Keogh plans.
  - Enter on line 7a the annual amount to be invested between now and retirement.
  - On line 7b, enter the estimated pretax rate of return on your annual investments.
  - On line 7c, enter the number of years from now until retirement.
  - On line 7d, enter the appropriate factor from Table 2 in Appendix I.
  - On line 7e, estimate the value of additional capital by multiplying the amount on line 7a by the factor on line 7d.
  - Finally, add the totals across on line 7e to get the total estimated value of your additional capital at retirement.
- On line 8, enter your total estimated retirement capital from lines 6e and 7e.
- On line 9, enter the amount that results from subtracting the amount on line 8 from the amount on line 5b. If the amount is negative—because your estimated retirement capital exceeds your requirements—consider early retirement or look forward to a much more comfortable retirement lifestyle, or plan a really big retirement party. If you need additional capital to meet your needs, go to the next and final step.
- If the result on line 9 of the worksheet suggests you will need additional investment capital at retirement, then you will need to start putting even more funds aside each year for investment. How much you need to set aside can be computed on the worksheet.
  - On line 10a, enter the estimated pre-tax rate of return on your investments from now until retirement.
  - On line 10b, enter the number of years between now and retirement.
  - On line 10c, enter the compound factor from Table 2 in Appendix I.
  - On line 10d, compute the annual amount of additional funds required by dividing the amount of capital required on line 9 by the factor on line 10c.

In our example in Figure 12-1, the individual would have to invest about $1,360 for seven years at 10 percent to have the additional capital needed at retirement. Some clients with whom we have worked have a much greater annual investment requirement and say, "Are you kidding me?" If that is your case, you will need to reevaluate the variables in your plan and consider the choices you have.

YOUR RETIREMENT PLANNING CHOICES

What choices do you have between now and retirement that will help you meet your estimated retirement needs? Here are several you should consider:

- You can manage your investments and retirement funds more effectively to get a greater annual return.
- You can set aside more funds for annual investment by decreasing your current expenditures for other goals.
- You can plan to sell your personal residence at or before retirement and move into something less expensive to provide additional investment capital.
- You can plan to use some of your investment capital during retirement to handle your needs. Maybe the easiest estate planning is to spend your last dime as you take your last breath! Systematic use of investment capital during retirement may, in fact, be a very good choice for some people.

If, after considering the above choices, you still do not think it will be feasible to retire when you want to and still maintain a desired standard of living, you may have to hang in there and continue to work for your living.

THINKING OF EARLY RETIREMENT?

Many people think about retiring at an early age, such as 50 or 55. It's an appealing idea, but one that should be considered carefully if you want to avoid frustration, anger, and financial problems. The advice we would give to anyone who is not independently wealthy is the following:

- Do not retire early unless you are free of major financial obligations, such as putting your children through college or paying off your mortgage.
- Do not retire early unless you have a vested pension—meaning one that belongs to you—as well as substantial savings or investments.
- Do not retire early if you have not qualified to receive sizable Social Security payments at the age of 62 or 65.
- Be wary if your retirement benefits are heavily dependent on the stock market.
- Try to negotiate any extra benefits your employer may be willing to give you because you take early retirement.
- Make sure the terms of your retirement plan will not prevent you from working elsewhere if you so desire.
- Have a plan to use your time effectively.

A RETIREMENT PLANNING CHECKLIST

As you approach your retirement date, you should do the following:

- Call your local Social Security office to find out what you must do to apply for benefits and enroll in Medicare.
- Make an appointment with the official in your company who is responsible for your pension and profit-sharing benefits. Find out what payment plans are available to you, and consider which of the payment options would be most beneficial to you.
- Discuss the tax consequences of your retirement payment options with your tax advisor.
- Review your life insurance coverage. In retirement you may need less than your present coverage. If you have and want to keep a company-paid or company-sponsored group policy, check the options available to you.
- Review your health care coverage. Find out what Medicare provides. If you need supplemental coverage, shop around. If you have a company plan, find out whether you can convert it to an individual plan.
- Review your will and your estate plan. You may wish to meet with your attorney or accountant to evaluate estate-planning ideas.
- Find out about senior citizens' programs and discounts in the locality you choose for your retirement.

13

LIFE INSURANCE

Most of our financial planning is based on the assumption that we will continue to live for a long time and thus can provide a continuing stream of income for as long as we choose. There is a possibility, though, that we won't live to a ripe old age, and good planning must take this risk into account. If our premature deaths would disrupt or dry up the income stream needed to maintain our dependents, then life insurance should be used to prevent such financial disruption.

Our insurance needs will go up and down as our income and responsibilities go up and down and as our investments grow. Without children, insurance requirements are not great. Children and a mortgage mean increased responsibilities and a greater need for insurance protection. As children near college age, insurance needs normally reach a maximum. As the children become financially independent, the need for insurance declines. At retirement, insurance again may not be a big factor, except for providing the necessary liquidity when it comes to settling the decedent's estate. At that point, your investment assets should be sufficient to provide your surviving spouse with the required income.

Because the need for protection changes, we strongly recommend that you evaluate your insurance every three years at the least, and that you buy insurance policies that allow you to change your protection coverage.

In essence, all life insurance policies say the same thing: In return for premiums duly received, the insurance company will pay the *face amount* (the promised benefit) of the policy to the beneficiary upon receiving proof of the insured person's death. The death benefits are paid out very quickly and are not taxable to the beneficiary. To provide flexibility to the beneficiary, the proceeds received should be put into the beneficiary's own account, not into an account held jointly with the late spouse or parent.

In order to assess whether your present life insurance coverage is adequate, inadequate, or excessive, you have to envisage the needs and resources of your dependents in the event of your or your spouse's unexpected death. Which dependents, if any, will require financial support? When will they need it, how much will they need, and for how long? What income will be available from other sources? How much income will the proceeds of the life insurance have to provide?

DO YOU REALLY NEED LIFE INSURANCE?

The only purpose of insuring your life is to provide income for your dependents after your death. Therefore, the first question to ask yourself is, "Do I have any dependents for whom I should provide after my death?"

There may be none, and therefore little or no need for life insurance, if you are single, or married but without children or mortgage and both of you are working. Similarly, there may be little or no point in paying for the safety net of life insurance once your children are independent and you have ample net worth. However, if your spouse, children, and/or parents depend on your earnings, you may have to insure your life quite heavily.

As your financial responsibilities and circumstances change, so will your need for life insurance. You can see this illustrated in Figure 13-1, which shows the insurance needs of people at different life stages. The six selected points on the graph correspond to the following stages:

- Point A: single young person. Normally, this person has no dependents, and therefore little or no need for insurance. About the only things that may have to be covered by insurance are funeral expenses or loans outstanding, such as education loans.
- Point B: a childless couple. When both spouses are employed, they each have the best kind of insurance—a job; but if they have purchased a house or condominium, insurance to cover the mortgage would be a good idea. If their lifestyle depends on their combined incomes, they may want $25,000 to $50,000 of insurance on each other's life. Often this can be provided through a group term policy offered by their employers.
- Point C: a 30-year-old couple with two small children and a heavily mortgaged house. There are three good reasons why the amount of life insurance needed is relatively high:

FIGURE 13-1
CHANGING NEED FOR LIFE INSURANCE

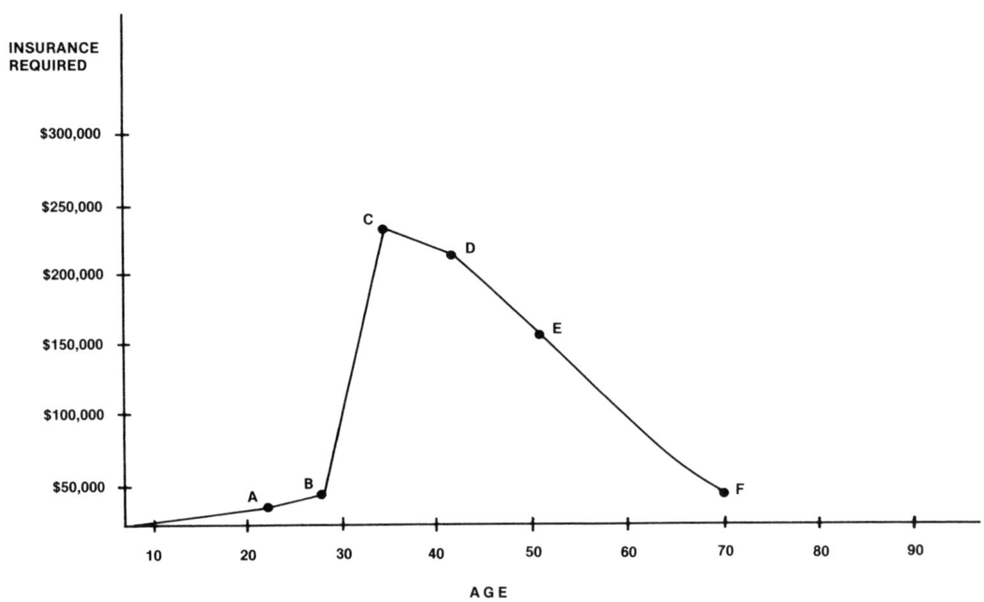

1. The investment assets of a couple at the age of 30 are usually not sufficient to cover the living expenses of the surviving spouse and two small children.
2. The living expenses are relatively high because the surviving spouse, aged 30, has many more years to live, so the lump sum required to pay his or her expenses for a long time is large.
3. The cost of raising and educating the children adds significantly to the required living expenses of the surviving spouse; it may be desirable to set up an education fund from the insurance proceeds.

- Point D: a 40-year-old couple with dependent children and dependent parents. They have relatively high life insurance needs for much the same reasons as the 30-year-old couple. They still have to cover significant living expenses for the surviving spouse (usually the wife) and for dependent parents; in addition, there are the costs of educating the children. Most couples of this age and in this situation have not amassed enough investment assets to cover these various requirements.
- Point E: a 50-year-old couple whose two children have completed their formal education and will soon be financially independent. The surviving spouse does not have as long to live as a spouse at the age of 30 or 40, and child-rearing expenses are few. In addition, a 50-year-old couple will usually have greater investment assets than a couple of 30 or 40, so their investments can provide some of the needed income.
- Point F: a 70-year-old couple whose children are financially independent. The amount needed for the living expenses of the surviving spouse is relatively small because there are not as many years for which provision must be made, and the investment assets of the couple may be sufficient to cover those needs.

FORM 28—YOUR PRESENT LIFE INSURANCE COVERAGE

The obvious way to begin your insurance review is by listing the significant aspects of any insurance you presently carry on your life and the life of your spouse. You will be able to obtain the necessary information from the actual policy or policies or from your insurance agent.

Under *Type of Policy*, identify each policy as either whole life, individual term, group term, endowment, or whatever other description is appropriate.

Under *Cash Surrender Value* and *Loan on Policy*, the total amounts should agree with those on your net worth statement (Form 4).

Under *Owner of Policy*, indicate who owns the policy. Usually, the insured is the owner. But, for estate tax planning, your spouse may be the owner of some or all of the policies on your life.

HOW MUCH INSURANCE DO YOU NEED?

Before you can tell how much life insurance you should carry, you have to forecast the financial needs of your dependents and should have a good idea of the amount and liquidity of your assets.

Your dependents' financial needs will normally fall into the following categories:

- Cash to pay immediate obligations, including estate taxes
- Money to pay the mortgage
- Money for education
- Cash to cover living expenses

It may be a good idea for the survivors to set up four separate funds in separate accounts to cover these four different needs.

IMMEDIATE CASH REQUIREMENTS

Many of the expenses that come into existence at death are expenses that simply did not exist before. Cash is required for funeral expenses, for current bills (including medical bills and administrative expenses), for an emergency fund, and possibly for estate taxes. Funeral costs vary depending on whether you want your ashes spread at sea (about $250) or wish to be buried with your ship and other accessories for the life hereafter, as the Vikings did in the Middle Ages. The average cost of death is about $3,000, which includes the funeral and burial in a cemetery.

An emergency fund is required to cover living expenses during the period when the estate is being settled and the nature and amount of assets to be received by the survivors may be uncertain. Since most of us do not plan to die soon, there may not be enough liquid assets available to your survivors to take care of the cash requirements in the first months following your death, and life insurance could fill this gap.

MORTGAGES

In this age of buying expensive homes and financing the purchase with a large mortgage, many breadwinners die leaving their families indebted to a lending institution. With regard to the money involved, it may not make much difference whether the mortgage is paid off immediately or is covered by a "living expenses fund" in the insurance; but for the peace of mind of the survivors, it may be important to have a mortgage insurance fund for clearing your home of debt.

If your mortgage interest rate is low—say, 7 or 8 percent—the survivor should consider keeping the mortgage, because the after-tax cost of the mortgage may be significantly lower than the after-tax return from employing the funds elsewhere. Suppose the survivor is in a tax bracket of 40 percent and has a mortgage rate of 8 percent; then the after-tax cost of the mortgage would be 4.8 percent. It would be wise to invest the mortgage fund elsewhere, rather than use it to pay off the mortgage, if a return of 5 or more percent after taxes could be obtained by investing it elsewhere.

EDUCATION COSTS

Education, like a mortgage, can be paid for from the living expenses fund; but your children may find it reassuring to have a specific fund set aside for educational purposes. The amount of the fund must depend on several factors: type of college; length of education; the children's ability to generate money for their education; availability of scholarships; and your views on providing support for the children after you die.

LIVING EXPENSES

The calculation of living expenses raises the fundamental question of how well the family should be provided for. Most of us would like our dependents to maintain the standard of living to which they are accustomed. Maintaining this same standard of living should not, however, require the same level of expenditure. With one member of the family gone, some expenses will either be reduced or eliminated, since this person will no longer need any clothes, transportation, or food. Some life insurance premiums will also be eliminated. Income taxes will be lower, and mortgage payments will be eliminated if a special mortgage fund has been set up.

If the mortgage is paid off or paid from a separate mortgage fund, the surviving spouse and children will need about 60 percent of the gross income that the family needed when it was complete. If the mortgage payments are part of the general living costs, then they will need closer to 75 percent of the complete family's gross income.

Some families may be able to meet their expenses with the income from accumulated assets, Social Security benefits, and the surviving spouse's income. A housewife who survives her husband may need to find a job outside the home after her husband's death. Some income may also be generated by teenage children.

FORM 29—TOTAL LIFE INSURANCE REQUIRED

Before or while you complete this form, it might be helpful to look at an example of the completed form as shown in Figure 13-2.

- Line 1a: The average present cost of funeral and interment is about $3,000.
- Line 1b: If you frequently have large debts outstanding on your credit cards, take that into consideration. If it seems probable that the insured person will die of a major illness not fully covered by your medical insurance, allow for that also.
- Line 1c: Such fees will generally amount to 3 percent of your net worth (see Form 4).
- Line 1d: Enter 50 percent of the insured spouse's annual gross income.
- Line 1e: If, upon death, the decedent's entire estate will be passed to the other spouse, put zero on this line. If not, and if decedent's taxable estate will significantly exceed $300,000, you might ask your attorney or your accountant for an estimate.
- Line 2a: Enter the lump-sum total of life insurance benefits to be paid when the insured spouse dies, as shown on Form 28 .
- Line 2b: Enter the death benefits payable from retirement programs. Most retirement programs do not provide significant death benefits until the employee reaches a certain age, such as 55 years or older; so check out the death benefits of your retirement programs.
- Line 2c: Enter your liquid assets total, as shown on your net worth statement, Form 4, but don't include the cash value of the insured spouse's life insurance.
- Line 3: Subtract line 1f from line 2e. If you get a negative figure, indicate this by showing it in parentheses. Most people who have any life insurance program or liquid assets will get a positive figure here.
- Line 4a: Discuss with your spouse whether, when you die, the mortgage(s) should be paid off. If you have a low balance on your mortgage, chances are you are paying a low rate of interest on the mortgage, and then it may be wiser for the surviving spouse not to pay off the mortgage. If the mortgage balance is large and the rate of interest high, and if your spouse cannot generate a lot of earned income, it may be better to pay off the mortgage.

FIGURE 13-2

File Under INSURANCE

Date: 9/25

FORM 29 TOTAL LIFE INSURANCE REQUIRED

1	Cash Required Immediately		
	a. Funeral	$3,000	
	b. Current bills	—	
	c. Administrative	15,000	
	d. Emergency fund	40,000	
	e. Estate taxes	—	
	f. TOTAL	$58,000	
2	Cash Available Immediately		
	a. Insurance proceeds	155,000	
	b. Death benefits of retirement programs	1,000	
	c. Liquid assets	26,500	
	d. Other	—	
	e. TOTAL	$182,500	
3	Net Cash Available (or Required)		$124,500
4	Assets Required for Mortgage and Children's Education		
	a. Mortgage outstanding	—	
	b. Education	45,000	
	c. TOTAL	$45,000	
5	Assets Available for Mortgage and Children's Education		
	a. Investment assets	$262,800	
	b. Personal assets convertible into cash	—	
	c. Other	—	
	d. TOTAL	$262,800	
6	Net Resources Available (or Required)		$217,800
7	Total Resources Available (or Required)		$342,300

FIGURE 13-2, cont'd.

8	Annual Living Expenses		$60,000
9	Annual Income Available for Living Expenses		
	a. Income from assets	$34,200	
	b. Employment income of spouse	10,000	
	c. Other	—	
	d. TOTAL	$44,200	
10	Annual Income Excess (or Deficiency)		$(15,800)
11	Additional Insurance Required		
	a. Negative amount from line 7	—	
	b. Negative amount from line 10 divided by 10%	158,000	
	c. TOTAL	$158,000	

- Line 4b: Use today's dollars, and base your figures on your estimates on Form 23—*College Costs*.
- Line 5a: Exclude the assets you listed on line 2c.
- Line 5b: Consider such items as a second car, a boat, and the odd Rembrandt you may own.
- Line 6: Subtract line 4c from line 5d. If you get a negative figure, indicate this by showing it in parentheses.
- Line 7: Add lines 6 and 3. If the result is a positive figure, there are some resources to cover the annual living expenses. If the result is a negative figure, then additional insurance is needed equal to the negative amount on line 7. Additional insurance will also be needed to cover the annual living expenses, which will be the next thing you assess.
- Line 8: If the living expenses are to include mortgage payments, list 75 percent of the gross income presently earned by the family. If mortgage payments will not be part of the annual living expenses, list 60 percent of the gross income presently needed by the family.
- Line 9a: If you have a positive figure on line 7, estimate the annual pretax income these assets might generate.
- Line 9b: If your spouse is employed, or would, in the event of your death, be in a position to seek gainful employment, estimate the annual income from such employment.
- Line 10: Subtract line 8 from line 9d. If the result is a positive figure, you probably have too much insurance. To determine how much excess insurance you have, multiply the amount on this line by 10. If the result on line 10 is a negative figure, you need additional insurance, and should now determine how much more.
- Line 11a: Enter the amount on line 7 if that is a negative amount.
- Line 11b: Enter ten times the negative amount on line 10.
- Line 11c: Add lines 11a and 11b. The resulting sum is the additional insurance you need.

Once you have completed this analysis and determined that you are either overinsured or underinsured, you should review your analysis with your insurance agent and then take the appropriate action.

LIFE INSURANCE POLICIES

There are two basic types of life insurance policies: pure insurance, called *term insurance*, and life insurance combined with a savings program. These two basic types can be further subdivided according to some of their special features.

TERM INSURANCE Term life insurance is like the automobile insurance, fire insurance, and health insurance you have in that it protects you for a limited specified time. If, as you hope, you are still living at the end of the specified time, your protection ceases, just as a fire insurance policy expires, and there is no residual value in that policy. Term policies are ideal for providing a large amount of protection for a limited time at the lowest premium outlay.

By paying an additional premium, term insurance may be renewable or convertible or both. If the policy is renewed or another term policy is issued to replace it, a higher premium is charged because the policy holder is now older and has a greater chance of dying than in the previous period.

Renewable term policies include an option permitting you to renew the contract for a number of specified periods—five, ten, fifteen, or twenty years, or to a certain age, such as 60, 65, or 70—without further medical examination. Term policies may allow you to convert the full amount of insurance to a *straight life, limited payment life,* or *endowment* policy without medical reexamination at any time while your insurance is still in force.

Term policies have several advantages. Term offers the lowest cost for pure protection. The needs of a family tend to change over the years, so term insurance can be very useful for providing the funds for temporary needs, such as college education or mortgage payments. With the flexibility of its renewable policies and its low premiums, term insurance has a definite place in all well-planned life insurance programs.

There are three kinds of term policies: *annual renewable term, decreasing term,* and *level term.*

ANNUAL RENEWABLE TERM

With an annual renewable term policy, the face amount of your insurance remains the same, and the premium increases every year.

DECREASING TERM

Your premium remains the same with a decreasing term policy, but the face amount of the insurance decreases. Typically, your insurance needs decline as you grow older, so decreasing term insurance can fit that situation very well. A mortgage insurance, which some people buy, is really a decreasing term policy.

LEVEL TERM

With a level term policy, the face amount of the policy remains the same for a chosen period of time—five, ten, fifteen, twenty, twenty-five, or thirty years, or until you reach the age of 65. The premium remains level throughout the period, and it approximates the average of the annual renewable term rates for the specified number of years. If you chose a twenty-year level term policy, for example, the insurance company would essentially add up the renewable term rates for twenty years and divide the total by twenty, and you would pay the same annual rate for each of the twenty years.

LIFE INSURANCE COMBINED WITH A SAVINGS PROGRAM

Some policies provide a savings program as well as protection. With such policies, you normally buy a level face amount of insurance—say, $10,000—but the premiums you pay go for protection *and* for a low-interest savings account. In reality, you are buying a form of decreasing term insurance, for as your savings account increases, your protection goes down.

You can obtain the cash from your savings account in two ways. You can stop paying premiums at any time, take the cash value, and terminate the policy. Alternatively, you can borrow from the cash value. Then your insurance coverage will be reduced by the amount you borrowed until the loan is repaid. You can repay your policy loan at any time, but you are never required to do so. In recent years, the cost of borrowing against the cash value of insurance policies, ranging from 5 to 8 percent, has been much lower than the cost of borrowing from a bank.

When you hold a life insurance policy that has a cash value, you can do any of the following things with your cash value:

- You can convert the contract to paid-up life insurance for a lesser amount than the original face amount.

- You can have the original face amount continued as term insurance for a specified period. The length of the period will depend on the amount of the cash value and on the face amount of the original policy.
- You can arrange for a minimum deposit plan that will allow you to take part of your annual dividend in the form of additional term insurance, instead of taking it all as cash. The additional term insurance is sold at a lower price than regular term insurance.

OTHER TYPES OF LIFE INSURANCE POLICIES

Three other insurance products have recently been introduced and deserve some mention. One is *universal life insurance,* which includes a tax-sheltered cash value accumulation fund similar to a tax-deferred annuity. This policy provides a high cash value return from which expense charges and the term insurance premium are deducted. The advantage of such a policy is its high return and the purchase of term insurance with untaxed earnings.

Another relatively new product is *variable whole life insurance.* Here cash values are invested in either a money market fund or a common stock fund, and both the return on the cash value and the amount of the death benefit vary with investment performance.

The third recent product is *survivorship life insurance.* Here the death benefit is paid when both of the people initially insured are dead. This type of coverage may be appropriate when each spouse leaves his or her estate to the surviving spouse, thereby postponing federal estate taxes until the other spouse dies. The death benefit of the survivorship policy would then be available to pay all or a portion of the estate taxes due.

SELECTING THE INSURANCE COMPANY

There are thousands of life insurance companies in the United States. Selecting the one that is right for you requires evaluation of three important factors:

- The financial strength and integrity of the company
- Service
- The cost of the policy

FINANCIAL STRENGTH AND INTEGRITY

Life insurance involves a long-term financial guarantee, so you should be concerned about the company's ability to fulfill its obligations to you whenever it is called upon to do so—tomorrow, or fifty years from now.

For information on the financial strength and integrity of insurance companies, we suggest that you look at a copy of *Best's Insurance Reports.* This hefty volume is available in the reference rooms of most metropolitan public libraries, and it contains a report on each life insurance company in the United States and on many Canadian ones as well. It will give you detailed financial information about a company, an analysis of the company's investments, a brief history of the company and its growth, and a description of the company's method of operation.

Best's Insurance Reports also includes a policyholder's rating for most insurance companies. The classifications used are:

A+ and A	Excellent
B+	Very Good
B	Good
C+	Fairly Good
D	Fair

SERVICE If you are not able to plan and maintain your insurance program yourself, you will probably rely on the advice of an insurance company's local representative. You should seek an agent who has competence and integrity. Ask your friends or associates whether they can recommend any such person working for companies that you know have financial strength and stability. Talk to several agents and find out about their experience and approach to determining your needs. Obtain a proposal and a sample policy; then study their provisions thoroughly at your leisure. Make sure you understand what insurance policy you are buying, and why, before you sign the application.

COST Cost is probably the most important factor in deciding from which company you will buy your life insurance. In any company, the cost of a policy depends on such factors as the company's investment performance, its selection of policyholders, its efficiency of operation, and its costs of acquiring new policyholders. These factors have to be managed, and the net result of company management is the cost of the insurance policy. Since management performance differs from company to company, so do costs. As more than one consumer-oriented insurance publication has suggested: Shop for your life insurance!

To help you compare the net costs of different insurers' policies, insurers provide interest-adjusted cost estimates, which apply an interest factor to the yearly premiums, dividends, and increases in cash value. When you are shopping for life insurance, ask the insurance agents to provide you with interest-adjusted cost estimates for any policy you are considering, and don't do any business with an agent who refuses to supply such indexes.

The interest-adjusted cost estimates given by different insurance companies differ greatly for the same benefit and type of policy. A recent study published by the American Institute for Economic Research, *Life Insurance from the Buyer's Point of View,** included a cost ranking of companies that had a Best's rating of A or A+ (excellent) and insurance contracts totaling $1 billion or more. To rank the companies, this study used the interest-adjusted annual cost of a $25,000 whole life policy for a man 35 years of age. The findings showed a difference of $4,505 between the least costly and the most costly company. This study only included those companies that were rated excellent. If all companies had been analyzed, the cost difference would have been even greater.

SHOULD YOU DISCONTINUE OR REPLACE OLD POLICIES?

Should you discontinue old policies? If your insurance analysis indicates that you have too much insurance, the answer is yes. When you decide to drop some of your policies, drop those with the highest cost per $1,000 of insurance protection—a calculation discussed in the next section.

*Available from the American Institute for Economic Research, Great Barrington, Massachusetts 01230.

As for replacing old policies with new ones, you should know that the cost of new policies has dropped substantially in recent years. You should, therefore, analyze the cost per $1,000 of benefits of your old policies and compare them with the costs of new policies.

Determining the cost per $1,000 of benefits for term insurance is quite easy. Merely divide the annual premium by one-thousandth of the face amount. For example, if you have a group term policy with a face amount of $100,000 and your premium is $600 a year, then the cost per thousand is $6 ($600 ÷ 100). For whole life policies, it is a little more complicated to determine the cost per thousand—but by completing Form 30, you can do so.

FORM 30—WHOLE LIFE POLICY: INSURANCE COST PER $1,000

- Line 1: Enter the face amount of your present policy as listed on Form 28.
- Line 2: Enter the cash surrender value for the policy as listed on Form 28.
- Line 3: Subtract line 2 from line 1 to get the net insurance protection provided by your policy.
- Line 4: Enter the present gross premium amount before dividends on your policy.
- Line 5: Enter the increase in the cash value of your policy during the current year. This can be determined by looking at the cash value table in your policy contract or by asking your agent.
- Line 6: Enter the dividend you received for the current year. This is normally shown on your premium payment notice.
- Line 7: Enter 5 percent of the amount on line 2.
- Line 8: If you have borrowed your cash value and are investing the funds, enter 5 percent of the borrowed cash value.
- Line 9: Add line 7 to line 4; then subtract lines 5, 6, and 8 from the result. You now have the total annual cost of your present policy.
- Line 10: Divide line 9 by one-thousandth of line 3.

14

ESTATE PLANNING

In conversations about worldly wealth, it is often remarked that "you can't take it with you" when you depart. Some unknown cynic has elaborated on this statement, saying, "The reason you can't take it with you is that *it* goes before *you* go." We will assume, though, that with the help of this book, yours won't go before you go, and so you may want your heirs to receive the maximum of your estate with a minimum of aggravation.

Since a smooth transfer of your property is by no means automatic, you should plan and organize your estate now in order to prevent needless delays and losses later on. The preparation of Your Financial Planner should be very helpful in estate planning. Obviously, the first step in the estate-planning process must be to ascertain what you own and can thus regard as your gross estate.

OWNERSHIP OF PROPERTY

Your gross estate consists of the assets to which you have title or legal rights of ownership. These rights depend on the method by which you acquired the property, and they also depend on state statutes governing marital property. Some states consider marital property to be community property, while others do not.

COMMUNITY PROPERTY STATES

The essential characteristic of community property is that each spouse is deemed to own one-half of any such property. Thus, if a couple's entire assets are community property, each one would have a gross estate equal to half the couple's total assets and liabilities. Not only do both spouses in community property states have equal rights of ownership in their acquired physical property and its earnings, but they also share such equal ownership rights in the income that one or both derive from salaries, wages, or other compensation for services.

Even in community property states, the property that you acquire prior to marriage, or by inheritance or gift before or during marriage, together with the earnings thereon, is classified as separate property. All other types of property acquired by either spouse while married and residing in a community property state are classified as community property, and so are the earnings and reinvestments of community property.

Once you are married, care should be taken to keep property separate (if that is desired), or else it will become community property over time. Separate property should be segregated through separate record-keeping, separate accounts, separate securities registration, etc. Dividends, interest, and other forms of income on separate property should be kept separate as well.

Beyond sharing their community property on an equal basis, spouses can also own their separate property and/or their half of the community property jointly with someone other than their spouse.

NON-COMMUNITY PROPERTY STATES

While there is no assumption of equally divided spousal property in these states, they all have joint property provisions that allow you to achieve the same results. Joint ownership is frequently chosen as a means of transferring title to such assets as the family's home or bank accounts to another member of the family in the event of one owner's death.

The most common forms of joint property ownership are *joint tenancy, tenancy by the entirety, and tenancy in common*. For all jointly held property, only one-half of the property is included in the decedent's estate. Property can be jointly owned in community property states as well.

JOINT TENANCY

Joint tenancy is co-ownership by husband and wife or by any other persons, related or unrelated, of real estate or other property, such as stocks and bonds. Each co-owner may dispose of his or her share without the permission of the other owner or owners. Upon the death of one co-owner, this person's share of the property will automatically pass to the surviving co-owner or co-owners.

TENANCY BY THE ENTIRETY

Tenancy by the entirety is a joint ownership that can be held only by a husband and wife, and in many states it applies only to the ownership of real estate. With this type of ownership, neither spouse may dispose of his or her share without the other spouse's permission. When one spouse dies, the ownership of the entire property passes to the surviving spouse.

TENANCY IN COMMON

Tenancy in common extends to two or more co-owners of real or personal property and permits any one of them to dispose of his or her share without the permission of the other co-owner or co-owners. There are no rights of survivorship with this type of ownership. When one of the owners dies, that person's share passes to the person's heirs or beneficiaries, who may or may not be the other owner or owners. For purposes of assessing estate taxes on such a share, the co-owner's share of the property is assessed as though it were a separate property.

FORM 31—PROPERTY OWNERSHIP AND GROSS ESTATE

On this form you will arrange your and your spouse's estate assets according to ownership and determine your and your spouse's gross estate. That is the starting point for any estate planning. Before you complete this form, it may be helpful to review Figure 14-1, which shows an example of the completed form.

- For lines 1a through 1d, use the information you listed on Form 4—*Statement of Net Worth*.
- On lines 2a and 2b, list the death benefits from life insurance on your

FIGURE 14-1

File Under ESTATE PLANNING　　　　　　　　Date: 11/15

FORM 31 PROPERTY OWNERSHIP AND GROSS ESTATE

PROPERTY		OWNERSHIP			
	Est. Current Value	Community	Joint	Solely Yours	Solely Spouse's
1 NET WORTH					
a. Liquid Assets Other Than Cash Value of Life Insurance	$26,500		$26,500		
b. Investment Assets, Other Than Retirement Funds	237,400	151,800	58,600		27,000
c. Personal Assets	404,500	404,500			
d. Total Assets	668,400	556,300	85,100		27,000
e. Liabilities	(123,300)	(123,300)	—		—
f. TOTAL	545,100	433,000	85,100		27,000
2 INSURANCE OWNED					
a. On Your Life	200,000				200,000
b. On Your Spouse's Life	50,000			50,000	
c. TOTAL	250,000			50,000	200,000
3 OTHER ESTATE ASSETS					
a. Retirement Plans	180,400	180,400			
b. Other	—				
c. TOTAL	180,400	180,400			
4 TOTAL GROSS ESTATE	975,500	613,400	85,100	50,000	227,000
5 TOTAL GROSS ESTATE FOR YOU AND YOUR SPOUSE					
a. Your Gross Estate	399,250	306,700	42,550	50,000	
b. Your Spouse's Gross Estate	576,250	306,700	42,550		227,000
c. TOTAL	975,500	613,400	85,100	50,000	227,000

life and your spouse's life as shown on Form 28—*Your Present Life Insurance Coverage*. Depending on the ownership of each policy, list its face amount either under *Solely Yours* or under *Solely Spouse's*.

- Complete lines 3a, 3b, and 3c for other assets that may be includable in your and your spouse's estates. Normally, such assets include the present value of death benefits from employer retirement plans, Keogh plans, and IRAs. Remember, some employer retirement plans do not provide any death benefits until you are at or near retirement age.
- On line 4, total the amounts on lines 1f, 2c, and 3c. The combined totals of the *Ownership* columns should agree with the total of the *Estimated Current Value* column. The total of the *Estimated Current Value* column shows your and your spouse's combined gross estates.
- On lines 5a and 5b, start with the *Community* column. Halve the amount above it on line 4 and enter one-half on line 5a, the other half on line 5b. In the same way, take the total on line 4 in the *Joint* column and put one-half of it on line 5a and the other half on line 5b.
- Under *Solely Yours*, put the amount you showed on line 4 on line 5a. Under *Solely Spouse's*, put the amount you showed on line 4 on line 5b.
- Add all the amounts in the *Ownership* columns on line 5a and enter the result in the *Estimated Current Value* column on line 5a. This figure represents your own gross estate. Arrive at your spouse's gross estate by adding all the amounts in the *Ownership* columns on line 5b, and enter this figure in the *Estimated Current Value* column on line 5b.
- To check your arithmetic, in each column add lines 5a and 5b. The result should always be the amount listed above it on line 4.

Your and your spouse's gross estates, as shown in the first column on lines 5a and 5b, will be the starting points for Form 32—*Estimated Federal Estate Tax*. Before we launch you on that, however, you should know something about the way the federal estate tax is computed and about the basic estate-planning techniques you can use to minimize estate taxes.

STATE INHERITANCE TAXES

There are two kinds of death taxes: estate taxes and inheritance taxes. While the federal government imposes an estate tax, which is payable by the estate of the deceased, most but not all of the states impose an inheritance tax, which is payable by the recipient of an inheritance. The amount that the state exacts from the heir is determined by the amount the heir inherits and by the heir's relationship to the deceased.

FEDERAL ESTATE AND GIFT TAXES

There is a combined federal estate and gift tax. The federal estate tax is imposed on the transfer of a decedent's taxable estate, and the federal gift tax is imposed on transfers of income through gifts made by an individual during his or her lifetime. Although they are separate taxes, the federal estate tax and federal gift tax are integrated under a single rate, as shown in Table 14-1.

TABLE 14-1
ESTATE AND GIFT TAXES, UNIFIED TAX RATE SCHEDULE

If the Taxable Amount Is:		Tentative Tax Is:		
From	To	Tax on Amount in First Column	+ %	On Excess Over
$ —	$ 10,000	$ —	18	$ —
10,000	20,000	1,800	20	10,000
20,000	40,000	3,800	22	20,000
40,000	60,000	8,200	24	40,000
60,000	80,000	13,000	26	60,000
80,000	100,000	18,200	28	80,000
100,000	150,000	23,800	30	100,000
150,000	250,000	38,800	32	150,000
250,000	500,000	70,800	34	250,000
500,000	750,000	155,800	37	500,000
750,000	1,000,000	248,300	39	750,000
1,000,000	1,250,000	345,800	41	1,000,000
1,250,000	1,500,000	448,300	43	1,250,000
1,500,000	2,000,000	555,800	45	1,500,000
2,000,000	2,500,000	780,800	49	2,000,000
2,500,000*	3,000,000	1,025,800	53	2,500,000
3,000,000	3,500,000	1,290,800	57	3,000,000
3,500,000	and over	1,575,800	60	3,500,000

*Beginning in 1985, the maximum rate of taxation for individuals will be 50 percent for taxable amounts of $2,500,000 and more. The rates on all lower amounts will remain the same.

As you can see in the table, the unified estate and gift tax rates are progressive, from 18 to 60 percent in 1983, from 18 to 50 percent in 1985. The tax can be reduced by a unified credit, which is $79,300 in 1983 and which will have increased to $192,800 by 1987 (see Table 14-2). Thus, if a person who dies in 1983 has a taxable estate of $275,000, the tentative estate tax would be $79,300 ($70,800 plus 34 percent of $25,000); but the credit against the tentative tax would be $79,300, and therefore the federal estate tax would be reduced to zero. The amount of a decedent's taxable estate that

TABLE 14-2
UNIFIED CREDIT FOR ESTATE AND GIFT TAXES

For estates of persons dying in 1983 and thereafter, the credit is phased in as follows:

Year	Amount of Credit	Amount of Exemption Equivalent
1983	$ 79,300	$275,000
1984	96,300	325,000
1985	121,800	400,000
1986	155,800	500,000
1987 and thereafter	192,800	600,000

can pass tax-free in 1983 is $275,000, but by 1987 the tax-free amount will be $600,000 (see Table 14-2).

No federal estate tax is ever payable by the recipient of a legacy. It is only the estate of the decedent that may have to pay federal estate taxes.

To illustrate the basic federal estate tax computation, assume that Dan Danderoo dies in 1985, never having made any taxable gifts. Assume that Dan's taxable estate is $420,000. Table 14-1 shows that the tax on this would be $70,800 plus 34 percent on the excess over $250,000. Thus the total tax (before credits) would be $130,600. From this, a credit of $121,800 can be deducted (see Table 14-2), leaving a total of $8,800 in estate taxes due the federal government.

We will discuss the terms *taxable estate* and *taxable gifts* later. For now, consider how the gift and estate taxes are integrated.

Assume that our Dan Danderoo made a taxable gift of $100,000 in 1983. Since he had made no prior taxable gifts, the gift tax would be computed as follows:

Tax on $100,000 (from Table 14-1)	$ 23,800
Less: Credit in 1983 (from Table 14-2)	(79,300)
TAX DUE	$ 0

The credit is not a credit of $79,300 per year, nor is it one credit of $79,300 for lifetime gifts and another credit of $79,300 for transfers at death. Gifts are cumulative, meaning that current gifts are added to prior gifts for purposes of the progressive rate computation.

Taking the subject of gifts a step further, assume that Dan makes another taxable gift in 1984, and that the amount of it is $250,000. The tax is computed as follows:

Current year's taxable gifts	$250,000
Prior years' taxable gifts	100,000
	$350,000
Tax (from Table 14-1)	104,800
Less: Credit in 1984 (from Table 14-2)	(96,300)
GIFT TAX DUE	$ 8,500

Now assume that Dan makes no further gifts and dies in 1985 with a taxable estate of $80,000. The estate tax will be calculated as follows:

Taxable estate					$ 80,000
Taxable gifts during life					350,000
TOTAL					$ 430,000
Tax on $430,000					132,000
Less	Tax previously paid		$ 8,500		
	Unified credit (1985)	+	121,800	=	$(130,300)
TAX DUE					$ 1,700

The $192,800 credit available in 1987 and thereafter means that no estate or gift tax is due until total transfers during your lifetime and at your death exceed $600,000. Few people will then leave estates for which a federal

FIGURE 14-2
COMPUTATION OF THE TAXABLE ESTATE

Your Gross Estate:

Less Deductions:
- Funeral expenses
- Administrative expenses
- Marital deduction
- Charitable deduction

Equals Taxable Estate:

estate tax return will have to be filed. For those few with sufficient assets to have a possible estate tax liability, it will be important to make plans for minimizing the estate tax and the costs of administering their estates.

To minimize federal estate taxes, one should implement the basic estate planning techniques discussed in the next section of this chapter. Before we discuss them, we want to summarize briefly the computation of the taxable estate. As shown in Figure 14-2, it starts with your gross estate from Form 31 and ends with your taxable estate after certain deductions are subtracted from your gross estate. The two most important deductions from an estate-planning standpoint are the marital deduction and the charitable deduction. Briefly, the marital deduction is equal to the amount left by the decedent to his or her surviving spouse. The charitable deduction is for all amounts left by a decedent to religious, charitable, scientific, literary, and educational organizations.

BASIC ESTATE-PLANNING TECHNIQUES

There are several basic estate-planning techniques:

- Lifetime gifts
- Use of the maximum allowable marital deduction
- Use of charitable beneficiaries
- Transfer of ownership of life insurance
- Exclusion of the maximum allowable portion of your retirement plans
- Use of trust devices to prevent transfer taxes from depleting capital from one generation to another

The use of these techniques may eliminate federal estate taxes completely on the estate of the spouse who dies first and minimize taxes on the estate of the spouse who dies second.

LIFETIME GIFTS

Any person can make an annual gift of $10,000 or less to anyone in the whole wide world without any gift tax consequence. This $10,000 exclusion is known as the *annual exclusion*. This means you could give millions of dollars to relatives, your friendly C.P.A., and others without incurring any liability for gift taxes, provided that no one donee received more than $10,000 from you in one year.

To illustrate, take a married couple, aged 50, with three married children. Each parent can be a donor; each child and each child's spouse can be a donee. The parents can give away $60,000 per year free of gift taxes if they keep their gifts in the blood line (2 donors × 3 children × $10,000), and $120,000 per year if they give to their children's spouses as well. In 20 years, if they gave money only to their own offspring, the parents would transfer a total of $1,200,000 tax-free.

In addition, the appreciation on the transferred capital would not be included in the parents' estate. Let's say the parents gave stock to the children, and the stock appreciated at a compounded annual rate of 10 percent for 20 years. The stock would be worth $3,436,500 at the end of 20 years—a tidy sum for the children, and completely free of gift or estate taxes. If, on the other hand, the parents had retained the stock and not made lifetime gifts, the stock would remain in their estates and would be subject to substantial estate taxes when they died. Taking advantage of the $10,000 annual gift exclusion, particularly through gifts to children, is a basic estate-planning technique.

If you give away more than $10,000 to someone in one year, the gift is a taxable gift and may be subject to a gift tax. The transfer tax due on a gift is payable by the person who makes the gift (the donor) and not by the person who receives it (the donee). But as we discussed, the application of the unified credit means there is no tax due until a substantial cumulative sum has been transferred.

The amount of the gift is the value of the transferred property at date of gift. The taxable amount of the gift is computed by subtracting the amount of the annual exclusion and any marital deduction available from the value of the gift.

Because of the appreciation potential, annual gifts of more than $10,000 may be important to consider when parents have a sizable estate. For example, let's assume a couple aged 55 owns a summer home worth $150,000 and wants to transfer this property to their two children when they die. If the property appreciates at 10 percent per year, it will be worth approximately $1,600,000 in 25 years. If it is then transferred to the children upon the death of the parents, it will be subject to substantial estate taxes. But if 60 percent of the property ($90,000) is transferred in 1984, the taxable gift would be $50,000 ($90,000 minus the $20,000 annual exclusion each parent gets for two donees). Each parent would therefore be making a taxable gift of $25,000. The gift tax on $25,000 would be $4,900 (see Table 14-1), but the parents could each use $4,900 of their available unified credit ($96,300 for each in 1984) to reduce the gift tax to zero. The portion they gave as a taxable gift in 1984 might well be worth $975,000 at their deaths 25 years later ($90,000 compounded at 10 percent), and at that point the estate tax would be no laughing matter.

MARITAL DEDUCTION

Money or property transferred from one spouse to the other, either in life or at death, is not subject to gift or estate tax, provided the following conditions are met:

- The receiving spouse must be entitled to all the income from the property for life.
- The income from the property must be paid at least annually.
- No one may have the power to appoint any part of the property to anyone other than the receiving spouse while the receiving spouse is alive.

Everybody can see the point of transferring property to one's spouse at death; but why, you may wonder, would anyone want to transfer some while both spouses are still alive? The answer is, primarily, to equalize the estates of both spouses, and to take advantage of the "poorer" spouse's unified credit.

Optimum tax results are achieved when the estates of both spouses are subject to the same marginal tax rate. A greater combined estate tax is paid if one of the estates is subject to a higher marginal rate than the other. As for spousal gifts and the use of the marital deduction, it is very advantageous when one spouse has an estate that is smaller than the exemption equivalent of the unified credit. Assume, for example, that the wife's estate is worth $900,000, while the husband's estate is worth only $50,000. Let's further assume that husband and wife want to leave the maximum tax-free amounts to their children as soon as one parent dies. If the husband dies first, there would be only $50,000 in his taxable estate to leave to the children, and the remaining $275,000 of tax-free transfer (the maximum tax-free transfer in 1984 is $325,000) would be wasted. Therefore, the wife should consider giving her husband $275,000 in 1984 to bring his estate up to the exemption equivalent and to maximize his unified credit. If now the husband died in 1984, he could leave $325,000 to the children, and none of it would be taxable to his estate.

There is no limit to the amount of property that can be transferred tax-free from one spouse to the other; but this does not mean that it is best for all people to leave all their property to their surviving spouse. Let us use two examples to illustrate this point.

Example 1: A husband and wife with two children have a combined gross estate of $500,000. The husband's estate is $400,000; the wife's is $100,000. Assume the husband dies in 1984. If he left his $400,000 estate to his wife, his taxable estate would be zero because of the marital deduction. After that, the wife would have a gross estate of $500,000, which will present few or no estate tax problems when she dies. So here the maximum use of the marital deduction makes good sense.

Example 2: A husband and wife with two children have a combined gross estate of $1,000,000. The wife's estate is $800,000; the husband's is $200,000. Assume the wife dies in 1984. If she left her $800,000 estate to her husband, her taxable estate would be zero because of the marital deduction. After that, the husband would have a gross estate of $1,000,000, which certainly will present estate tax problems after his death. In this case, it would have been wiser for the wife to leave some of her estate to the children, either outright or in trust. She could have left as much as $325,000 of her estate to the children in 1984 without incurring any estate tax, and the remaining $475,000 she could have left to her husband. Now let us go through this computation, but without regard to funeral and administrative expenses.

Wife's Gross Estate		$800,000
Marital Deduction for Amount Left to Husband		(475,000)
Taxable Estate		$325,000
Federal Estate Tax (see Table 14-1)		
On first $250,000	—$70,800	
On remaining $75,000	— 25,500	96,300
Wife's Unified Credit in 1984 (see Table 14-2)		(96,300)
Federal Estate Tax Due		$ 0

TRANSFERS THAT QUALIFY FOR MARITAL DEDUCTION

To be classed as marital deductions and thus exempt from federal estate tax, transfers of property from the deceased spouse to the surviving spouse must be accomplished by one of the following means.

- Transfer through joint ownership of property. With this method, ownership of the entire property passes to the surviving spouse.
- Transfer through a deceased spouse's contract that provides for benefits payable to the surviving spouse. Examples of such contracts are life insurance, deferred compensation, employer pension and profit-sharing plans, and Keogh and IRA plans.
- Transfer through a will by which property passes to the surviving spouse, either outright or through a Qualified Terminable Interest Property (QTIP) trust. If the property is transferred to a QTIP trust, the surviving spouse must be given the interest income for life, and this must be payable at least once a year. In addition, no one, not even the surviving spouse, may have the power to appoint any part of the trust property to anyone else while the surviving spouse is alive.

CHARITABLE TRANSFERS

As we showed in Figure 14-2, a decedent's gross estate can be reduced by transfers to a surviving spouse—the marital deduction—and by the charitable deduction for transfers to religious, charitable, scientific, literary, or educational organizations.

Normally, such transfers occur in estates of very wealthy individuals or in estates of individuals with no surviving spouse and children.

LIFE INSURANCE

If you are the insured, and you own the life insurance contract yourself, and the premiums are paid out of your *separate* property, the death benefits paid to a beneficiary upon your death will be includable in your estate. If you are the insured, and you own the insurance contract yourself, and the premiums are paid out of *community* property, one-half of the death benefits paid upon your death are includable in your estate.

If your spouse is the beneficiary of any life insurance death benefits includable in your estate, the amount of such benefits will qualify for a marital deduction from your gross estate.

To keep the insurance death benefits out of your gross estate to begin with, someone else—for example, your spouse or a life insurance trust—must own the policy. For existing policies that you own, you can transfer the ownership by assigning the policy to someone else and giving up *all and any* powers over the policy and its benefits, such as the power to change the beneficiary, to surrender or cancel the policy, to assign it, to pledge the policy for a loan, or to borrow the cash value. Your life insurance agent has forms for assigning the ownership of policies. If you assign policies with cash values, there may be gift tax consequences. So check on this with an attorney or an accountant before you make any commitment.

RETIREMENT PLANS

Employee retirement plans and individual retirement plans such as IRAs and Keoghs may be a significant part of your estate. Suppose that when you retire at age 65 your employee retirement plan benefits are $4,000 a month for your life and your surviving spouse's life; then the present value of such payments might be close to $400,000. Add to that your IRA and any death benefits from your other retirement plans.

Only $100,000 of the present value of any benefits paid to survivors from your retirement plans is excludable from your estate. If the death benefits includable in your estate will be paid to your surviving spouse, it will, of course, qualify for the marital deduction. So check your employee retirement plan and your IRA plan to determine exactly how your death benefit is worded. If the proceeds are payable to your spouse alone, they will qualify for the marital deduction and will not be taxable in your estate. If your plan calls for outright payments to your spouse over a period of years and for a continuation of payments to your children in case your spouse dies before all payments are received, it will not qualify for the marital deduction. If payments remaining after your spouse's death are to pass to your spouse's estate, it will qualify.

You may not be entitled to any death benefits from the plan before you retire. Check your employee retirement plan to see what death benefits accrue to you at what age.

EXEMPTION-EQUIVALENT TRUST

With most married couples, the primary concern in the event of one spouse's death is the financial well-being of the surviving spouse. That objective can be achieved by leaving everything outright to the surviving spouse. The marital deduction can reduce the estate taxes on the first decedent's estate to zero. It may be important, however, to look at the potential estate tax consequences for both spouses.

Where the combined gross estate of both spouses is $600,000 or less, it generally makes good sense for each spouse to leave his or her whole estate to the other spouse. Where the combined estates exceed $600,000, consideration should be given to using the exemption-equivalent trust as well as the unlimited marital deduction.

The primary feature of an exemption-equivalent trust is that the surviving spouse gets all the annual income from the trust and can also draw on the trust principal in the event that other resources are not sufficient to maintain the surviving spouse's standard of living. Whatever assets remain in the trust upon the death of the surviving spouse will then pass free of estate tax to the beneficiaries of the trust, such as the deceased couple's children.

Now look at some examples that illustrate when and how an exemption-equivalent trust would be used to save taxes on both estates and thus to pass greater assets on to a couple's beneficiaries. All the examples will assume that the first spouse to die will be the husband (denoted by the letter H), and that he will die in 1987, when the unified credit of $192,800 is the equivalent of a tax-free transfer of $600,000.

EXAMPLE 1

Gross Estate of H	$ 500,000
Marital Deduction	(500,000)
Taxable Estate	$ 0
Estate Tax Due	$ 0
Gross Estate of W at H's Death	$ 100,000
Received from H	500,000
Taxable Estate (assuming no marital deduction or charitable deduction)	$ 600,000
Estate Tax	$ 192,800
Unified Credit	(192,800)
Estate Tax Due	$ 0

If the combined gross estates are greater than $600,000, then leaving everything outright to the spouse may result in a tax on the wife's estate, as shown in Example 2, where the combined gross estate after the husband's death is $800,000.

EXAMPLE 2

Gross Estate of H	$ 400,000
Marital Deduction	(400,000)
Taxable Estate	$ 0
Estate Tax Due	$ 0
Gross Estate of W at H's Death	$ 400,000
Received from H	400,000
Taxable Estate	$ 800,000
Estate Tax	$ 266,800
Unified Credit	($192,000)
Estate Tax Due	$ 74,000

In both examples you can see that the husband's estate did not use any of his unified credit because he left everything outright to his spouse.

In each example, the husband could have left some portion of his estate to other than his spouse—say, a trust for the spouse's benefit—without having to pay any estate tax. Therein lies the advantage of using an exemption-equivalent trust. Such a trust could be set up in your will to receive any amount up to $600,000 (in 1987) transferred in the will to the trust. The amount transferred into the trust would be includable in your estate, but as long as it was $600,000 or less, the amount would not be taxed because of the unified credit available (assuming no credits were used in making taxable gifts in prior years).

Let's use Example 3 to illustrate the use of an exemption-equivalent trust for the situation in Example 2. The use of the trust would result in estate tax savings of $74,000.

EXAMPLE 3

Gross Estate of H	$400,000
Marital Deduction	(200,000)
Taxable Estate (to put in exemption-equivalent trust at H's death)	$200,000
Estate Tax	$ 54,800
Unified Credit	(192,800)
Estate Tax Due	$ 0
Gross Estate of W	$400,000
Received from H	200,000
Taxable Estate at W's Death	$600,000
Estate Tax	$192,800
Unified Credit	(192,800)
Estate Tax Due	$ 0

In Example 4, we start with a combined gross estate of $1,200,000 and see how an exemption-equivalent trust could be used to avoid taxes on both estates.

EXAMPLE 4

Gross Estate of H	$800,000
Marital Deduction	(200,000)
Taxable Estate (in exemption-equivalent trust at H's death)	$600,000
Estate Tax	$192,800
Unified Credit	(192,800)
Estate Tax Due	$ 0
Gross Estate of W	$400,000
Received from H	200,000
Taxable Estate at W's Death	$600,000
Estate Tax	$192,800
Unified Credit	(192,800)
Estate Tax Due	$ 0

One of the primary features of the exemption-equivalent trust is that the surviving spouse could have all of the income from the trust each year *and* could still obtain any amount of trust principal needed to maintain his or her standard of living in the event that other resources were not sufficient.

The assets not used, and therefore remaining in the trust upon the death of the surviving spouse, will pass free of estate tax to the trust beneficiaries, such as the children.

So the surviving spouse can receive a good deal of financial benefit from an exemption-equivalent trust during her lifetime and can avoid having any federal estate taxes paid from her estate on such a trust when she dies. Result—significant estate tax savings.

DISPOSING OF YOUR ESTATE

The term *gross estate* refers to all the property included in the decedent's estate for estate tax purposes. If the decedent has made a will, then part of the gross estate, called the *probate estate,* is transferred under the terms of the will. Items that will be or have been transferred through operation of contract law to specific beneficiaries do not become part of the probate estate. Thus, the following items, which transfer "outside the will," are not included in the probate estate:

- Insurance death benefits paid to a named beneficiary (other than the estate) who survives the decedent—the surviving spouse, for example.
- Jointly owned accounts, real estate, and securities held with rights of survivorship.
- Death benefits from retirement plans or annuity contracts payable to a designated and surviving beneficiary.
- Any property the decedent gave away while alive.

The only assets that are part of the probate estate are those transferred according to a will. If you do not have a will, your probate assets (those that could have been passed by a will) are distributed according to the "intestacy" law of the state in which you live. In effect, the state makes a will for those who die without one, and the state's disposition of your property may not be what you wanted or what you thought it would be.

WILLS Should everybody have a will? Maybe not everybody, but if you have a spouse and children, or some interest in the eventual disposition of your property, then making a will is essential unless you want a probate judge in your state to determine who will be the guardian of your children and how your estate will be disposed of. Most wills are drawn up for persons of modest wealth with relatively simple estate plans whose needs are met by a "simple" will. The following points should be remembered in drawing up a will:

- Your (the testator's) identity and address.
- Revocation of prior wills and codicils (revisions to prior wills).
- Burial instructions or other disposition of your body (such as donating it for medical purposes).
- Specific bequests (gifts) of identifiable real or personal property, sums of money, or shares of stock to a specified beneficiary, such as your spouse, your children, or charities. Specific bequests to your spouse qualify for the marital deduction; bequests to charities qualify for the charitable deduction.
- Bequests of tangible personal property, such as personal and household effects, jewelry, and cars, to friends or charities.
- Residuary bequests of assets that have not been specifically bequeathed. In small estates, such assets are usually left outright to the surviving spouse or children. In large estates, the residual assets are more important and their disposition is more complicated, often involving trusts and matters requiring legal advice. When there is no close family or surviving spouse, the residual assets are often left to charities.
- Survivorship provisions that establish a presumed order of death in case you and your spouse or other beneficiary die in the same accident and there is no proof of which one died first. This component in the will should also include provisions that will serve to avoid the expense of double administration in case two parties, one inheriting from the other, die within a short time of each other.
- A clause designating funds or assets from which federal estate and state inheritance taxes should be paid.
- Appointment of a guardian for your minor children in the event that you and your spouse die at the same time.
- Appointment of executor(s).
- Appointment of trustee(s) when the will contains a trust.

CHANGING YOUR WILL Keep your will in a safe place where your executor, spouse, or closest beneficiary can get to it quickly and easily. The original will might best be kept in your attorney's safe. Another copy can be kept in your safe deposit box, but if you plan to do so, find out first what procedures would have to be followed to open the box after your death. Keep another copy with your financial records at home for easy reference. It might be a good idea also to summarize and discuss the important provisions of your will with persons affected by it.

Once you have a will, you should review it every few years to make sure that it still fits your situation. Changes in your financial position—an inheritance or a large gift—or changes in your personal life—marriage, divorce, a new child, a move to another state—might affect your will. There may also be changes in the tax laws that affect your will.

Never make changes on the face of your will. If you need to make only a few changes in your will, add a codicil. A codicil is a document that explains, adds, or deletes provisions in your existing will. The codicil should also identify the will that is being amended and confirm the portions of the will that it does not change. When you need to make a lot of changes, it is best to draw up a new will, which should include a clause revoking all your earlier wills and codicils.

REVOCABLE LIVING TRUSTS

A revocable living trust is one of the most flexible devices available in estate planning. It offers little in the way of income or estate tax advantages, but offers substantial nontaxable advantages. Many estate planners offer it as a substitute for a will. The essence of the arrangement is that the estate owner, sometimes called the trust grantor, during his or her lifetime transfers assets to a trust, reserving, during lifetime, all the beneficial rights in the trust, including the right to revoke. Upon the death of the grantor, the trust becomes irrevocable. The trust assets are administered and distributed in accordance with the provisions of the trust.

The assets of a living trust are considered to be controlled by the trust grantor, and therefore the income of the trust is income of the grantor and subject to income tax. Upon the grantor's death, the value of the trust's assets is added to the grantor's gross estate and is subject to federal estate tax. The trust assets are distributed according to the trust provisions.

The trust can be used to provide lifetime management of the grantor's property and to test the capacity of various trustees to manage the grantor's property after his or her death. The trust assets need not be probated at the grantor's death, an important advantage if you wish to avoid probate and the potential publicity of your probate estate (probate estates are matters of public record). The trust may include any of a wide variety of plans for the administration of the property following the grantor's death, depending on the age, experience, and needs of the grantor's surviving spouse and children.

Because a revocable living trust can be revoked or terminated by the grantor at any time during his or her lifetime, the trust income will be taxable to the grantor. Also, the trust property will be included in the grantor's gross estate at death.

COSTS OF DISPOSING OF YOUR ESTATE

There are costs to consider in disposing of your estate. When you die, your estate is subject to two types of costs that should be considered: probate and administrative costs, and taxes, federal as well as state.

PROBATE AND ADMINISTRATIVE COSTS

Probate, which is a court proceeding, is the process of proving the validity of your will. In recent years, the cost and delay of probate proceedings have been reduced by streamlined estate administration procedures such as the Uniform Probate Code.

One of the probate provisions is the mandatory filing of creditors' claims within a statutory period—usually four months from the first publication of notice to creditors. After that date, creditors' claims are barred. Thus, for the estate of someone in business or the professions, the probate process might be important because it clearly cuts off lingering liabilities.

The costs of administering an estate normally include probate court fees, accountants' fees, attorneys' fees, and executors' fees and expenses. Normally, these fees run between 4 and 8 percent of the decedent's gross estate. These costs can be minimized by taking steps to minimize the probate process (to be discussed later) and by having good records of your estate assets and liabilities such as would be contained in Your Financial Planner.

WHO WILL BE YOUR EXECUTOR?

What could be better than to have your spouse or relative serve as the executor of your estate? After all, he or she is most likely to know exactly what you would have done if you were still alive. However, you might be better off having a professional take on the job of executor.

The job of executor is complicated because of new tax laws, inheritance rules, and probate regulations. It makes sense to evaluate the following checklist before choosing an executor. One solution is to name a bank or attorney and have your spouse or a relative as coexecutor.

Your executor should do the following:

- Choose the tax year that will best suit the income tax situations of your estate and your heirs
- Complete your estate's federal income tax return so that taxes are minimized
- Complete and file your final personal income tax return using the same tax-saving opportunities you would have used if you were still alive
- Determine the value of your property for federal estate tax purposes, both at the time of your death and at the "alternate valuation date" six months thereafter
- Calculate your federal estate tax
- Elect to defer the payment of your estate's taxes, if your estate is eligible for such deferral and if such a step is desirable in the overall context of your estate
- Make other elections and decisions that may ease the overall tax burden on your estate and your heirs
- File state death tax returns as required
- Determine your heirs' basis in property they have inherited

Were you able to check off each item comfortably? An executor's tax-related responsibilities are numerous, as this partial listing indicates. There are many tax-saving opportunities available to your executor. Knowledge and experience are essential.

FORM 32—ESTIMATED FEDERAL ESTATE TAX

To determine the potential federal tax on your estate, complete Form 32—*Estimated Federal Estate Tax*. This form has two pages: page A for your estate, and page B for your spouse's estate.

Before or while you complete this form, it may be helpful to look at Figure 14-3, which is an example of the completed page A, and at Figure 14-4, which is an example of the completed page B. The examples are based on the amounts shown in Figure 14-1. They show what would happen if one spouse died and left all personal assets and retirement plans in his or her estate outright to his or her spouse.

In the example situation we show in Figures 14-3 and 14-4, the couple should give some serious thought to increasing the taxable estate of the spouse in question and then to putting the maximum amount into an exemption-equivalent trust for the children. This would avoid the substantial estate tax on the surviving spouse's estate and would also allow the income from the trust to be used by the surviving spouse during his or her lifetime.

The whole point of your completing Form 32 is to estimate what the potential estate tax will be, based on your present estate and on your present dispositions. If you do not like the tax that would be payable on your and your spouse's estimated estates, then do some estate planning and try to apply the techniques that have been discussed in this chapter.

PAGE A—YOUR ESTATE

- Line 1: Enter the amount of your gross estate as shown in the column *Estimated Current Value*, line 5, on Form 31—*Property Ownership and Gross Estate*.
- Lines 2a and 2b: Enter the estimated funeral and administrative costs and total on line 2c.
- Lines 3a-c: Enter the amounts you will leave to your spouse outright and/or in a QTIP trust.
- Line 3d: Add up lines 3a, 3b, and 3c
- Line 4: Enter any amounts you plan to leave to charities.
- Line 5: Add lines 2c, 3d and 4.
- Line 6: Subtract lines 2a, 2b, and 5 from line 1.
- Line 7: Enter the total of any post-1976 taxable gifts you have made.
- Line 8: Add lines 6 and 7.
- Line 9: Determine the tentative federal estate tax for the amount on line 8 by using Table 14-1 and enter that amount.
- Line 10a: Enter any gift tax paid on taxable gifts you made after 1976.
- Line 10b: Enter the appropriate unified credit, as shown on Table 14-2. (For 1984, the unified credit is $96,300.)
- Line 10c: Add lines 10a and 10b. Enter the resulting sum in both columns.
- Line 11: Subtract line 10c from line 9.

PAGE B—YOUR SPOUSE'S ESTATE

On this page, follow the procedures you used for page A, except for the following lines:

- Line 1: Add your spouse's gross estate, as shown on Form 31, line 6, in the column *Estimated Current Value*, and the amount you will leave to your spouse, as shown on Form 32, page A, line 3d.
- Line 3: Make no entries here unless your spouse plans to remarry. Continue with the rest of the form.

FIGURE 14-3

File Under ESTATE PLANNING   Date: 11/16

FORM 32A ESTIMATED FEDERAL ESTATE TAX

YOUR ESTATE

1	Gross Estate		$399,250
2	Deductions		
a.	Funeral Expenses	$ 3000	
b.	Administrative Expenses	15,000	
c.	TOTAL Expenses	18,000	
3	Marital Deduction for Property Passing to Spouse:		
a.	Jointly Held Property	42,550	
b.	Transferred by Contract (retirement plan)	90,200	
c.	Transferred by Will or Living Trust	202,250 (personal assets)	
d.	TOTAL Marital Deductions	335,000	
4	Charitable Deduction	—	
5	TOTAL Deductions		(353,000)
6	Tentative Taxable Estate		46,250
7	Post-1976 Taxable Gifts Other Than Gifts Includible in Gross Estate		—
8	TOTAL Taxable Estate		46,250
9	Tentative Federal Estate Tax		7,700
10	Less:		
a.	Gift Taxes Paid on Post-1976 Gifts		
b.	Unified Credit	96,300 (1984)	
c.	TOTAL		(96,300)
11	Federal Estate Tax		0

FIGURE 14-4

File Under ESTATE PLANNING Date: 11/16

FORM 32B ESTIMATED FEDERAL ESTATE TAX

SPOUSE'S ESTATE

1	Gross Estate	$576,250 (Form 31) 335,000 (Form 32A)	$911,250
2	Deductions		
	a. Funeral Expenses	$3,000	
	b. Administrative Expenses	27,000	
	c. TOTAL Expenses	30,000	
3	Marital Deduction for Property Passing to Spouse:		
	a. Jointly Held Property		
	b. Transferred by Contract		
	c. Transferred by Will or Living Trust		
	d. TOTAL Marital Deductions		
4	Charitable Deduction		
5	TOTAL Deductions		(30,000)
6	Tentative Taxable Estate		$881,250
7	Post-1976 Taxable Gifts Other Than Gifts Includible in Gross Estate		—
8	TOTAL Taxable Estate		881,250
9	Tentative Federal Estate Tax		299,500
10	Less:		
	a. Gift Taxes Paid on Post-1976 Gifts	—	
	b. Unified Credit	$192,800 (1987)	
	c. TOTAL		$192,800
11	Federal Estate Tax		$106,700

CLOSING OBSERVATIONS

You work hard—maybe a total of 80,000 hours during your lifetime—to earn your money and to invest it intelligently. It would be a shame if, at your death, your nearest and dearest were to suffer financially because you did not give sufficient consideration to the transfer of your estate. We hope you have taken the time to outline your family's existing estate situation, to forecast how the estate would be transferred under your present ownership arrangements and will provisions, and to estimate what the potential estate tax consequences would be. We hope you will analyze what impact the estate-planning techniques we outlined in this chapter might have on the transfer of your estate.

Suppose, for example, you worked out that in 1987 you and your spouse would have a combined estate of $1,200,000. What do you think you should do? Here are some recommendations:

- Take advantage of the exemption-equivalent trust up to $600,000.
- Use the marital deduction for the amount by which each spouse's taxable estate exceeds $600,000.
- Have the surviving spouse manage his or her resources by making gifts of appreciating assets and by consumption—conspicuous or otherwise—to minimize his or her taxable estate at death.

We know that estate planning can sometimes become quite complicated. If that's how it seems to be in your own case, we would suggest that you seek some good professional advice to help you conserve the maximum of your estate.

15

TAKE ACTION

This book has given you a structure for analyzing your personal finances, for envisaging your financial future, and for identifying the financial steps that can bring you closer to your various objectives in life. This, in itself, may well prevent you from taking some ill-considered step you might have taken without it; but to reap major benefits from the knowledge and insight you have acquired, you must apply it by taking the appropriate positive action.

The first thing to do is to ask and answer questions such as:

- How much do you want or can you afford to put aside for your long-term objectives of education, retirement, extended travel, remodeling, and so forth?
- Do your current and projected budgets permit you to set aside enough for your longer-term objectives?
- What are the trade-offs to make between your current lifestyle and future objectives?

Before you answer such questions and prepare a projection for next year, here are some general guidelines for people of varying ages.

IN YOUR THIRTIES

Take care of the four firsts: an annual income, normally secured by a job; a place to live; a reserve fund that can be used in an emergency; and low-cost life insurance—a source of future income should you die.

The first two, an annual income and a place to live, have far-reaching implications for long-term financial planning. Income obviously is a big factor in providing sufficient resources for accumulating assets and establishing a comfortable standard of living. However, it is not necessarily true that the larger the income, the larger the resources accumulated or the estate developed. Maintaining an income level sets in motion complicated problems of living up to one's career position. Many people of significant income have lifestyle expenses as great as if not greater than their income, and they never seem to accumulate assets for future needs.

So during your thirties, concentrate on your income and basic lifestyle expenditures—housing, transportation, food, and clothing. Resist the instant gratification craze and get in the habit of saving something for investment. Consider starting an education fund if you have children.

IN YOUR FORTIES

Control the increase in lifestyle expenditures. Look for investments, other than your personal residence, that the family can use and enjoy—vacation property, a boat, a computer. Concentrate on education funds and try to shift income to your children to pay for their education. Start thinking about a retirement program. Focus on growth and tax savings in selecting your investments.

IN YOUR FIFTIES

The children, you hope, are educated and on their own. You might even be able to decrease your basic lifestyle expenditures at this stage. Focus on new personal growth activities, such as travel, photography, or art collecting. Concentrate on retirement planning and increasing your investment assets and retirement funds to make your retirement years golden. Pay off your home mortgage.

IN YOUR SIXTIES

Pare your basic lifestyle costs. Get those retirement activities lined up and going. Concentrate on being active and continue your zest for life. Get out of debt and manage your investment assets to stay even with inflation. Get your estate in order and keep your financial affairs simple.

FORM 33—INCOME AND EXPENDITURE PROJECTION

To complete this form, you need to refer to forms you previously completed about your objectives and to follow the steps below:

- Enter in the *Last Year* column your actual income and expenditures from Forms 6, 7, 8, and 9.
- Enter on lines 1, 2, 3, and 4 in the *Next Year* column your estimates of next year's expenditures for long-term objectives.
- On line 1, enter the amount for each of your children from line 11 of Form 23—*College and Graduate School Costs*. Using the example shown in Figure 11-1 for Form 23, you would enter $19,000 on line 1 of Form 33.
- On line 2, enter the amounts from lines 7a and 10d of Form 27—*Retirement Income*. Using the example in Figure 12-1 for Form 27, you would enter $9,900 on line 2 of Form 33.
- On line 3, enter your answer to question 5 of Form 22—*Your Investment Strategy*. Using the example shown in Figure 10-3 for Form 22, you would enter $10,000 on line 3 of Form 33.
- On line 4, enter the amounts for next year of the major discretionary expenditures you listed on Form 17—*Income and Expenditure Objectives*.
- On line 5, enter the totals of lines 1 through 4 to get the amount you would like to set aside next year for long-term objectives.

- On line 6a in the *Next Year* column, enter your estimate of employment income for next year. Review lines 1 and 2 of Form 17 for an estimate you previously prepared.
- On line 6b, enter your estimate of investment income for next year. Review information on Form 11—*Tax-Planning Worksheet* as a starting point here. Total your estimated income for next year on line 6c.
- On line 7, enter your estimate of basic lifestyle expenditures for next year. Review Form 7—*Basic Lifestyle Expenditures* as a starting point; remember that some very significant basic expenditures may not increase—for example, your mortgage payment. Remember also that whether these expenditures increase is up to you—the quality of your future lifestyle is not necessarily dependent on more quantity, more expenditures.
- On line 8, enter your estimate of discretionary expenditures. Review Form 8—*Discretionary Expenditures* as a starting point.
- On line 9a, enter your estimate of federal income tax from Form 11—*Tax-Planning Worksheet*. On lines 9b and 9c, enter your estimates of state income tax and employment tax. Total your estimated taxes on line 9d.
- On line 10, enter the totals from lines 7, 8, and 9d.
- On line 11, enter the amount that results from subtracting line 10 from line 6c.

At this point, compare the amount on line 5 to the amount on line 11. If the amount on line 11 is less than the amount on line 5, determine what changes you need to make in your financial situation to achieve your long-term objectives. Can you increase your income? Can you reduce your discretionary expenditures? Can you manage your taxes more effectively? These are choices you can make to increase the amount available for long-term objectives. If you are unwilling or unable to increase the amount on line 11, then you will have to revise the amounts you can set aside next year for long-term goals.

Once you have evaluated your choices and trade-offs, get the amounts on line 5 and line 11 in balance. Then commit yourself to making your projections a reality. The income and expenditure projection then becomes a blueprint for the first year of your financial future.

FORM 34—YOUR ACTION STEPS

Have you been noting your potential action steps for next year as you were working on various other forms? If not, let us remind you of the planning areas into which they might fall.

- Net worth planning
- Controlling or reducing expenditures
- Increasing earned income
- Reducing taxes
- Increasing investments and return on investments
- Financing your children's education
- Retirement planning

- Life insurance
- Estate planning

In listing your action steps on Form 34, try to be as specific as you can. Decide on the type of action to take, on the amount of money involved, and on the date by which the action should be accomplished. Something vague like "My wife and I want to set aside some funds for retirement this year" is less likely to be translated into action than "My wife and I want to contribute $4,000 to an IRA program by May 31 this year," which sets you a specific and presumably well-considered target.

As has been mentioned earlier, it is unrealistic to assume that you can accomplish more than ten such action steps in one year. Therefore, select the most feasible of your proposed action steps and make a commitment to complete them.

To keep to your timetable, and to make sure that nothing is left undone because it just slipped your mind, take a look at this form once a month, and transfer the appropriate action step(s) onto your everyday list of things you must remember to do.

PROFESSIONAL ADVICE

As you face the increasing complexity of our tax laws and a multitude of investment opportunities, you may feel a need for professional guidance or confirmation before you make some weighty financial decision. Depending on your particular concerns—income tax planning, retirement or estate planning, investments, or life insurance—you might want to consult a professional advisor in an accounting firm, a bank, a brokerage, a financial counseling firm, or an insurance company, or in a law firm.

The institution or organization you consult should be experienced in the particular field of your inquiry, and you should ask how clients with problems similar to your own have been counseled. Get references on the quality of the organization's work in this field, and find out what professional training your prospective counselor has had.

The majority of these counseling services will charge you a fee, but that fee is tax-deductible unless it was paid for some aspects of estate-planning services. Certain commercial banks, brokerages, and insurance companies may provide some financial counseling. These organizations may be primarily in the business of selling products, and they may offer free counseling services in order to make their products more attractive or to promote their sale.

Any professional advisor you choose will find the analyses you have made of your financial holdings, needs, objectives, and expectations enormously helpful; and wherever the advisor's fee is determined by the time spent on your behalf, the work you have done on your forms will reduce such a fee, perhaps by 40 to 50 percent. If there is going to be a fee, agree on the terms of it beforehand, and make sure you will get an itemized bill.

Except in matters of law, rules, and regulations, which the advisor should know insofar as they relate to the advisor's specialty, the professional guidance you receive will not be based on certainties but on estimates of probabilities. On the whole, the professional's estimates should be correct more often than your own. Even so, any professional advice that is based on an estimate of probabilities should not be followed blindly, nor should you ever take financial action on the basis of rationales that you do not understand. A good advisor will be ready to explain the reasons for any advice or recommendation.

For those who might want to consult an advisor, the following paragraphs will give a brief description of the organizations that provide various types of financial advisors.

ACCOUNTING FIRMS

Personal financial planning services are offered by some medium-sized accounting firms and by all of the large ones, such as our partnership, Touche Ross. As well as helping you to formulate financial plans and goals, they can advise you on particular concerns like tax planning, tax shelters, investment planning and performance, educational financing, and retirement and estate planning. Their unique expertise lies in the field of taxation, and this is quite crucial, since tax considerations enter into just about every phase of financial planning and management. To ascertain which combination of variables will be the most advantageous for you, they make extensive use of computer analysis, in addition to their knowledge of the tax laws.

The advice you get from an accounting firm will not be colored by self-interest. Accounting firms don't ever act as brokers or sell insurance on the side. If they suggest that you buy or sell some product, it will not be because they receive a commission on it. They don't. They work for a fee based on hourly rates, and before entering into an engagement with you, they should give you an estimate of their fee. They will also be able to put you in touch with competent and reliable firms of stockbrokers, insurers, or whatever else you may need to put your financial plans in action.

BANKS

Recently banks—commercial and savings banks—have started to provide a variety of financial planning services to primarily affluent customers. These services include tailor-made loans, estate planning, asset management, trust services, stock purchases, and financial counseling.

INVESTMENT COUNSELORS

Most investment counselors provide investment management of a portfolio of securities. Many firms will not handle portfolios below some minimum size—from $100,000 to $250,000. Also, their financial advice does not come cheap. They will charge some percentage of the value of the portfolio. This percentage may run from 1 or 2 percent of the minimum portfolio to 0.5 percent of larger portfolios.

In using an investment counseling firm, it normally makes sense to give the professional manager the power to buy and sell investments without your consent. Remember, the professional counseling firm is being paid for its judgment. If you do not want the firm to exercise its judgment, you should probably not pay for investment management. If you do choose to let an investment counseling firm handle your investments, you should review its performance periodically and either retain or dismiss the firm, based on its performance.

Since there are so many investment counseling firms available, one of the biggest problems is to select the right firm for you. One approach is to check the banks in your area to see if they provide an investment counseling service. Often they do. If they do not, they might be able to give you a list of investment advisors who may help you. In addition, your C.P.A. and attorney should know of investment counseling firms they can recommend to you. Sometimes stockbrokerage firms know of investment firms, since investment counseling firms have to work through a stockbroker in order to buy and sell securities for their clients.

MUTUAL FUNDS

For those who do not have sufficient investments to interest a personal investment counselor, consider mutual funds. A mutual fund is an enterprise that obtains money from institutional and individual investors and invests the money in securities selected to achieve certain financial objectives. By pooling the funds of many investors, the mutual fund provides diversification, professional management, and continuous supervision of investments.

There are hundreds of mutual funds from which to choose, varying in size, purpose, and policy. Mutual funds generally fall into five basic categories.

Money market funds are those funds that invest in short-term investments and provide liquidity and current income to the investors.

Balanced funds attempt to provide current income and long-term growth to the investors. They attempt to achieve these goals by investing some money in common stocks and some in bonds and preferred stocks. Balanced funds seek to maintain certain levels of speculative and conservative common stocks and different classes of fixed-income securities.

Income funds strive for good dividend and interest income through investments in bonds and preferred stocks.

Common stock funds assume that the best way to make your money grow is by placing your bets on the growth of the economy. Such funds keep most of their assets in common stock at all times. Most emphasize long-term capital growth. Some also try to provide a fair dividend return.

Growth stock funds are sometimes called capital gain funds. Typically, most buyers of such funds are not interested in dividends, but are more interested in investing in growth companies that put earnings to work to produce more growth and presumably stock value appreciation. The growth funds usually have the objective of maximizing capital gain.

LOAD AND NO-LOAD FUNDS

Load funds are funds that charge a commission, or "load," of about 8 percent, which is deducted immediately from the sum invested. This load is used to finance the heavy outlay made for staff sales and sales promotions. While all funds assess their shareholders an annual management fee, a number of the funds charge no commission to new investors; these are called "no-load" funds. These funds are not promoted by any salesman, and must be discovered by the investor himself or herself through advertisements in financial publications or word-of-mouth. In addition, they may be obtained by writing to Investment Company Institute, 1775 K Street N.W., Washington, D.C. 20006.

Given the fact that load funds charge a pretty hefty commission, why invest in load funds when no-load funds are available? The answer can only be performance. Perhaps the most widely used measure of performance of investment companies is determined by

- comparing the net asset value or market value of the fund's share at the beginning and end of the period under review and ascertaining the increase or decrease; and
- adding the amount of all dividends paid during the period.

The following example may serve to illustrate this calculation:

	Fund A	**Fund B**
Asset value at beginning of period	\$15	\$15
Asset value at end of period	\$22	\$12
Dividends paid during period	\$ 3	\$ 9
Increase	67%	40%

Once you have selected a measure of performance, you have to consider the relevant performance period. Some analysts argue that the performance period should be sufficiently long to include at least one and preferably several complete cycles. In addition, performance comparisons should be made among a broad cross-section of funds and against a recognized measure of stock-price averages.

There are several sources of information on the performance of mutual funds.

Perhaps the bible of the industry is *Wiesenberger Investment Companies Annual*, published by Wiesenberger Investment Companies Services. This book contains detailed information on specific funds, together with much useful information about the general subject of investment companies. The annual publication is kept up-to-date by monthly and quarterly supplements. This service is authoritative, very objective, and available in most public libraries.

In addition, there are other sources of information that you may wish to use:

- *Forbes Magazine* publishes an annual mutual fund survey in late August or early September. The survey includes easy-to-grasp performance comparisons for specific periods of time and for up and down markets.
- *Mutual Fund Performance Analysis*, published by Lipper Analytical, Inc. This publication provides weekly and quarterly performance figures and a computer comparison of the relative standing of funds.

BROKERAGE HOUSES

In recent years, brokerage houses have established financial planning departments staffed with investment counselors, CPAs, attorneys, and insurance specialists. They provide comprehensive services and charge a fee for the services. Some of them have arrangements whereby if the client buys investment products from the brokerage home, the brokerage commissions are deducted from the financial planning fees.

Of course, brokerage houses are organized primarily to provide investment products, ranging from money market funds, stocks, and bonds to real estate or oil and gas tax shelters. A good broker should first perform an analysis of your investment needs, including your present assets and your investment objectives. The broker should know whether you wish to emphasize capital gains or income, short-term or long-term investments, safety or speculation, and so forth. In essence, the broker attempts to find out what types of investments you would feel comfortable with. After reviewing your personal data, present financial situation, and investment objectives, the stockbroker should develop an appropriate investment plan based on what you consider to be a desirable or acceptable rate of risk and return.

Full-service brokerage houses provide research reports on specific securities, reference libraries, and safekeeping services for your securities. Of course, they buy and sell securities, for which they charge a commission. A full-service brokerage house charges a higher commission than a discount brokerage house because of the extensive services it offers. Discount brokers do nothing more than buy and sell securities.

FINANCIAL PLANNERS

Recently, two new designations in the financial planning field have emerged. One is the Certified Financial Planner (CFP); the other is the Chartered Financial Consultant (CFC). Both of these designations are awarded to people who have completed a comprehensive educational program in areas of financial planning. Typically, a CFP or CFC has experience in a specific financial field such as selling stocks or insurance. Some financial planners are independent and objective in their analyses and recommendations and charge a fee for their services; others do not charge a fee and hence will tend to recommend the products that they sell on commission.

INSURANCE ADVISORS Primarily, insurance advisors provide professional assistance in the broad area of insurance—health, disability, casualty, and life insurance. Such an advisor often acts as a catalyst in the financial planning process, bringing the client together with whomever is needed—a CPA, an attorney, or an investment broker.

Presumably, a good insurance advisor will review the client's financial affairs and will call in these other financial advisors when appropriate. If the client's business transactions too complex for the insurance agent to handle, it is to be hoped that the agent will consult the proper specialist—a C.P.A. about possible tax advantages, a trust department or attorney about changing a client's will or the setting up of a trust.

The role of the life insurance agent as a financial advisor is a difficult one because of the obvious conflict of interest. The insurance agent is expected to make an objective analysis of the client's need and to recommend the appropriate insurance coverage, but the agent is compensated on a commission basis: The more insurance the agent sells, the greater the agent's income.

KEEPING UP WITH CURRENT FINANCIAL INFORMATION

PERIODICALS There are several daily and weekly sources of financial information and analyses.

The Wall Street Journal (daily)
200 Burnett Road
Chicopee, Massachusetts 01021
(in every Monday issue is a column entitled "Your Money Matters")

Business Week (weekly)
McGraw-Hill Inc.
1221 Avenue of the Americas
New York, New York 10020
(has a "Personal Business" column, in addition to articles covering many economic areas)

Changing Times (monthly)
1729 H Street N.W.
Washington, D.C. 20006
(articles of consumer interest)

Consumer Views (10 times a year)
Citibank
399 Park Avenue
New York, New York 10043
(a four-page publication on topics of consumer interest)

Executive Wealth Advisory (biweekly)
The Research Institute of America, Inc.
589 Fifth Avenue
New York, New York 10017

Forbes (biweekly)
60 Fifth Avenue
New York, New York 10011
(includes a "Personal Affairs" column as well as several money and investments columns in each issue. Also has an annual mutual fund analysis in August or September issue)

Fortune (biweekly)
541 North Fairbanks Court
Chicago, Illinois 60611
(has a "Personal Investing" column, in addition to comprehensive business articles)

Medical Economics (biweekly)
680 Kinderkamack Road
Oradell, New Jersey 07649
(although oriented toward physicians, this publication contains many articles on tax planning, estate planning, and investment opportunities relevant to other affluent professional people; has a year-end financial planning issue)

Money (monthly)
Time, Inc.
541 North Fairbanks Court
Chicago, Illinois 60611
(includes articles on many personal financial matters with a how-to-do-it approach; includes a regular article on "one family's finances" that discusses specific financial recommendations)

In addition to the above periodicals, there are several booklets on current economics and personal finance published by the American Institute for Economic Research, Great Barrington, Massachusetts 01230. This organization has many low-cost publications that are extremely valuable to those who wish to gain first-hand knowledge about economics and money matters. A partial list of their publications follows:

Annuities From the Buyer's Point of View

Life Insurance From the Buyer's Point of View

Homeowner or Tenant? How to Make a Wise Choice

How to Avoid Financial Tangles
- Section A: Elementary Property Problems and Important Financial Relationships (Including Wills, Trusts, and Insurance)
- Section B: Taxes, Gifts, and Help for the Widow
- Section C: Trusts May Be More Useful Than Many Realize

Why Gold?

NEWSLETTERS There are many newsletters available. Many brokerage houses provide letters to their clients, as do investment counseling firms. Some specialize in certain kinds of investments. Many of these newsletters are advertised in general financial media such as *The Wall Street Journal*. If you are interested in one that seems to fit your objectives, we suggest you write and ask for a sample copy.

Touche Ross publishes a quarterly newsletter, *Personal Financial Management*, that covers one or two topics in some depth each issue. Topics covered in recent issues have included tax-saving strategies, educational financing, tax shelters, and basic estate-planning techniques. Contact the office nearest you to get on the mailing list.

TELEVISION There are television news programs and talk shows that stress money matters. Cable News Network features a daily program, "Money Line," that covers current financial issues. "Wall Street Week" is a half-hour Public Broadcasting System production that ranges over a variety of current investment ideas and products.

SEMINARS There are a variety of financial planning seminars—some free, some expensive—offered by universities, community colleges, investment firms, and accounting firms. For example, Touche Ross regularly provides seminars ranging from one hour to two days on financial and tax matters. Contact the office in your area to get on the mailing list for seminars offered.

16

YOUR ANNUAL FINANCIAL CHECKUP

Congratulations to all of you who have worked your way through this book and filled in all its forms. At this point, you know what you own, what you need, what you want, what you can reasonably expect, and what you can do. You have made some choices, evaluated the consequences, committed yourself to some action, and are in control of your financial affairs. In addition, you have saved $2,000 to $3,000 in professional fees by putting Your Financial Planner together. You have earned the laurels and might like to wear them around the house for a month or so.

Beware of resting on your laurels, though. Time marches on, and therefore some of your current records and plans will inevitably become out-of-date records and plans. So you should periodically update everything that has some bearing on your financial plans and dispositions.

Some of the forms you have completed may merely need to be reviewed and amended where necessary. Others should be completed anew.

Because few people can or want to update their affairs in one sitting, we suggest that you do your updating systematically and do it over the course of the year. In our experience, the following timetable is the best and most convenient.

JANUARY—FEBRUARY

In these first months of the year, make some inroads on the tax returns due in April by assembling all data pertaining to your financial transactions in the last calendar year. Put this information into a "tax organizer," which you can buy if you do not have a tax advisor like Touche Ross to make you a present of it.

When you have finished with that, review and update the following forms:

- Form 1—*Family Data* (Chapter 2), filed under *Family Data* in Your Financial Planner. The information listed here will not change greatly from year to year, so merely check your completed form and amend it as necessary.

- Form 2—*Financial Documents* (Chapter 2), filed under *Financial Documents* in Your Financial Planner. Use your completed form. Make sure the listings are complete and that the documents are in their listed locations. Go over this list with your spouse and also let someone else in your family know that this list exists and where to find it.
- Form 3—*Financial Advisors* (Chapter 2), filed under *Financial Documents* in Your Financial Planner. Use your filled-in form. Evaluate your original choices and amend them if that seems advisable.
- Form 4—*Statement of Net Worth* and Form 5—*Analysis of Net Worth* (Chapter 3), filed under *Financial Profile* in Your Financial Planner. Here your filled-in forms are out of date by up to one year. Since you can now take some of the required data from your original form and the rest from the data collected for your tax return, this second time around will be much easier than the first.
- Form 6—*Income Sources* (Chapter 4), filed under *Financial Profile*. Take a copy of this form and complete it with the information you have collected for your tax return. Compare it with your original form and set some goals for the current year.
- Form 7—*Basic Lifestyle Expenditures* and Form 8—*Discretionary Expenditures* (Chapter 4), filed under *Financial Profile*. Update these forms with data for the last calendar year. Then challenge your expenditure patterns and set some goals for the current year.

MARCH

Focus on completing your tax return for last year by mid-March. If you want a tax accountant to review or prepare your return, stay away from the April 15 scramble. You are likely to get much better service before April, and to obtain that, you must give your accountant the necessary data by early March. Be sure to keep a copy of your tax return.

When you have mailed your tax return to the Internal Revenue Service, update the following forms:

- Form 9—*Income and Employment Taxes* (Chapter 4), filed under *Financial Profile* in Your Financial Planner. Use a duplicate of this form, and take your figures from your newly completed tax return. Find your top tax rate from the appropriate schedule in Appendix II. Find your average tax rate by adding lines 2 and 3 and then dividing the result by line 1.
- Form 10—*Analysis of Earned Income and Expenditures* (Chapter 4), filed under *Financial Profile* in Your Financial Planner. Use a copy of this form, and take your figures from your newly completed Form 6, Form 7, Form 8, and Form 9.

So now, after updating and/or completing anew Forms 1 through 10, you have an updated financial profile and are again in a position to do some planning for the future.

APRIL—MAY

Now that you have completed and mailed your last year's tax return, prepare a tax plan for this year on Form 11—*Tax-Planning Worksheet*. You may wish to use a tax professional to help you prepare your taxable year plan and to identify tax-saving ideas (Form 12). Finally, you should prepare an estimate of this year's tax liability. Make sure you understand how much tax will be withheld from your paychecks and/or the estimated tax payments you will need to make on April 15, June 15, and September 15 of this year and January 15 of next year.

Before the summer rolls around, you can do a little more reviewing and updating. Use extra copies for updating the following forms.

- Form 16—*Financial Security* (Chapter 9), filed under *Financial Objectives* in Your Financial Planner.
- Form 17—*Income and Expenditure Objectives* (Chapter 9), filed under *Financial Objectives* in Your Financial Planner.
- Form 20—*Investment Objectives* (Chapter 9), filed under *Investment Strategy* in Your Financial Planner. Review your completed form and amend it as necessary.
- Form 21—*Review of Your Present Investments* (Chapter 10), filed under *Investment Strategy* in Your Financial Planner. Review your completed form and amend it as necessary.
- Form 22—*Your Investment Strategy* (Chapter 10), filed under *Investment Strategy* in Your Financial Planner. Review your completed form and amend it as necessary.
- If you have many assets and liabilities, try to complete the forms in Appendix III—*Supporting Details*. Once you complete these forms, you will have readily available all the information you need on your assets and liabilities. Completing them is a marvelous way to spend a rainy April day.
- Form 33—*Income and Expenditure Projection* (Chapter 15), filed under *Summary Plan* in Your Financial Planner. Use the copy of this form and update your projections for this year.

JUNE—AUGUST

Even the most conscientious financial planners must take time off to recharge their batteries. Try to relax during these months, and temper your financial planning with lots of sunshine, hikes, vacation trips, sailing, or whatever gives you a break from work and gets you closer to your family and friends.

SEPTEMBER—OCTOBER

Imagine how boring fall would be if you had no financial planning to do—nothing but falling leaves, apples, pumpkins, and football games! As a change from all that, you will want to update the following forms:

- Form 28—*Your Present Life Insurance Coverage* (Chapter 13), filed under *Insurance* in Your Financial Planner. Review your completed form and amend it as necessary.
- Form 29—*Total Life Insurance Required* (Chapter 13), filed under *Insurance* in Your Financial Planner. Review your completed form and amend it as necessary.

- Form 13—*Capital Gains and Losses* (Chapter 8), filed under *Tax Planning* in Your Financial Planner. Use a copy of this form and complete it with your transactions for the current year.
- Form 14—*Your Year-End Tax Plan* (Chapter 8), filed under *Tax Planning* in Your Financial Planner. Use a copy of this form and complete it with your data for the current year.
- Form 15—*Year-End Tax Action* (Chapter 8), filed under *Tax Planning* in Your Financial Planner. Use a copy of this form, and try to render as little as possible unto Caesar—legally, of course.

NOVEMBER—DECEMBER

Continue to implement your year-end tax action steps through December.

If you have had any second thoughts about your financial retirement needs, make the appropriate changes in your completed Form 24—*Estimated Basic Lifestyle Expenditures at Retirement* or Form 25—*Estimated Discretionary Expenditures at Retirement* (Chapter 12), filed under *Retirement Planning* in Your Financial Planner. If there is any change in your expectable retirement income, amend your completed Form 27—*Retirement Income* (Chapter 12), filed under *Retirement Planning* in Your Financial Planner.

Unless the secret of immortality has been discovered and is available to you by the time you read this, review the following forms, and use copies to complete them anew if there are any changes.

- Form 31—*Property Ownership and Gross Estate* (Chapter 14), filed under *Estate Planning* in Your Financial Planner.
- Form 32—*Estimated Federal Estate Tax* (Chapter 14), filed under *Estate Planning* in Your Financial Planner.

And finally, now that you have finished updating all of the forms, review Your Financial Planner and complete Form 34—*Your Action Steps* (Chapter 15), filed under *Action* in Your Financial Planner.

COMPUTERIZED UPDATE

If you own or have access to a microcomputer, you may be interested in the personal financial planning package we have developed. The package is based on the process and the forms we have discussed in this book. The computerized package is just an easier way to maintain and update Your Financial Planner. If you are interested in receiving more information on the package, complete and mail the card attached.

CONCLUDING OBSERVATIONS

You have prepared Your Financial Planner and are well on your way to financial control and financial security. Spend according to your plan and invest in those assets that are tailored to your objectives. Evaluate your plan at least once a year and update it for changes in your objectives, the economic situation, and other events that affect you financially. But by all means, remember to have a good life. May you grow old gracefully and with a good deal of prosperity.

APPENDIX I

COMPOUND INTEREST TABLES

TABLE 1
FUTURE WORTH OF ONE DOLLAR WITH AMOUNT OF RETURN COMPOUNDED ANNUALLY

	Annual Rate of Return										
Year	**5%**	**6%**	**7%**	**8%**	**9%**	**10%**	**11%**	**12%**	**13%**	**14%**	**15%**
1	1.05	1.06	1.07	1.08	1.09	1.10	1.11	1.12	1.13	1.14	1.15
2	1.10	1.12	1.15	1.17	1.19	1.21	1.23	1.25	1.28	1.30	1.32
3	1.16	1.19	1.23	1.26	1.30	1.33	1.37	1.40	1.44	1.48	1.52
4	1.22	1.26	1.31	1.36	1.41	1.46	1.52	1.57	1.63	1.69	1.75
5	1.28	1.34	1.40	1.47	1.54	1.61	1.69	1.76	1.84	1.93	2.01
6	1.34	1.42	1.50	1.59	1.68	1.77	1.87	1.97	2.08	2.20	2.31
7	1.41	1.50	1.61	1.71	1.83	1.95	2.08	2.21	2.35	2.50	2.66
8	1.48	1.59	1.72	1.85	1.99	2.14	2.31	2.48	2.66	2.85	3.06
9	1.55	1.69	1.84	2.00	2.17	2.36	2.56	2.77	3.00	3.25	3.52
10	1.63	1.79	1.97	2.16	2.37	2.59	2.84	3.10	3.40	3.71	4.05
11	1.71	1.90	2.11	2.33	2.58	2.85	3.15	3.48	3.84	4.23	4.65
12	1.80	2.01	2.25	2.52	2.81	3.14	3.50	3.90	4.34	4.82	5.35
13	1.89	2.13	2.41	2.72	3.07	3.45	3.88	4.36	4.90	5.50	6.15
14	1.98	2.26	2.58	2.94	3.34	3.80	4.31	4.89	5.54	6.26	7.08
15	2.08	2.40	2.76	3.17	3.64	4.18	4.79	5.47	6.25	7.14	8.14
16	2.18	2.54	2.95	3.43	3.97	4.60	5.31	6.13	7.07	8.14	9.36
17	2.30	2.69	3.16	3.70	4.33	5.05	5.90	6.87	7.99	9.28	10.76
18	2.41	2.85	3.38	4.00	4.72	5.56	6.54	7.69	9.02	10.58	12.38
19	2.53	3.03	3.62	4.32	5.14	6.12	7.26	8.61	10.20	12.06	14.23
20	2.65	3.21	3.87	4.67	5.60	6.73	8.06	9.65	11.52	13.74	16.37
21	2.79	3.40	4.14	5.03	6.11	7.40	8.95	10.80	13.02	15.67	18.82
22	2.93	3.60	4.43	5.44	6.66	8.14	9.93	12.10	14.71	17.86	21.65
23	3.07	3.82	4.74	5.87	7.26	8.95	11.03	13.55	16.63	20.36	24.89
24	3.23	4.05	5.07	6.34	7.91	9.85	12.24	15.18	18.79	23.21	28.63
25	3.39	4.29	5.43	6.86	8.62	10.83	13.59	17.00	21.23	26.46	32.92
26	3.56	4.55	5.81	7.40	9.40	11.92	13.08	19.04	23.99	30.17	37.86
27	3.73	4.82	6.21	7.99	10.25	13.11	16.74	21.33	27.11	34.39	43.54
28	3.92	5.11	6.65	8.63	11.17	14.42	18.58	23.88	30.63	39.20	50.07
29	4.12	5.42	7.11	9.32	12.17	15.86	20.62	26.75	34.62	44.69	57.58
30	4.32	5.74	7.61	10.06	13.27	17.45	22.90	29.96	39.12	50.95	66.21
31	4.54	6.09	8.15	10.87	14.46	19.19	25.41	33.56	44.20	58.08	76.14
32	4.77	6.45	8.72	11.74	15.76	21.11	28.21	37.58	49.95	66.22	87.57
33	5.00	6.84	9.33	12.68	17.18	23.23	31.31	42.09	56.44	75.49	100.70
34	5.25	7.25	9.98	13.69	18.73	25.55	34.75	47.14	63.78	86.05	115.81
35	5.52	7.69	10.68	14.79	20.41	28.10	38.58	52.80	72.07	98.10	133.18
36	5.79	8.15	11.42	15.97	22.25	30.91	42.82	59.14	81.44	111.83	153.15
37	6.08	8.64	12.22	17.25	24.25	34.00	47.53	66.23	92.02	127.49	176.13
38	6.39	9.15	13.08	18.63	26.44	37.40	52.76	74.18	103.99	145.34	202.54
39	6.71	9.70	14.00	20.12	28.82	41.15	58.56	83.08	117.51	165.69	232.93
40	7.04	10.29	14.97	21.73	31.41	45.26	65.00	93.05	132.78	188.88	267.86

TABLE 2
FUTURE WORTH OF ONE DOLLAR INVESTED EACH YEAR WITH INTEREST (RETURN) PAYABLE AND REINVESTED AT END OF EACH YEAR

Year	5%	6%	7%	8%	9%	10%	11%	12%	13%	14%	15%
					Annual Rate of Return						
1	1.00	1.00	1.00	1.00	1.00	1.00	1.00	1.00	1.00	1.00	1.00
2	2.05	2.06	2.07	2.08	2.09	2.10	2.11	2.12	2.13	2.14	2.15
3	3.15	3.18	3.22	3.25	3.28	3.31	3.34	3.37	3.41	3.44	3.47
4	4.31	4.37	4.44	4.50	4.57	4.64	4.71	4.78	4.85	4.92	4.99
	5.53	5.64	5.75	5.87	5.99	6.10	6.23	6.35	6.48	6.61	6.74
6	6.80	6.98	7.15	7.33	7.52	7.71	7.91	8.11	8.32	8.54	8.75
7	8.14	8.39	8.65	8.92	9.20	9.49	9.78	10.09	10.41	10.73	11.07
8	9.55	9.90	10.26	10.64	11.03	11.43	11.86	12.30	12.76	13.23	13.73
9	11.03	11.49	11.98	12.49	13.02	13.58	14.16	14.77	15.42	16.09	16.78
10	12.58	13.18	13.82	14.49	15.19	15.94	16.72	17.55	18.42	19.34	20.30
11	14.21	14.97	15.78	16.65	17.56	18.53	19.56	20.66	21.81	23.05	24.35
12	15.92	16.87	17.89	18.98	20.14	21.38	22.71	24.13	25.65	27.27	29.00
13	17.71	18.88	20.14	21.50	22.95	24.52	26.21	28.03	29.99	32.09	34.35
14	19.60	21.02	22.55	24.22	26.02	27.98	30.10	32.39	34.88	37.58	40.51
15	21.58	23.27	25.13	27.15	29.36	31.77	34.41	37.28	40.42	43.84	47.58
16	23.66	23.67	27.89	30.32	33.00	35.95	39.19	42.75	46.67	50.98	55.72
17	25.84	28.21	30.84	33.75	36.97	40.55	44.50	48.88	53.74	59.12	65.08
18	28.13	30.91	34.00	37.45	41.30	45.60	50.40	55.75	61.73	68.39	75.84
19	30.54	33.76	37.38	41.45	46.02	51.16	56.94	63.44	70.75	78.97	88.21
20	33.07	36.78	41.00	45.76	51.16	37.27	64.20	72.05	80.95	91.03	102.44
21	35.72	39.99	44.87	50.42	56.77	64.00	72.27	81.70	92.47	104.77	118.81
22	38.51	43.39	49.01	55.46	62.87	71.40	81.21	92.50	105.49	120.44	137.63
23	41.43	47.00	53.44	60.89	69.53	79.54	91.15	104.60	120.21	138.30	159.28
24	44.50	50.82	58.18	66.77	76.79	88.50	102.17	118.16	136.83	158.66	184.17
25	47.73	54.86	63.25	73.10	84.70	98.35	114.41	133.33	155.62	181.87	212.79
26	51.11	59.16	68.88	79.95	93.32	109.18	128.00	150.33	176.85	208.33	245.71
27	54.67	63.71	74.48	87.35	102.72	121.10	143.08	169.37	200.84	238.50	283.57
28	58.40	68.53	80.70	95.34	112.97	134.21	159.82	190.70	227.95	272.89	327.10
29	62.32	73.64	87.35	103.97	124.14	148.63	178.40	214.58	258.58	312.09	377.17
30	66.44	79.06	94.46	113.28	136.31	164.49	199.02	241.33	293.20	356.79	434.75
31	70.76	84.80	102.07	123.35	149.58	181.94	221.91	271.29	332.32	407.74	500.96
32	75.30	90.89	110.22	134.21	164.04	201.14	247.32	304.85	376.52	465.82	577.10
33	80.06	97.34	118.93	145.95	179.80	222.25	275.53	342.43	426.46	532.04	664.67
34	85.07	104.18	128.26	158.63	196.98	245.48	306.84	384.52	482.90	607.52	765.37
35	90.32	111.44	138.24	172.32	215.71	271.02	341.59	431.66	546.68	693.57	881.17
36	95.84	119.12	148.91	187.10	236.13	299.13	380.16	484.46	618.75	791.67	1,014.35
37	101.63	127.27	160.34	203.07	258.38	330.04	422.98	543.60	700.19	903.51	1,167.50
38	107.71	135.90	172.56	220.32	282.63	364.04	470.51	609.83	792.21	1,031.00	1,343.62
39	114.10	145.06	185.64	238.94	309.07	401.45	523.27	684.01	896.20	1,176.34	1,546.17
40	120.80	154.76	199.64	259.06	337.88	442.59	581.83	767.09	1,013.70	1,342.03	1,779.09

TABLE 3
$10,000 LUMP-SUM INVESTMENT COMPOUNDED ANNUALLY END-OF-YEAR VALUES

End of Year	Annual Rate of Return 5%	6%	7%	8%	9%	10%	11%	12%	13%	14%	15%
1	10,500	10,600	10,700	10,800	10,900	11,000	11,100	11,200	11,300	11,400	11,500
2	11,025	11,236	11,449	11,664	11,881	12,100	12,321	12,544	12,769	12,996	13,225
3	11,576	11,910	12,250	12,597	12,950	13,310	13,676	14,049	14,428	14,815	15,208
4	12,155	12,624	13,107	13,604	14,155	14,641	15,180	15,735	16,304	16,889	17,490
5	12,763	13,382	14,025	14,693	15,386	16,105	16,850	17,623	18,424	19,254	20,113
6	13,401	14,185	15,007	15,868	16,771	17,715	18,704	19,738	20,819	21,949	23,130
7	14,071	15,036	16,057	17,138	18,280	19,487	20,761	22,106	23,526	25,022	26,600
8	14,775	15,938	17,181	18,509	19,925	21,435	23,045	24,759	26,584	28,525	30,590
9	15,513	16,894	18,384	19,990	21,718	23,579	25,580	27,730	30,040	32,519	35,178
10	16,289	17,908	19,671	21,589	23,673	25,937	28,394	31,058	33,945	37,072	40,455
11	17,103	18,982	21,048	23,316	25,804	28,531	31,517	34,785	38,358	42,262	46,523
12	17,959	20,121	22,521	25,181	28,126	31,384	34,984	38,959	43,345	48,179	53,502
13	18,856	21,329	24,098	27,196	30,658	34,522	38,832	43,634	48,980	54,924	61,527
14	19,799	22,609	25,785	29,371	33,417	37,974	43,104	48,871	55,347	62,613	70,757
15	20,789	23,965	27,590	31,721	36,424	41,772	47,845	54,735	62,542	71,379	81,370
16	21,829	25,403	29,521	34,259	39,703	45,949	53,108	61,303	70,673	81,372	93,576
17	22,920	26,927	31,588	37,000	43,276	50,544	58,590	68,660	79,860	92,764	107,612
18	24,066	28,543	33,799	39,960	47,171	55,599	65,435	76,899	90,242	105,751	123,754
19	25,270	30,255	36,165	43,157	51,416	61,159	72,633	86,127	101,974	120,556	142,317
20	26,533	32,071	38,696	46,609	56,044	67,274	80,623	96,462	115,230	137,434	163,665
21	27,860	33,995	41,405	50,338	61,088	74,002	89,491	108,038	130,210	156,675	188,215
22	29,253	36,035	44,304	54,365	66,586	81,402	99,335	121,003	147,138	178,610	216,447
23	30,715	38,197	47,405	58,714	72,578	89,543	110,262	135,523	166,266	203,615	248,914
24	32,251	40,489	50,723	63,411	79,110	98,497	122,391	151,786	187,880	232,122	286,251
25	33,864	42,918	54,274	68,484	86,230	108,347	135,854	170,000	212,305	264,619	329,189
26	35,557	45,493	58,073	73,963	93,991	119,181	150,798	190,400	239,905	301,665	378,567
27	37,335	48,223	62,138	79,880	102,450	131,099	167,386	213,248	271,092	343,899	435,353
28	39,201	51,116	66,488	86,271	111,671	144,209	185,799	238,838	306,334	392,044	500,656
29	41,161	54,183	71,142	93,172	121,721	158,630	206,236	267,499	346,158	446,931	575,754
30	43,219	57,434	76,122	100,626	132,676	174,494	228,922	299,599	391,158	509,501	662,117
31	45,380	60,881	81,451	108,676	144,617	191,943	254,104	335,551	442,009	580,831	761,435
32	47,649	64,533	87,152	117,370	157,633	211,137	282,055	375,817	499,470	662,148	875,650
33	50,032	68,405	93,253	126,760	171,820	232,251	313,082	420,915	564,402	754,849	1,006,998
34	52,533	72,510	99,781	136,901	187,284	255,476	347,521	471,425	637,774	860,527	1,158,048
35	55,160	76,860	106,765	147,853	204,139	281,024	385,748	527,996	720,685	981,001	1,331,775
40	70,399	102,857	149,744	217,245	314,094	452,592	650,008	930,509	1,327,815	1,888,835	2,678,635

TABLE 4
FUTURE WORTH OF $1,200 INVESTED EACH YEAR AT VARYING RATES COMPOUNDED EACH YEAR

Rate of Return	End of Year 5	10	15	20	25	30	35	40
5%	6,631	15,093	25,894	39,679	57,272	79,727	108,384	144,960
6%	6,764	15,817	27,931	44,143	65,837	94,870	133,722	185,714
7%	6,901	16,580	30,155	49,194	75,891	113,353	165,884	239,562
8%	7,040	17,384	32,583	54,914	87,727	135,940	206,780	310,868
9%	7,182	18,231	35,233	61,392	101,641	163,569	258,853	405,459
10%	7,326	19,125	38,127	68,730	118,016	197,393	325,229	531,111
11%	7,473	20,066	41,286	77,043	137,296	238,825	409,907	698,191
12%	7,623	21,058	44,736	86,463	160,001	289,599	517,996	920,510
13%	7,776	22,104	48,501	97,136	186,743	351,839	656,017	1,216,445
14%	7,932	23,205	52,611	109,230	218,245	428,144	832,287	1,610,430
15%	8,091	24,364	57,096	122,932	255,352	521,694	1,057,404	2,134,908

TABLE 5
RATES OF RETURN AND THE INVESTMENT AMOUNTS REQUIRED TO HAVE $100,000 AVAILABLE AT END OF SPECIFIED PERIOD

Rate of Return	End of Year 5	10	15	20	25	30	35	40
5%	78,353	61,391	48,102	37,689	29,530	23,138	18,129	14,205
6%	74,726	55,839	41,727	31,180	23,300	17,411	13,011	9,722
7%	71,299	50,835	36,245	25,842	18,425	13,137	9,367	6,678
8%	68,058	46,319	31,524	21,455	14,602	9,938	6,763	4,603
9%	64,993	42,241	27,454	17,843	11,597	7,537	4,899	3,184
10%	62,092	38,554	23,940	14,864	9,230	5,731	3,558	2,209
11%	59,345	35,218	20,900	12,403	7,361	4,368	2,592	1,538
12%	56,743	32,197	18,270	10,367	5,882	3,340	1,894	1,075
13%	54,276	29,460	15,989	8,678	4,710	2,557	1,388	753.12
14%	51,937	26,974	14,010	7,276	3,780	1,963	1,019	529.43
15%	49,718	24,718	12,289	6,110	3,040	1,510	750.89	373.32
16%	47,611	22,683	10,792	5,139	2,447	1,165	554.59	264.05
17%	45,611	20,804	9,489	4,329	1,974	900.38	410.67	187.31
18%	43,711	19,107	8,352	3,651	1,596	697.49	304.88	133.27
19%	41,905	17,560	7,359	3,084	1,292	541.49	226.91	95.10
20%	40,188	16,151	6,491	2,610	1,048	421.27	169.30	68.04
21%	38,554	14,864	5,731	2,209	851.85	328.43	126.62	48.82
22%	37,000	13,690	5,065	1,874	693.43	256.57	94.93	35.12
23%	35,520	12,617	4,482	1,592	565.42	200.84	71.34	25.34
24%	34,112	11,635	3,969	1,354	461.80	157.52	53.72	18.33

TABLE 6
APPROXIMATE ANNUAL INVESTMENT REQUIRED TO EQUAL $100,000 AT VARYING RATES

Rate of Return	End of Year 5	10	15	20	25	30	35	40
5%	17,236	7,572	4,414	2,880	1,966	1,433	1,054	788
6%	16,736	7,157	4,053	2,565	1,720	1,193	847	610
7%	16,254	6,764	3,719	2,280	1,478	989	656	468
8%	15,783	6,392	3,410	2,024	1,267	817	537	357
9%	15,332	6,039	3,125	1,793	1,083	673	425	272
10%	14,890	5,704	2,861	1,587	924	552	335	205
11%	14,467	5,388	2,618	1,403	787	453	263	155
12%	14,055	5,088	2,395	1,239	670	370	206	116
13%	13,658	4,805	2,190	1,070	569	302	168	87
14%	13,270	4,536	2,001	964	482	246	126	65
15%	12,898	4,283	1,828	849	409	200	99	49

APPENDIX II

TAX RATE SCHEDULES

I. SINGLE TAXPAYERS

For Tax Year 1982

If taxable income is:	The tax is:
Not over $2,300	No tax
Over $2,300 but not over $3,400	12% of the amount over $2,300
Over $3,400 but not over $4,400	$132 + 14% of the amount over $3,400
Over $4,400 but not over $6,500	$272 + 16% of the amount over $4,400
Over $6,500 but not over $8,500	$608 + 17% of the amount over $6,500
Over $8,500 but not over $10,800	$948 + 19% of the amount over $8,500
Over $10,800 but not over $12,900	$1,385 + 22% of the amount over $10,800
Over $12,900 but not over $15,000	$1,847 + 23% of the amount over $12,900
Over $15,000 but not over $18,200	$2,330 + 27% of the amount over $15,000
Over $18,200 but not over $23,500	$3,194 + 31% of the amount over $18,200
Over $23,500 but not over $28,800	$4,837 + 35% of the amount over $23,500
Over $28,800 but not over $34,100	$6,692 + 40% of the amount over $28,800
Over $34,100 but not over $41,500	$8,812 + 44% of the amount over $34,100
Over $41,500	$12,068 + 50% of the amount over $41,500

For Tax Year 1983

If taxable income is:	The tax is:
Not over $2,300	No tax
Over $2,300 but not over $3,400	11% of the amount over $2,300
Over $3,400 but not over $4,400	$121 + 13% of the amount over $3,400
Over $4,400 but not over $8,500	$251 + 15% of the amount over $4,400
Over $8,500 but not over $10,800	$866 + 17% of the amount over $8,500
Over $10,800 but not over $12,900	$1,257 + 19% of the amount over $10,800
Over $12,900 but not over $15,000	$1,656 + 21% of the amount over $12,900
Over $15,000 but not over $18,200	$2,097 + 24% of the amount over $15,000
Over $18,200 but not over $23,500	$2,865 + 28% of the amount over $18,200
Over $23,500 but not over $28,800	$4,349 + 32% of the amount over $23,500
Over $28,800 but not over $34,100	$6,045 + 36% of the amount over $28,800
Over $34,100 but not over $41,500	$7,953 + 40% of the amount over $34,100
Over $41,500 but not over $55,300	$10,913 + 45% of the amount over $41,500
Over $55,300	$17,123 + 50% of the amount over $55,300

For Tax Years After 1983

If taxable income is:	The tax is:
Not over $2,300	No tax
Over $2,300 but not over $3,400	11% of the amount over $2,300
Over $3,400 but not over $4,400	$121 + 12% of the amount over $3,400
Over $4,400 but not over $6,500	$241 + 14% of the amount over $4,400
Over $6,500 but not over $8,500	$535 + 15% of the amount over $6,500
Over $8,500 but not over $10,800	$835 + 16% of the amount over $8,500
Over $10,800 but not over $12,900	$1,203 + 18% of the amount over $10,800
Over $12,900 but not over $15,000	$1,581 + 20% of the amount over $12,900
Over $15,000 but not over $18,200	$2,001 + 23% of the amount over $15,000
Over $18,200 but not over $23,500	$2,737 + 26% of the amount over $18,200
Over $23,500 but not over $28,800	$4,115 + 30% of the amount over $23,500
Over $28,800 but not over $34,100	$5,705 + 34% of the amount over $28,800
Over $34,100 but not over $41,500	$7,507 + 38% of the amount over $34,100
Over $41,500 but not over $55,300	$10,319 + 42% of the amount over $41,500
Over $55,300 but not over $81,800	$16,115 + 48% of the amount over $55,300
Over $81,800	$28,835 + 50% of the amount over $81,800

Source: Internal Revenue Code Section 1, PL 97-34, section 101, enacted August 13, 1981

II. MARRIED TAXPAYERS FILING JOINT RETURNS

For Tax Year 1982

If taxable income is:	The tax is:
Not over $3,400	No tax
Over $3,400 but not over $5,500	12% of the amount over $3,400
Over $5,500 but not over $7,600	$252 + 14% of the amount over $5,500
Over $7,600 but not over $11,900	$546 + 16% of the amount over $7,600
Over $11,900 but not over $16,000	$1,234 + 19% of the amount over $11,900
Over $16,000 but not over $20,200	$2,013 + 22% of the amount over $16,000
Over $20,200 but not over $24,600	$2,937 + 25% of the amount over $20,200
Over $24,600 but not over $29,900	$4,037 + 29% of the amount over $24,600
Over $29,900 but not over $35,200	$5,574 + 33% of the amount over $29,900
Over $35,200 but not over $45,800	$7,323 + 39% of the amount over $35,200
Over $45,800 but not over $60,000	$11,457 + 44% of the amount over $45,800
Over $60,000 but not over $85,600	$17,705 + 49% of the amount over $60,000
Over $85,600	$30,249 + 50% of the amount over $85,600

For Tax Year 1983

If taxable income is:	The tax is:
Not over $3,400	No tax
Over $3,400 but not over $5,500	11% of the amount over $3,400
Over $5,500 but not over $7,600	$231 + 13% of the amount over $5,500
Over $7,600 but not over $11,900	$504 + 15% of the amount over $7,600
Over $11,900 but not over $16,000	$1,149 + 17% of the amount over $11,900
Over $16,000 but not over $20,200	$1,846 + 19% of the amount over $16,000
Over $20,200 but not over $24,600	$2,644 + 23% of the amount over $20,200
Over $24,600 but not over $29,900	$3,656 + 26% of the amount over $24,600
Over $29,900 but not over $35,200	$5,034 + 30% of the amount over $29,900
Over $35,200 but not over $45,800	$6,624 + 35% of the amount over $35,200
Over $45,800 but not over $60,000	$10,334 + 40% of the amount over $45,800
Over $60,000 but not over $85,600	$16,014 + 44% of the amount over $60,000
Over $85,600 but not over $109,400	$27,278 + 48% of the amount over $85,600
Over $109,400	$38,702 + 50% of the amount over $109,400

For Tax Years After 1983

If taxable income is:	The tax is:
Not over $3,400	No tax
Over $3,400 but not over $5,500	11% of the amount over $3,400
Over $5,500 but not over $7,600	$231 + 12% of the amount over $5,500
Over $7,600 but not over $11,900	$483 + 14% of the amount over $7,600
Over $11,900 but not over $16,000	$1,085 + 16% of the amount over $11,900
Over $16,000 but not over $20,200	$1,741 + 18% of the amount over $16,000
Over $20,200 but not over $24,600	$2,497 + 22% of the amount over $20,200
Over $24,600 but not over $29,900	$3,465 + 25% of the amount over $24,600
Over $29,900 but not over $35,200	$4,790 + 28% of the amount over $29,900
Over $35,200 but not over $45,800	$6,274 + 33% of the amount over $35,200
Over $45,800 but not over $60,000	$9,772 + 38% of the amount over $45,800
Over $60,000 but not over $85,600	$15,168 + 42% of the amount over $60,000
Over $85,600 but not over $109,400	$25,920 + 45% of the amount over $85,600
Over $109,400 but not over $162,400	$36,630 + 49% of the amount over $109,400
Over $162,400	$62,600 + 50% of the amount over $162,400

Source: Internal Revenue Code Section 1, PL 97-34, section 101, enacted August 13, 1981

III. MARRIED TAXPAYERS FILING SEPARATE RETURNS

For Tax Year 1982

If taxable income is:	The tax is:
Not over $1,700	No tax
Over $1,700 but not over $2,750	12% of the amount over $1,700
Over $2,750 but not over $3,800	$126 + 14% of the amount over $2,750
Over $3,800 but not over $5,950	$273 + 16% of the amount over $3,800
Over $5,950 but not over $8,000	$617 + 19% of the amount over $5,950
Over $8,000 but not over $10,100	$1,006 + 22% of the amount over $8,000
Over $10,100 but not over $12,300	$1,468 + 25% of the amount over $10,100
Over $12,300 but not over $14,950	$2,018 + 29% of the amount over $12,300
Over $14,950 but not over $17,600	$2,787 + 33% of the amount over $14,950
Over $17,600 but not over $22,900	$3,661 + 39% of the amount over $17,600
Over $22,900 but not over $30,000	$5,728 + 44% of the amount over $22,900
Over $30,000 but not over $42,800	$8,852 + 49% of the amount over $30,000
Over $42,800	$15,124 + 50% of the amount over $42,800

For Tax Year 1983

If taxable income is:	The tax is:
Not over $1,700	No tax
Over $1,700 but not over $2,750	11% of the amount over $1,700
Over $2,750 but not over $3,800	$115 + 13% of the amount over $2,750
Over $3,800 but not over $5,950	$252 + 15% of the amount over $3,800
Over $5,950 but not over $8,000	$574 + 17% of the amount over $5,950
Over $8,000 but not over $10,100	$923 + 19% of the amount over $8,000
Over $10,100 but not over $12,300	$1,322 + 23% of the amount over $10,100
Over $12,300 but not over $14,950	$1,828 + 26% of the amount over $12,300
Over $14,950 but not over $17,600	$2,517 + 30% of the amount over $14,950
Over $17,600 but not over $22,900	$3,312 + 35% of the amount over $17,600
Over $22,900 but not over $30,000	$5,167 + 40% of the amount over $22,900
Over $30,000 but not over $42,800	$8,007 + 44% of the amount over $30,000
Over $42,800 but not over $54,700	$13,639 + 48% of the amount over $42,800
Over $54,700	$19,351 + 50% of the amount over $54,700

For Tax Years After 1983

If taxable income is:	The tax is:
Not over $1,700	No tax
Over $1,700 but not over $2,750	11% of the amount over $1,700
Over $2,750 but not over $3,800	$115 + 12% of the amount over $2,750
Over $3,800 but not over $5,950	$241 + 14% of the amount over $3,800
Over $5,950 but not over $8,000	$542 + 16% of the amount over $5,950
Over $8,000 but not over $10,100	$870 + 18% of the amount over $8,000
Over $10,100 but not over $12,300	$1,248 + 22% of the amount over $10,100
Over $12,300 but not over $14,950	$1,732 + 25% of the amount over $12,300
Over $14,950 but not over $17,600	$2,395 + 28% of the amount over $14,950
Over $17,600 but not over $22,900	$3,137 + 33% of the amount over $17,600
Over $22,900 but not over $30,000	$4,886 + 38% of the amount over $22,900
Over $30,000 but not over $42,800	$7,584 + 42% of the amount over $30,000
Over $42,800 but not over $54,700	$12,960 + 45% of the amount over $42,800
Over $54,700 but not over $81,200	$18,315 + 49% of the amount over $54,700
Over $81,200	$31,300 + 50% of the amount over $81,200

Source: Internal Revenue Code Section 1, PL 97-34, section 101, enacted August 13, 1981

IV. UNMARRIED HEADS OF HOUSEHOLD

For Tax Year 1982

If taxable income is:	The tax is:
Not over $2,300	No tax
Over $2,300 but not over $4,400	12% of the amount over $2,300
Over $4,400 but not over $6,500	$252 + 14% of the amount over $4,400
Over $6,500 but not over $8,700	$546 + 16% of the amount over $6,500
Over $8,700 but not over $11,800	$898 + 20% of the amount over $8,700
Over $11,800 but not over $15,000	$1,518 + 22% of the amount over $1,800
Over $15,000 but not over $18,200	$2,222 + 23% of the amount over $15,000
Over $18,200 but not over $23,500	$2,958 + 28% of the amount over $18,200
Over $23,500 but not over $28,800	$4,442 + 32% of the amount over $23,500
Over $28,800 but not over $34,100	$6,138 + 38% of the amount over $28,800
Over $34,100 but not over $44,700	$8,152 + 41% of the amount over $34,100
Over $44,700 but not over $60,600	$12,498 + 49% of the amount over $44,700
Over $60,600	$20,289 + 50% of the amount over $60,600

For Tax Year 1983

If taxable income is:	The tax is:
Not over $2,300	No tax
Over $2,300 but not over $4,400	11% of the amount over $2,300
Over $4,400 but not over $6,500	$231 + 13% of the amount over $4,400
Over $6,500 but not over $8,700	$504 + 15% of the amount over $6,500
Over $8,700 but not over $11,800	$834 + 18% of the amount over $8,700
Over $11,800 but not over $15,000	$1,392 + 19% of the amount over $11,800
Over $15,000 but not over $18,200	$2,000 + 21% of the amount over $15,000
Over $18,200 but not over $23,500	$2,672 + 25% of the amount over $18,200
Over $23,500 but not over $28,800	$3,997 + 29% of the amount over $23,500
Over $28,800 but not over $34,100	$5,534 + 34% of the amount over $28,800
Over $34,100 but not over $44,700	$7,336 + 37% of the amount over $34,100
Over $44,700 but not over $60,600	$11,258 + 44% of the amount over $44,700
Over $60,600 but not over $81,800	$18,254 + 48% of the amount over $60,600
Over $81,800	$28,430 + 50% of the amount over $81,800

For Tax Years After 1983

If taxable income is:	The tax is:
Not over $2,300	No tax
Over $2,300 but not over $4,400	11% of the amount over $2,300
Over $4,400 but not over $6,500	$231 + 12% of the amount over $4,400
Over $6,500 but not over $8,700	$483 + 14% of the amount over $6,500
Over $8,700 but not over $11,800	$791 + 17% of the amount over $8,700
Over $11,800 but not over $15,000	$1,318 + 18% of the amount over $11,800
Over $15,000 but not over $18,200	$1,894 + 20% of the amount over $15,000
Over $18,200 but not over $23,500	$2,534 + 24% of the amount over $18,200
Over $23,500 but not over $28,800	$3,806 + 28% of the amount over $23,500
Over $28,800 but not over $34,100	$5,290 + 32% of the amount over $28,800
Over $34,100 but not over $44,700	$6,986 + 35% of the amount over $34,100
Over $44,700 but not over $60,600	$10,696 + 42% of the amount over $44,700
Over $60,600 but not over $81,800	$17,374 + 45% of the amount over $60,600
Over $81,800 but not over $108,300	$26,914 + 48% of the amount over $81,800
Over $108,300	$39,634 + 50% of the amount over $108,300

Source: Internal Revenue Code Section 1, PL 97-34, section 101, enacted August 13, 1981

APPENDIX III

SUPPORTING DETAILS

CASH

Financial Institution	Account Number	Separate		Joint, with Right of Survivorship	Community Property
		You	Spouse		
Checking accounts:					
		$	$	$	$
Total		$	$	$	$

	Account Number	Separate		Joint, with Right of Survivorship	Community Property	Type of Account (regular, 90 day, one year, etc.)	Restriction on Withdrawals
		You	Spouse				
Savings accounts:							
		$	$	$	$		
Total		$	$	$	$		

SHORT-TERM INVESTMENTS

I. Certificates of deposit, treasury bills, bankers' acceptances, money market certificates:

Financial Institution	Type of Investment	Separate		Joint, with Right of Survivorship	Community Property	Maturity Date
		You	Spouse			
		$	$	$	$	

II. Money market funds:

Fund	Separate		Joint, with Right of Survivorship	Community Property
	You	Spouse		
	$	$	$	$

LOANS RECEIVABLE

Note is due from: ____

Current principal balance: $__________ How is title to note held?

Original principal balance: $__________ __________ Joint, with right of survivorship

Interest rate: __________% __________ Community property

Date of acquisition of note: __________ __________ Your separate property

Due date of note: __________ __________ Spouse's separate property

Amount of periodic payment: $__________ __________ Other (please specify)

Payment mode:
____ Monthly
____ Quarterly
____ Semiannually
____ Annually
____ Lump Sum

What percent of funds which were loaned belong to:
You ____%
Spouse ____%

Note is due from: ____

Current principal balance: $__________ How is title to note held?

Original principal balance: $__________ __________ Joint, with right of survivorship

Interest rate: __________% __________ Community property

Date of acquisition of note: __________ __________ Your separate property

Due date of note: __________ __________ Spouse's separate property

Amount of periodic payment: $__________ __________ Other (please specify)

Payment mode:
____ Monthly
____ Quarterly
____ Semiannually
____ Annually
____ Lump Sum

What percent of funds which were loaned belong to:
You ____%
Spouse ____%

SECURITIES—STOCK

Security description	Security ownership*	No. of shares	Present market value per share	Acquisition date	Purchase price per share	Liquidation at death (yes or no)	What percent?	Pledged? If so, to whom?	Annual dividend income per share

*Separate property—yours, spouse's; joint with right of survivorship; community property.

SECURITIES—BONDS

Security description (include coupon rate and maturity date)	Security ownership*	No. of units	Present market value per share	Acquisition date	Purchase price per share	Liquidation at death (yes or no)	What percent?	Pledged? If so, to whom?	Annual interest income per share

*Separate property—yours, spouse's; joint with right of survivorship; community property.

SECURITIES—OTHER

Security description	Security ownership*	No. of shares	Present market value per share	Acquisition date	Purchase price per share	Liquidation at death (yes or no)	What percent?	Pledged? If so, to whom?	Annual dividend income per share

*Separate property—yours, spouse's; joint with right of survivorship; community property.

PERSONAL REAL ESTATE
PRIMARY RESIDENCE

Description: ______________________________

Address: ______________________________

Date acquired: ______________ Purchase price: ______________

Improvements made: ______________________________

(amounts and dates) ______________________________

____

Current market value: ______________

How is ownership of the property titled?

____ Joint, with right of survivorship

____ Community property

____ Your separate property

____ Spouse's separate property

____ Other (please specify)

What percent of the funds used for the purchase of the residence belong to:

You ____%

Spouse ____%

How many mortgages, contracts, or other liabilities are there on the property? ______________________________

(Please provide details of each on the next page)

Expenses

Annual taxes: ______________

Other (amounts and ______________________________

nature of expenses: ______________________________

PRIMARY RESIDENCE
MORTGAGES, NOTES, CONTRACTS

Lien holder: ______________________________

Date obligation incurred: ______________ Due date: ____________

Original balance: $______________ Present balance: $____________

Periodic payment: $______________

Interest rate: ________%

Collateral (if none, please write none): ______________________________

Lien holder: ______________________________

Date obligation incurred: ______________ Due date: ____________

Original balance: $______________ Present balance: $____________

Periodic payment: $______________

Interest rate: ________%

Collateral (if none, please write none): ______________________________

Lien holder: ______________________________

Date obligation incurred: ______________ Due date: ____________

Original balance: $______________ Present balance: $____________

Periodic payment: $______________

Interest rate: ________%

Collateral (if none, please write none): ______________________________

PERSONAL REAL ESTATE
VACATION PROPERTY

Description: ______________________________

Address: ______________________________

Date acquired: ______________ Purchase price: $______________

Improvements made: ______________________________

(amounts and dates) ______________________________

____

Current market value: ______________ Present monthly rental income, if any: $______________

How is ownership of the property titled?

____ Joint, with right of survivorship

____ Community property

____ Your separate property

____ Spouse's separate property

____ Other (please specify)

What percent of funds used for the purchase of the residence belong to:

You ____%

Spouse ____%

How many mortgages, contracts, or other liabilities are there on the property? ______________________________

(Please provide details of each on the next page)

Expenses

Annual taxes: ______________

Other (amounts and nature of expenses): ______________________________

____

VACATION RESIDENCE
MORTGAGES, NOTES, CONTRACTS

Lien holder: ______________________________

Date obligation incurred: ______________ Due date: ______________

Original balance: $______________ Present balance: $______________

Periodic payment: $______________

Interest rate: ________%

Collateral (if none, please write none): ______________________________

Lien holder: ______________________________

Date obligation incurred: ______________ Due date: ______________

Original balance: $______________ Present balance: $______________

Periodic payment: $______________

Interest rate: ________%

Collateral (if none, please write none): ______________________________

Lien holder: ______________________________

Date obligation incurred: ______________ Due date: ______________

Original balance: $______________ Present balance: $______________

Periodic payment: $______________

Interest rate: ________%

Collateral (if none, please write none): ______________________________

OTHER REAL ESTATE

(Use separate sheet for each property)

Description: ______________________________

Address: ______________________________

Date acquired: ______________ Purchase price: $______________

Improvements made: ______________________________

(amounts and dates) ______________________________

____

Current market value: ______________ Present monthly rental income, if any: $______________

How is ownership of the property titled?

____ Joint, with right of survivorship

____ Community property

____ Your separate property

____ Spouse's separate property

____ Other (please specify)

What percent of the funds used for the purchase of the residence belong to:

You ____%

Spouse ____%

How many mortgages, contracts, or other liabilities are there on the property? ______________________________

(Please provide details of each on the next page)

Expenses

Annual taxes: ______________

Other (amounts and nature of expenses): ______________________________

____

OTHER REAL ESTATE
MORTGAGES, NOTES, CONTRACTS

Lien holder: ____

Date obligation incurred: ______________ Due date: ____________

Original balance: $__________________ Present balance: $____________

Periodic payment: $__________________

Interest rate: _______%

Collateral (if none, please write none): ______________________________

Lien holder: ____

Date obligation incurred: ______________ Due date: ____________

Original balance: $__________________ Present balance: $____________

Periodic payment: $__________________

Interest rate: _______%

Collateral (if none, please write none): ______________________________

Lien holder: ____

Date obligation incurred: ______________ Due date: ____________

Original balance: $__________________ Present balance: $____________

Periodic payment: $__________________

Interest rate: _______%

Collateral (if none, please write none): ______________________________

TAX-INCENTIVE INVESTMENT

(Use separate sheet for each property)

Tax-incentive investments are those investments in which there is normally some tax-favored treatment for the investor. Common tax-incentive investments include oil and gas exploration, real estate, equipment leasing.

Also, another common feature of such investments is that the form of ownership is a limited partnership in which the investor is one of several limited partners along with a general partner who normally handles administration and management of the investments.

Investment

Name of investment: ______________________________

Description: ______________________________

Date acquired: ______________

Amount of initial investment: $______________

Amount of subsequent investments: $______________ Date ______________

Present market value: $______________

Anticipated cash distribution for the current year: $______________

Anticipated taxable income (or loss) for the current year: $______________

Investment ownership* ______________________________

*Separate property—yours, spouse's; joint with right of survivorship; community property.

TAX-INCENTIVE INVESTMENT

(Use separate sheet for each property)

Tax-incentive investments are those investments in which there is normally some tax-favored treatment for the investor. Common tax-incentive investments include oil and gas exploration, real estate, equipment leasing.

Also, another common feature of such investments is that the form of ownership is a limited partnership in which the investor is one of several limited partners along with a general partner who normally handles administration and management of the investments.

Investment

Name of investment: ______________________________

Description: ______________________________

Date acquired: ______________

Amount of initial investment: $ ______________

Amount of subsequent investments: $ ______________ Date ______________

Present market value: $ ______________
Anticipated cash distribution for the current year: $ ______________
Anticipated taxable income (or loss) for the current year: $ ______________

Investment ownership* ______________________________

*Separate property—yours, spouse's; joint with right of survivorship; community property.

TAX-INCENTIVE INVESTMENT

(Use separate sheet for each property)

Tax-incentive investments are those investments in which there is normally some tax-favored treatment for the investor. Common tax-incentive investments include oil and gas exploration, real estate, equipment leasing.

Also, another common feature of such investments is that the form of ownership is a limited partnership in which the investor is one of several limited partners along with a general partner who normally handles administration and management of the investments.

Investment

Name of investment: ______________________________

Description: ______________________________

Date acquired: ______________

Amount of initial investment: $ ______________

Amount of subsequent investments: $ ______________ Date ______________

Present market value: $ ______________

Anticipated cash distribution for the current year: $ ______________

Anticipated taxable income (or loss) for the current year: $ ______________

Investment ownership* ______________________________

*Separate property—yours, spouse's; joint with right of survivorship, community property.

OTHER INVESTMENTS

(Other investments of value not previously listed, excluding personal assets)

(Use a separate sheet for each asset)

Name of asset: ______________________________

Market value: $______________________

Acquisition date: ______________________

Is there a loan against this asset? __________

Current balance of loan: $______________

Original balance of loan: $______________

Who is the lender? ______________________

____

Date loan incurred: ______________________

Date loan due: ______________________

Periodic loan payment: $______________

Interest rate: ______________________

Original purchase price: $______________

How is ownership of this asset titled?

Joint, with right of survivorship __________

Community property __________

Your separate property __________

Spouse's separate property __________

Other (please specify) ______________

____

What percent of the funds used for the purchase of this asset belong to:

You _____%

Spouse _____%

What collateral, if any: ______________________________

OTHER INVESTMENTS

(Other investments of value not previously listed, excluding personal assets)

(Use a separate sheet for each asset)

Name of asset: ______________________________

Market value: $______________________

Original purchase price: $______________________

Acquisition date: ______________________

How is ownership of this asset titled?

Is there a loan against this asset? __________

Joint, with right of survivorship __________

Current balance of loan: $______________________

Community property __________

Original balance of loan: $______________________

Your separate property __________

Who is the lender? ______________________

Spouse's separate property __________

____

Other (please specify) ______________________

____

Date loan incurred: ______________________

Date loan due: ______________________

What percent of the funds used for the purchase of this asset belong to:

You _____%

Spouse _____%

Periodic loan payment: $______________________

Interest rate: ______________________

What collateral, if any: ______________________________

OTHER INVESTMENTS

(Other investments of value not previously listed, excluding personal assets)

(Use a separate sheet for each asset)

Name of asset: ______________________________

Market value: $______________

Acquisition date: ______________

Is there a loan against this asset? ________

Current balance of loan: $______________

Original balance of loan: $______________

Who is the lender? ______________

____

Date loan incurred: ______________

Date loan due: ______________

Periodic loan payment: $______________

Interest rate: ______________

Original purchase price: $______________

How is ownership of this asset titled?

Joint, with right of survivorship ________

Community property ________

Your separate property ________

Spouse's separate property ________

Other (please specify) ______________

____

What percent of the funds used for the purchase of this asset belong to:

You _____%

Spouse _____%

What collateral, if any: ______________________________

MISCELLANEOUS PERSONAL ASSETS

(Automobiles, boats, airplanes, furs, jewelry, household articles, antiques, etc.)

Description of property: ______________________________

Current market value: $____________

Purchase price: $____________

Date of acquisition: ____________

Is there a loan against this asset? ____________

Who is the lender? ____________

____

Original amount of loan: $____________

Current amount of loan: $____________

Loan interest rate: ____________%

Periodic loan payment: $____________

How is title to this asset held?

Joint, with right of survivorship ______

Community property ______

Your separate property ______

Spouse's separate property ______

Other (please specify) ____________

____

What percent of the funds used for the purchase of this asset belong to:

You ______%

Spouse ______%

MISCELLANEOUS PERSONAL ASSETS

(Automobiles, boats, airplanes, furs, jewelry, household articles, antiques, etc.)

Description of property: ____________________

Current market value: $__________

Purchase price: $__________

Date of acquisition: __________

Is there a loan against this asset? __________

Who is the lender? __________

____

Original amount of loan: $__________

Current amount of loan: $__________

Loan interest rate: ______%

Periodic loan payment: $__________

How is title to this asset held?

Joint, with right of survivorship ______

Community property ______

Your separate property ______

Spouse's separate property ______

Other (please specify) __________

____

What percent of the funds used for the purchase of this asset belong to:

You ____%

Spouse ____%

MISCELLANEOUS PERSONAL ASSETS

(Automobiles, boats, airplanes, furs, jewelry, household articles, antiques, etc.)

Description of property: ______________________________

Current market value: $______________

Purchase price: $______________

Date of acquisition: ______________

Is there a loan against this asset? ________

Who is the lender? ______________

____

Original amount of loan: $__________

Current amount of loan: $__________

Loan interest rate: __________%

Periodic loan payment: $__________

How is title to this asset held?

Joint, with right of survivorship ________

Community property ________

Your separate property ________

Spouse's separate property ________

Other (please specify) ______________

____

What percent of funds used for the purchase of this asset belong to:

You _____%

Spouse _____%

LIABILITIES

For all debts not previously listed, such as mortgages on real estate, margin loans on securities, automobile loans, and other secured debt, please describe below.

Payable to: ____________________

Obligation of: ____ You and Spouse ____ You ____ Spouse

Date incurred: ____________ Due date: ____________

Current principal balance: $____________ Original principal balance: $____________

Periodic payment: $____________ Interest rate: ____________%

What collateral, if any: ____________________

____

Payable to: ____________________

Obligation of: ____ You and Spouse ____ You ____ Spouse

Date incurred: ____________ Due date: ____________

Current principal balance: $____________ Original principal balance: $____________

Periodic payment: $____________ Interest rate: ____________%

What collateral, if any: ____________________

____

LIABILITIES

For all debts not previously listed, such as mortgages on real estate, margin loans on securities, automobile loans, and other secured debt, please describe below.

Payable to: ____

Obligation of: ____ You and Spouse ____ You ______ Spouse

Date incurred: ____________________ Due date: ____________________

Current principal balance: $____________ Original principal balance: $____________

Periodic payment: $________________ Interest rate: ________________%

What collateral, if any: ______________________________________

____

Payable to: ____

Obligation of: ____ You and Spouse ____ You ____ Spouse

Date incurred: ____________________ Due date: ____________________

Current principal balance: $____________ Original principal balance: $____________

Periodic payment: $________________ Interest rate: ________________%

What collateral, if any: ______________________________________

____

LIABILITIES

For all debts not previously listed, such as mortgages on real estate, margin loans on securities, automobile loans, and other secured debt, please describe below.

Payable to: ____________________

Obligation of: ____ You and Spouse ____ You ____ Spouse

Date incurred: ____________ Due date: ____________

Current principal balance: $__________ Original principal balance: $__________

Periodic payment: $__________ Interest rate: __________%

What collateral, if any: ____________________

____

Payable to: ____________________

Obligation of: ____ You and Spouse ____ You ____ Spouse

Date incurred: ____________ Due date: ____________

Current principal balance: $__________ Original principal balance: $__________

Periodic payment: $__________ Interest rate: __________%

What collateral, if any: ____________________

____

DEFERRED COMPENSATION, PENSION, AND PROFIT-SHARING PLANS

1. Deferred compensation:

   - How much deferred compensation? $____________________
   - When will it be paid? ____________________
   - What do you have to do to receive the deferred compensation?

     ____

   - Other summary provisions of the plan:

2. Stock options:

   - Date options granted: ____________________
   - Option price: ____________________
   - Exercise date: ____________________
   - Expiration date: ____________________
   - Type of option:

     Incentive Stock Option ____________________

     Restricted ____________________

     Nonqualified ____________________

   - Your plans for exercising options:

     When do you plan to exercise? ____________________

     How do you plan to finance them? ____________________

3. Other plans (please check):

   Individual Retirement Account ____________________

   Keogh plan ____________________

   Employee pension plan ____________________

   Employee profit-sharing plan ____________________

   Employee voluntary savings plan ____________________

   Salary savings plan ____________________

   Other (please describe) ____________________

For each item checked above, please complete the next sheet.

RETIREMENT PLANS

1. Plan description: ______________________________

2. What is the present value of your share of the plan? ______________________________

3. Do you contribute? Yes ____ No ____ If yes, how much each year? $______________

4. What is the total of your contributions to date? $______________________________

5. Who is the beneficiary of the retirement plan? ______________________________

6. What are the payment options available to you at retirement or to the beneficiary at your death?

   Lump sum ______________________________

   Installment ______________________________

   Other ______________________________

7. What are your present vested benefits (if you left the company, what amount would you get)? $______________________________

8. When will you be 100% vested? ______________________________

9. Expected value at retirement: $______________________________ At age: ____

10. Expected monthly income at retirement: $______________________________

11. Death benefit after retirement: $______________________________

RETIREMENT PLANS

1. Plan description: ____

2. What is the present value of your share of the plan? $________________________

3. Do you contribute? Yes ____ No ____ If yes, how much each year? $________________

4. What is the total of your contributions to date? $________________________

5. Who is the beneficiary of the retirement plan? ________________________

6. What are the payment options available to you at retirement or to the beneficiary at your death?

   Lump sum ____

   Installment ____

   Other ____

7. What are your present vested benefits (if you left the company, what amount

   would you get)? $____

8. When will you be 100% vested? ____

9. Expected value at retirement: $________________________ At age: ____

10. Expected monthly income at retirement: $________________________

11. Death benefit after retirement: $________________________________

RETIREMENT PLANS

1. Plan description: ______________________________

2. What is the present value of your share of the plan? $______________________

3. Do you contribute? Yes ____ No ____ If yes, how much each year? $____________

4. What is the total of your contributions to date? $______________________

5. Who is the beneficiary of the retirement plan? ______________________

6. What are the payment options available to you at retirement or to the beneficiary at your death?

   Lump sum ______________________________

   Installment ______________________________

   Other ______________________________

7. What are your present vested benefits (if you left the company, what amount would you get)? $______________________

8. When will you be 100% vested? ______________________

9. Expected value at retirement: $______________________ At age: ____

10. Expected monthly income at retirement: $______________________

11. Death benefit after retirement: $______________________

YOUR PERSONAL FINANCIAL PLANNER

File under PERSONAL DATA   Date: ________

FORM 1 PERSONAL AND FAMILY DATA

1 YOU

Name: ______________________ Birth Date: ________

SS#: ________

2 YOUR SPOUSE

Name: ______________________ Birth Date: ________

SS#: ________

3 YOUR PRESENT HOME

Address: ______________________

4 YOUR OCCUPATION

Business Address: ______________________

Employer's Name: ______________________

Address: ______________________

Phone: ______________________

Your Job Title: ______________________

5 SPOUSE'S OCCUPATION

Business Address: ______________________

Employer's Name: ______________________

Address: ______________________

Phone: ______________________

Spouse's Job Title: ______________________

6 CHILDREN

NAME	BIRTH DATE	SS#

7 GRANDCHILDREN

NAME	BIRTH DATE	SS#

8 OTHERS DEPENDENT ON YOU

NAME	RELATIONSHIP	SS#	AMOUNT OF ANNUAL SUPPORT

File under FINANCIAL DOCUMENTS Date: ___________

FORM 2 FINANCIAL DOCUMENTS

USE THE FOLLOWING LOCATION CODE:

TR Touche Ross files
SD Safe deposit box located at ___________________________
HF At home in fireproof file cabinet
HD At home in desk
HS At home in safe
AT Attorney's office
BR Broker's office
Other (describe)

__ ______________________________

__ ______________________________

__ ______________________________

	DESCRIPTION	LOCATION
Your Will	________________	____________
Spouse's Will	________________	____________
Trust Agreements	________________	____________
Mortgages	________________	____________
	________________	____________
	________________	____________
Property Deeds	________________	____________
	________________	____________
	________________	____________
Car Titles	________________	____________
	________________	____________
	________________	____________
Stock Certificates	________________	____________
	________________	____________
	________________	____________

Stock Options

Stock Purchase Plan

Bonds

Certificates of Dep.

Real Estate Contracts

Checking Accounts

Savings Passbooks

Life Insur. Policies

Insurance Policies

Retirement Agreements

Pension Plans

Profit Sharing Plans

Birth Certificates

Marriage License ______________________ ________________

Divorce Papers ______________________ ________________

Notes Receivable ______________________ ________________

Notes Payable ______________________ ________________

Employment Contracts ______________________ ________________

Income Tax Returns ______________________ ________________

______________________ ________________

______________________ ________________

Gift Tax Returns ______________________ ________________

Military Documents ______________________ ________________

Financial Surveys ______________________ ________________

Insurance Surveys ______________________ ________________

Safe Deposit Keys ______________________ ________________

Other Records and Valuables

________________ ______________________ ________________

________________ ______________________ ________________

________________ ______________________ ________________

________________ ______________________ ________________

Who has access to your safe deposit box? ____________________________

In whose name is the safe deposit box registered? ____________________

File under FINANCIAL DOCUMENTS Date: ___________

FORM 3 FINANCIAL ADVISORS

List advisors you currently use to assist in your financial affairs.

ATTORNEY

Name: ____________________ Street: ____________________

Firm: ____________________ City, State: ____________________

Phone: ____________________

Name: ____________________ Street: ____________________

Firm: ____________________ City, State: ____________________

Phone: ____________________

BANK OFFICER

Name: ____________________ Street: ____________________

Firm: ____________________ City, State: ____________________

Phone: ____________________

Name: ____________________ Street: ____________________

Firm: ____________________ City, State: ____________________

Phone: ____________________

BROKER

Name: ____________________ Street: ____________________

Firm: ____________________ City, State: ____________________

Phone: ____________________

Name: ____________________ Street: ____________________

Firm: ____________________ City, State: ____________________

Phone: ____________________

CPA

Name: ____________________ Street: ____________________

Firm: ____________________ City, State: ____________________

Phone: ____________________

Name: ____________________ Street: ____________________

Firm: ____________________ City, State: ____________________

Phone: ____________________

INSURANCE AGENT

Name: ____________________ Street: ____________________

Firm: ____________________ City, State: ____________________

Phone: ____________________

Name: ____________________ Street: ____________________

Firm: ____________________ City, State: ____________________

Phone: ____________________

INVESTMENT ADVISOR

Name: ____________________ Street: ____________________

Firm: ____________________ City, State: ____________________

Phone: ____________________

Name: ____________________ Street: ____________________

Firm: ____________________ City, State: ____________________

Phone: ____________________

OTHERS

Name: ____________________ Street: ____________________

Firm: ____________________ City, State: ____________________

Phone: ____________________

Name: ____________________ Street: ____________________

Firm: ____________________ City, State: ____________________

Phone: ____________________

To which of these would you turn to discuss a serious business problem or an important financial decision? ________________________________

File under FINANCIAL PROFILE   Date: ____________

FORM 4 STATEMENT OF NET WORTH

WHAT YOU OWN	CURRENT VALUE (EST.)	% OF TOTAL ASSET VALUE
1 Liquid Assets		
Cash (checking, savings accounts):	________	____
Short-Term Investments		
Treasury Bills:	________	____
Savings Certificates:	________	____
Money Market Funds	________	____
Cash Value of Life Insurance	________	____
TOTAL Liquid Assets	________	____
2 Investment Assets		
Notes Receivable	________	____
Marketable Securities		
Stocks	________	____
Bonds	________	____
Real Estate (investment)	________	____
Tax Incentive Investments	________	____
Other Investment Assets (describe below)		
a. ______________________________	________	____
b. ______________________________	________	____
c. ______________________________	________	____
d. ______________________________	________	____
Retirement Funds	________	____
TOTAL Investment Assets	________	____

3 Personal Assets

Residence	________	____
Vacation Property	________	____
Art, Antiques	________	____
Furnishings	________	____
Vehicles	________	____
Boats	________	____
Other	________	____
TOTAL Personal Assets	________	____
TOTAL ASSETS	________	____

WHAT YOU OWE	CURRENT VALUE (EST.)	INTEREST RATE
4 Short-Term Obligations		
Consumer Credit Obligations	________	____
Borrowings on Life Insurance	________	____
Installment Loans	________	____
Personal Loans	________	____
Accrued Income Taxes	________	____
Other Obligations (describe below)		
a. ______________________________	________	____
b. ______________________________	________	____
c. ______________________________	________	____
d. ______________________________	________	____
TOTAL Short-Term Obligations	________	____

5 Long-Term Obligations

Loans to purchase investment assets	________	____
Loans to purchase personal assets	________	____
Mortgage on personal residences	________	____
TOTAL Long-Term Obligations	________	____
TOTAL LIABILITIES	________	

TOTAL ASSETS ________

- TOTAL LIABILITIES ________

= NET WORTH ________

File under FINANCIAL PROFILE Date: ____________

FORM 5 ANALYSIS OF NET WORTH

			AMOUNT	PERCENT
LIQUIDITY				
1	Total Liquid Assets	________		
2	Total Short-Term Obligations	________		
3	Excess (deficiency) Of Liquid Assets		________	____
INVESTMENT ASSETS				
4	Total Investment Assets	________		
5	Total Long-Term Investment Loans	________		
6	Total Equity in Investment Assets		________	____
PERSONAL ASSETS				
7	Total Personal Assets	________		
8	Total Long-Term Personal Loans	________		
9	Total Equity In Personal Assets		________	____
10	TOTAL NET WORTH	________		

File Under FINANCIAL PROFILE Date: __________

FORM 6 INCOME SOURCES

	YOU	SPOUSE	TOTAL
1 Income from Employment			
Salary	________	________	________
Commissions	________	________	________
Self Employment	________	________	________
Other	________	________	________
TOTAL Employment Income	________	________	________
2 Investment Income			
Taxable Interest	________	________	________
Nontaxable Interest	________	________	________
Dividends	________	________	________
Rents (net of cash expenses)	________	________	________
Investment Partnerships	________	________	________
Social Security	________	________	________
Pension	________	________	________
Trust Fund	________	________	________
Other	________	________	________
TOTAL Income from Investments	________	________	________
TOTAL Income from All Sources	________	________	________

Investment Income as Percentage of Total Income ____

File under FINANCIAL PROFILE Date: ____________

FORM 7 BASIC LIFESTYLE EXPENDITURES

			AMOUNT	PERCENT
1	Housing			
	Mortgage or Rent	__________		____
	Property Taxes	__________		____
	Insurance	__________		____
	Utilities	__________		____
	Other Housing Costs	__________		____
	TOTAL Housing Costs		___________	____
2	Food		___________	____
3	Clothing		___________	____
4	Transportation			
	Installment Payments	__________		____
	Insurance	__________		____
	Fuel	__________		____
	Maintenance	__________		____
	Other Transportation	__________		____
	TOTAL Transportation Expenditures		___________	____
5	Phone		___________	____
6	Household Purchases and Supplies		___________	____
7	House Cleaning and Household Help		___________	____
8	Education (not secondary and college)		___________	____
9	Recreation and Club Membership		___________	____
10	Personal Care and Improvements		___________	____

11	Medical and Dental, Health and Disability Insur.	________	____
12	Life Insurance	________	____
13	Liability Insurance	________	____
14	Other Insurance	________	____
15	Yard Maintenance (including pool)	________	____
16	Debt Reduction (exclude home and autos)	________	____
17	Contributions	________	____
18	Other Basic Lifestyle Costs	________	____
	TOTAL Basic Lifestyle Expenditures	________	____
	Average Monthly Amount	________	

File under FINANCIAL PROFILE Date: ___________

FORM 8 DISCRETIONARY EXPENDITURES

		AMOUNT	PERCENT
1	Education (private secondary schools and college)	________	____
2	Entertainment and Eating Out	________	____
3	Regular Vacations	________	____
4	Extraordinary Charitable Expenditures	________	____
5	Hobbies	________	____
6	Personal Gifts	________	____
7	Support of Relatives and Others		
	Name ______________________________	________	____
	Name ______________________________	________	____
	Name ______________________________	________	____
8	Home Improvements	________	____
9	Purchase of Automobiles, Boats, etc.	________	____
10	Retirement Plans		
	Type ______________________________	________	____
	Type ______________________________	________	____
	Type ______________________________	________	____
11	Debt Reductions	________	____
12	Other		
	______________________________	________	____
	______________________________	________	____
	______________________________	________	____
	TOTAL Discretionary Expenditures	________	____
	AVERAGE Monthly Amount	________	

File under FINANCIAL PROFILE   Date: ____________

FORM 9 INCOME AND EMPLOYMENT TAXES

1	Taxable Income		__________
2	Federal Income Tax	__________	
3	State and City Taxes	__________	
4	Employment Taxes		
	Employee Social Security	__________	
	Self Employment Tax	__________	
5	TOTAL Income and Employment Taxes		__________

File under FINANCIAL PROFILE Date: ____________

FORM 10 ANALYSIS OF EARNED INCOME AND EXPENDITURES

		AMOUNT	AMOUNT	PERCENT OF TOTAL INCOME
1	TOTAL Income from Employment		________	100%
2	Expenditures			
	Basic Lifestyle	________		____
	Discretionary	________		____
	Taxes	________		____
3	TOTAL Expenditures		________	____
4	Excess (or Deficiency)		________	____

File under TAX PLANNING Date: ___________

FORM 11 TAX-PLANNING WORKSHEET

	LAST YR.	CURRENT YR.
1 Gross Income		
a. Taxable Wages/Salaries	________	________
b. Taxable Dividends and Interest	________	________
c. Net Business Income (Loss)	________	________
d. Net Taxable Long-Term Capital Gain (Loss)	________	________
e. Net Taxable Short-Term Capital Gain (Loss)	________	________
f. Net Rent Income (Loss)	________	________
g. Net Partnership Income (Loss)	________	________
h. Other Income (Loss)	________	________
i. TOTAL Gross Income	________	________
2 Adjustments to Gross Income		
a. Alimony Paid	________	________
b. IRA Payments	________	________
c. Keogh Plan Payments	________	________
d. Unreimbursed Business Expenses	________	________
e. Unreimbursed Moving Expenses	________	________
f. Deduction for Married Couple When Both Work	________	________
g. Other Adjustments	________	________
h. TOTAL Adjustments	________	________
3 Adjusted Gross Income	________	________

4 Itemized Deductions

a.	Medical	______	______
b.	Taxes	______	______
c.	Interest Paid	______	______
d.	Charitable Contributions	______	______
e.	Casualty and Theft Losses	______	______
f.	Miscellaneous Deductions	______	______
g.	TOTAL Itemized Deductions	______	______
h.	Standard (zero bracket) Deduction	______	______
5a.	Excess Deductions	______	______
b.	Exemptions	______	______
c.	TOTAL Deductions and Exemptions	______	______
6a.	Taxable Income	______	______
b.	Tax Bracket	______	______
7a.	Targeted Taxable Income		______
b.	Targeted Tax Bracket		______

File under TAX PLANNING   Date: ____________

FORM 12 TAX-SAVING IDEAS

TAX-SAVING IDEA

Tax-Free Income: ______________________________

____

Tax-Favored Income: ______________________________

____

Tax-Deferred Income: ______________________________

____

Tax-Sheltered Income: ______________________________

____

Shifting Income to Dependents: ______________________________

____

Tax-Deductible Expenditures: ______________________________

____

Action	Action Date	Funds Needed	Reduction of Taxable Income
Tax-Free Income	________	________	________
	________	________	________
Tax-Favored Income	________	________	________
	________	________	________
Tax-Deferred Income	________	________	________
	________	________	________
Tax-Sheltered Investments	________	________	________
	________	________	________

Shift Income to Dependents	________	________	________
	________	________	________
Tax Deductible Expenditures	________	________	________
	________	________	________
TOTALS		________	________

File under TAX PLANNING Date: ___________

FORM 13A CAPITAL GAINS AND LOSSES REALIZED TO DATE

Number Units	Investment Type	Date Acquired	Cost or Basis	Date Sold	Net Proceeds

CAPITAL GAINS AND LOSSES REALIZED

Investment Type	Short Term		Long Term	
	Gain	Loss	Gain	Loss
Subtotals	___	___	___	___
Capital Gain Dividends			___	
Short Term Capital Loss Carryovers		___		
Long Term Capital Loss Carryovers				___
TOTAL	___	___	___	___
NET Short Term Capital Gain or Loss	___	___		
NET Long Term Capital Gain or Loss			___	___

File under TAX PLANNING Date: ___________

FORM 13B UNREALIZED GAINS OR LOSSES IN CURRENT INVESTMENTS

Number Units	Investment Type	Date Acquired	Cost or Basis	Date of Becoming Long Term	Current Market Value

CAPITAL GAINS AND LOSSES UNREALIZED

Investment Type	Short Term Gain	Short Term Loss	Long Term Gain	Long Term Loss
TOTAL Unrealized Capital Gains and Losses				
NET Short Term Capital Gain or Loss				
NET Long Term Capital Gain or Loss				

File under TAX PLANNING Date: ____________

FORM 14 YEAR-END TAX PLAN

	ACTUAL TO DATE	ESTIMATES TO END YR.	ESTIMATES TOTAL YR.
1 Gross Income			
a. Taxable Wages/Salaries	________	________	________
b. Taxable Dividends and Interest	________	________	________
c. Net Business Income (Loss)	________	________	________
d. Net Taxable Long-Term Capital Gain (Loss)	________	________	________
e. Net Taxable Short-Term Capital Gain (Loss)	________	________	________
f. Net Rent Income (Loss)	________	________	________
g. Net Partnership Income (Loss)	________	________	________
h. Other Income (Loss)	________	________	________
i. TOTAL Gross Income	________	________	________
2 Adjustments to Gross Income			
a. Alimony Paid	________	________	________
b. IRA Payments	________	________	________
c. Keogh Plan Payments	________	________	________
d. Unreimbursed Business Expenses	________	________	________
e. Unreimbursed Moving Expenses	________	________	________
f. Deduction for Married Couple When Both Work	________	________	________
g. Other Adjustments	________	________	________
h. TOTAL Adjustments	________	________	________
3 Adjusted Gross Income	________	________	________

4 Itemized Deductions

a.	Medical	________	________	________
b.	Taxes	________	________	________
c.	Interest Paid	________	________	________
d.	Charitable Contributions	________	________	________
e.	Casualty and Theft Losses	________	________	________
f.	Miscellaneous Deductions	________	________	________
g.	TOTAL Itemized Deductions	________	________	________
h.	Standard (zero bracket) Deduction	________		________
5a.	Excess Deductions	________	________	________
b.	Exemptions	________	________	________
c.	TOTAL Deductions and Exemptions	________	________	________
6a.	Taxable Income	________	________	________
b.	Tax Bracket			________
7a.	Targeted Taxable Income			________
b.	Targeted Tax Bracket			________

File under TAX PLANNING | Date: ____________

FORM 15 YEAR-END TAX ACTION

Estimated Taxable Income Current Year (from Form 14, line 6a)	________
Targeted Taxable Income Current Year (from Form 14, line 7a)	________
Reduction in Taxable Income Required	________

YEAR-END TAX-PLANNING ACTIONS	CASH REQUIRED	REDUCTION TAXABLE INCOME CURRENT YR.
____________________	________	________
____________________	________	________
____________________	________	________
____________________	________	________
____________________	________	________
____________________	________	________
____________________	________	________
____________________	________	________
____________________	________	________
____________________	________	________
____________________	________	________
TOTALS	________	________

File under FINANCIAL OBJECTIVES   Date: ___________

FORM 16 FINANCIAL SECURITY

1 What does financial security mean to you?

____

____

____

	Amount
Annual Income (today's dollars)	_________
Investment Assets	_________
Net Worth	_________
Debt Level	_________
Other	
__________________________________	_________
__________________________________	_________
__________________________________	_________

2 In how many years from now would you like to achieve financial security? _____________

3 List the three greatest obstacles to your achieving financial security (as you defined it in Question 1):

____

____

____

File under FINANCIAL OBJECTIVES Date: ____________

FORM 17 INCOME AND EXPENDITURE OBJECTIVES

1 Estimate employment income for each year:

	CURRENT YEAR	NEXT YEAR	THIRD YEAR
Your Income	_________	_________	_________
Spouse's Income	_________	_________	_________

2 By what percentage could you reduce your basic lifestyle expenditures if you really wanted to? __________

3 By what percentage could you reduce your discretionary expenditures if you really wanted to? __________

4 What major discretionary expenditures other than education do you plan to incur in the next three years?

	AMOUNT	YEAR
Cars	_________	_____
Boat	_________	_____
Extended Travel	_________	_____
Major Home Improvements	_________	_____
Major Charitable Contributions	_________	_____
Other		
___________________________________	_________	_____
___________________________________	_________	_____
___________________________________	_________	_____

File under FINANCIAL OBJECTIVES Date: ____________

FORM 18 EDUCATION AND OTHER SUPPORT OF CHILDREN

1 PRIVATE ELEMENTARY AND SECONDARY SCHOOLS

CHILD	AGE	YEARS OF SCHOOLING	YEAR BEGINNING	YEARLY COST	TOTAL COST
____________	___	___	_____	_______	________
____________	___	___	_____	_______	________
____________	___	___	_____	_______	________
____________	___	___	_____	_______	________
____________	___	___	_____	_______	________
____________	___	___	_____	_______	________

TOTAL Estimated Cost __________

2 COLLEGE AND UNIVERSITY EDUCATION

CHILD	AGE	YEARS OF SCHOOLING	YEAR BEGINNING	YEARLY COST	TOTAL COST
____________	___	___	_____	_______	________
____________	___	___	_____	_______	________
____________	___	___	_____	_______	________
____________	___	___	_____	_______	________
____________	___	___	_____	_______	________
____________	___	___	_____	_______	________

TOTAL Estimated Cost __________

3 ASSETS SET ASIDE FOR EDUCATION

CHILD	TYPE OF ASSET	AMOUNT	HOW HELD

4 OTHER SUPPORT OF CHILDREN

CHILD	REASON FOR SUPPORT	NUMBER OF YEARS	YEARLY COST	TOTAL COST
	TOTAL Estimated Cost			

File under FINANCIAL OBJECTIVES Date: ___________

FORM 19 RETIREMENT PLANNING

1 When do you plan to retire? ______________________

Your age at retirement? ______________________

Number of years from now? ______________________

2 Do you or your spouse have any health problems that might make you retire at an earlier date?

Explain: ____

____

____

3 If you retired tomorrow, with all educational expenditures behind you, and no one depended on you, financially how much spendable after-tax income would you and your spouse need for one year at today's prices? __________

4 Estimate your retirement income from various sources.

SOURCE	ESTIMATED ANNUAL AMOUNT AT RETIREMENT AGE
Retirement plan from company	________
Retirement benefits from previous employer(s)	________
Social Security	________
Keogh Plan	________
IRA Plan	________
Spouse's Retirement Plan	________
Deferred Compensation	________
Investment Assets	________
Other Sources	
______________________________	________
______________________________	________
______________________________	________
TOTAL	________

5 What do you estimate your investment assets will be worth at retirement age? __________

6 When you retire, will you sell your home? __________
If yes, will you

Buy another? __________

Rent? __________

Relocate? __________

Based on your anticipated retirement age and housing arrangements, would your housing expenditures, at present prices, be higher or lower in retirement than they are today?

_____% higher _____% lower

Why? ____

File under INVESTMENT STRATEGY   Date: ____________

FORM 20 INVESTMENT OBJECTIVES

Indicate the relative importance you attribute to the following considerations by placing the appropriate number after each statement.

NOT IMPORTANT -- 1
MARGINALLY IMPORTANT -- 2
REASONABLY IMPORTANT -- 3
DEFINITELY IMPORTANT -- 4
MOST IMPORTANT -- 5

Diversification	How important is it for you to hedge against big losses by spreading your risks?	___
Liquidity	How important is it that you have cash available for emergencies or investment opportunities?	___
Safety	If we went into a deep economic depression, how important would it be for you to sell your investments at about the price you paid for them?	___
Current Income	How important is it that you get maximum income from your investments this year and next?	___
Future Appreciation	How important is it that your investment dollars keep pace with inflation or do better than inflation?	___
Tax Advantage	How important is it that you get all the tax relief that may be available to you?	___
Leverage	How important is it for you to use borrowed money in hopes of reaping a higher return on your investment?	___
Ease of Management	How important is it for you to have investments you do not have to watch or worry about?	___

File under INVESTMENT STRATEGY Date: ____________

FORM 21 REVIEW OF YOUR PRESENT INVESTMENTS

TYPE OF ASSET	CURRENT VALUE	% OF TOTAL	INVESTMENT OBJECTIVES	CURRENT INCOME	APPR'N (LOSS)	ANNUAL RATE OF RETURN
TOTAL						

File under INVESTMENT STRATEGY Date: ____________

FORM 22 YOUR INVESTMENT STRATEGY

1 What investment objectives (see Form 20) will be most important for you during the next three years? ________________________________

____

____

2 What is your assumption for the inflation rate during the next three years? ______

3 What overall annual pre-tax return on your investments do you want to achieve in the next three years? ______

4 What specific changes do you have to make in your present investments to achieve your objectives and overall rate of return in the next three years? ____________________________________

____

____

5 What annual amount do you believe you can set aside for investment during the next three years? __________

6 What investments will you make with your additional investment dollars? ____

____

____

File under EDUCATIONAL FINANCING Date: ____________

FORM 23 COLLEGE AND GRADUATE SCHOOL COSTS

1	Children's Names	______________	______________	______________
2	Ages of Children	______________	______________	______________
3	Number of Years Until College	______________	______________	______________
4	Est. Number of Years in College and Graduate School	______________	______________	______________
5	Number of Years for Inflation Adjustment	______________	______________	______________
6	Est. Annual Inflation Rate Between Now and End of Education	______________	______________	______________
7	Inflation Factor	______________	______________	______________
8	Est. Annual College Costs in Today's Dollars	______________	______________	______________
9	Est. Annual Costs Adjusted	______________	______________	______________
10	Est. TOTAL Costs Adjusted	______________	______________	______________
11	Est. After-Tax Rate of Return on Educational Funds	______________	______________	______________
12	Compound Factor for Rate of Return on Line 11	______________	______________	______________
13	Present Value of Funds Set Aside for Education	______________	______________	______________
14	Future Value of Funds Set Aside	______________	______________	______________
15	Annual Amount to Be Invested for Education	______________	______________	______________

File under RETIREMENT PLANNING Date: ____________

FORM 24 ESTIMATED LIFESTYLE EXPENDITURES AT RETIREMENT

	CURRENT YEAR	AT RETIREMENT
1 Housing		
Mortgage or Rent	______	______
Property Taxes	______	______
Insurance	______	______
Utilities	______	______
Other Housing Costs	______	______
TOTAL Housing Costs	______	______
2 Food	______	______
3 Clothing	______	______
4 Transportation		
Installment Payments	______	______
Insurance	______	______
Fuel	______	______
Maintenance	______	______
Other Transportation	______	______
TOTAL Transportation Expenditures	______	______
5 Phone	______	______
6 Household Purchases and Supplies	______	______
7 House Cleaning and Household Help	______	______
8 Education (not secondary and college)	______	______
9 Recreation and Club Membership	______	______
10 Personal Care and Improvements	______	______
11 Medical and Dental, Health and Disability	______	______
12 Life Insurance	______	______

13	Liability Insurance	________	________
14	Other Insurance	________	________
15	Yard Maintenance (including pool)	________	________
16	Debt Reduction (exclude home and autos)	________	________
17	Contributions	________	________
18	Other Basic Lifestyle costs	________	________
19	TOTAL Basic Lifestyle Expenditures	________	________
20	Number of Years to Retirement ____		
21	Average Annual Rate of Inflation ____		
22	Inflation Factor (from Table 1 in Appendix I) ____		
23	TOTAL of Projected Annual Basic Lifestyle Expenditures Adjusted for Inflation		________

File under RETIREMENT PLANNING Date: ____________

FORM 25 ESTIMATED DISCRETIONARY EXPENDITURES AT RETIREMENT

		CURRENT YEAR	AT RETIREMENT
1	Education (Private Secondary Schools and College)	________	________
2	Entertainment and Eating Out	________	________
3	Regular Vacations	________	________
4	Extraordinary Charitable Expenditures	________	________
5	Hobbies	________	________
6	Personal Gifts	________	________
7	Support of Relatives and Others:		
	________________________	________	________
	________________________	________	________
	________________________	________	________
8	Home Improvements	________	________
9	Purchase of Automobiles, Boat, etc.	________	________
10	Retirement Plans	________	________
11	Debt Reductions	________	________
12	Other:		
	________________________	________	________
	________________________	________	________
	________________________	________	________
13	TOTAL	________	________
14	Inflation Factor _____		
15	TOTAL Projected Annual Discretionary Expenditures Adjusted for Inflation		________

File under RETIREMENT PLANNING   Date: ____________

FORM 26 ESTIMATED RETIREMENT NEEDS, INCLUDING TAXES

		ANNUAL AMOUNT
1	Estimated Basic Lifestyle Expenditures	________
2	Estimated Discretionary Expenditures	________
3	TOTAL	________
4	Tax Factor (Percentage)	________
5	TOTAL Retirement Expenditures Including Taxes	________

File under RETIREMENT PLANNING   Date: __________

FORM 27 RETIREMENT INCOME

Projected Retirement Age: ____   Number of Years to Retirement: ____

1 Estimated Annual Retirement Needs __________

2 Estimated Annual Income from Retirement Plans (other than lump-sum distributions)

a. Social Security __________

b. Company Retirement Plan __________

c. Defered Compensation __________

d. Other Retirement Plans __________

3 TOTAL Annual Income from Retirement Plans __________

4 Annual Income Gap __________

5 Retirement Capital Required to Fill Gap

a. Estimated Pre-Tax Rate of Return __________

b. Retirement Capital Required __________

6 Sources of Retirement Capital	INVESTMENT ASSETS	LUMP SUMS FROM RETIREMENT PLANS	IRA/ KEOGH	TOTAL
a. Value of Present Investment Assets and and Retirement Accounts	__________		__________	__________
b. Estimated Rate of Return from Now until Retirement	__________		__________	
c. Years until Retirement	__________		__________	
d. Compound Factor from Table 1 (in Appendix I)	__________		__________	
e. Estimated Value of Your Investment Assets and Retirement Accounts at Retirement	__________	__________	__________	__________

		INVESTMENT ASSETS	IRA/ KEOGH	OTHER	TOTAL
7	Additional Capital from Annual Investments You Are Planning to Make				
a.	Annual Amount to Be Invested Between Now and Retirement	________	________	________	________
b.	Estimated Pre-Tax Rate of Return on Annual Investment	________	________	________	________
c.	Years until Retirement				
d.	Compound Factor from Table 2 (in Appendix I)	________	________	________	________
e.	Estimated Value of Additional Capital from Your Annual Investments	________	________	________	________
8	TOTAL Estimated Retirement Capital				________
9	Additional Capital Needed, if Any, to Provide Retirement Income				________
10	Additional Annual Investment Needed to Provide Capital on Line 9				
a.	Estimated Rate of Return from Now until Retirement			________	
b.	Years until Retirement			________	
c.	Compound Factor from Table 2 (in Appendix I)			________	
d.	Annual Amount Required				________

File Under INSURANCE

Date: ____________

FORM 28 YOUR PRESENT LIFE INSURANCE COVERAGE

INSURANCE ON YOUR LIFE

Name of Insurance Company	Policy Number	Beneficiary	Type of Policy	Face Value	Cash Surrender Value	Loan on Policy	Owner of Policy
			TOTAL				

INSURANCE ON SPOUSE'S LIFE

Name of Insurance Company	Policy Number	Beneficiary	Type of Policy	Face Value	Cash Surrender Value	Loan on Policy	Owner of Policy
			TOTAL				

File Under INSURANCE | Date: __________

FORM 29 TOTAL LIFE INSURANCE REQUIRED

1 Cash Required Immediately

a. Funeral	________	
b. Current bills	________	
c. Administrative	________	
d. Emergency fund	________	
e. Estate taxes	________	
f. TOTAL	(________)	

2 Cash Available Immediately

a. Insurance proceeds	________	
b. Death benefits of retirement programs	________	
c. Liquid assets	________	
d. Other	________	
e. TOTAL	________	

3 Net Cash Available (or Required) ________

4 Assets Required for Mortgage and Children's Education

a. Mortgage outstanding	________	
b. Education	________	
c. TOTAL	(________)	

5 Assets Available for Mortgage and Children's Education

a. Investment assets	________	
b. Personal assets convertible into cash	________	
c. Other	________	
d. TOTAL	________	

6 Net Resources Available (or Required) ________

7 Total Resources Available (or Required) ________

8 Annual Living Expenses ________

9 Annual Income Available for Living Expenses

a. Income from assets ________

b. Employment income of spouse ________

c. Other ________

d. TOTAL ________

10 Annual Income Excess (or Deficiency) ________

11 Additional Insurance Required

a. Negative amount from line 7 ________

b. Negative amount from line 10 divided by 10% ________

c. TOTAL ________

File Under INSURANCE

Date: ____________

FORM 30 WHOLE-LIFE POLICY INSURANCE COST PER $1000

PRESENT POLICY

1	Face Amount	________	
2	Cash Surrender Value (your savings element)	(________)	
3	Net Insurance Protection		________
4	Present Premium	________	
5	Cash Value Increase for Current Year	(________)	
6	Current Dividend	(________)	
7	Lost Earnings on Cash Value at 5%	________	
8	Earnings on Borrowed Cash Value at 5%	(________)	
9	Total Cost		________
10	Cost Per Thousand		________

File Under ESTATE PLANNING | Date: ____________

FORM 31 PROPERTY OWNERSHIP AND GROSS ESTATE

PROPERTY		OWNERSHIP			
	Est. Current Value	Community	Joint	Solely Yours	Solely Spouse's
1 NET WORTH					
a. Liquid Assets Other Than Cash Value of Life Insurance	_________	______	______	______	______
b. Investment Assets, Other Than Retirement Funds	_________	______	______	______	______
c. Personal Assets	_________	______	______	______	______
d. Total Assets	_________	______	______	______	______
e. Liabilities	_________	______	______	______	______
f. TOTAL	_________	______	______	______	______
2 INSURANCE OWNED					
a. On Your Life	_________	______	______	______	______
b. On Your Spouse's Life	_________	______	______	______	______
c. TOTAL	_________	______	______	______	______
3 OTHER ESTATE ASSETS					
a. Retirement Plans	_________	______	______	______	______
b. Other	_________	______	______	______	______
c. TOTAL	_________	______	______	______	______
4 TOTAL GROSS ESTATE	_________	______	______	______	______
5 TOTAL GROSS ESTATE FOR YOU AND YOUR SPOUSE					
a. Your Gross Estate	_________	______	______	______	______
b. Your Spouse's Gross Estate	_________	______	______	______	______
c. TOTAL	_________	______	______	______	______

File Under ESTATE PLANNING　　　　Date: ____________

FORM 32A ESTIMATED FEDERAL ESTATE TAX

YOUR ESTATE

1	Gross Estate		________
2	Deductions		
	a. Funeral Expenses	________	
	b. Administrative Expenses	________	
	c. TOTAL Expenses	________	
3	Marital Deduction for Property Passing to Spouse:		
	a. Jointly Held Property	________	
	b. Transferred by Contract	________	
	c. Transferred by Will or Living Trust	________	
	d. TOTAL Marital Deductions	________	
4	Charitable Deduction	________	
5	TOTAL Deductions		________
6	Tentative Taxable Estate		________
7	Post-1976 Taxable Gifts Other Than Gifts Includible in Gross Estate		________
8	TOTAL Taxable Estate		________
9	Tentative Federal Estate Tax		________
10	Less:		
	a. Gift Taxes Paid on Post-1976 Gifts	________	
	b. Unified Credit	________	
	c. TOTAL		________
11	Federal Estate Tax		________

File Under ESTATE PLANNING Date: ____________

FORM 32B ESTIMATED FEDERAL ESTATE TAX

SPOUSE'S ESTATE

1	Gross Estate		________
2	Deductions		
a.	Funeral Expenses	________	
b.	Administrative Expenses	________	
c.	TOTAL Expenses	________	
3	Marital Deduction for Property Passing to Spouse:		
a.	Jointly Held Property	________	
b.	Transferred by Contract	________	
c.	Transferred by Will or Living Trust	________	
d.	TOTAL Marital Deductions	________	
4	Charitable Deduction	________	
5	TOTAL Deductions		________
6	Tentative Taxable Estate		________
7	Post-1976 Taxable Gifts Other Than Gifts Includible in Gross Estate		________
8	TOTAL Taxable Estate		________
9	Tentative Federal Estate Tax		________
10	Less:		
a.	Gift Taxes Paid on Post-1976 Gifts	________	
b.	Unified Credit	________	
c.	TOTAL		________
11	Federal Estate Tax		________

File Under TAX PLANNING | Date: ____________

FORM 33 INCOME AND EXPENDITURE PROJECTION

Amount desired for long-term objectives:

	LAST YEAR	NEXT YEAR
1 Education and Support of Children	________	________
2 Retirement	________	________
3 Investments	________	________
4 Other	________	________
5 TOTAL	________	________

What's available for long-term objectives:

	LAST YEAR	NEXT YEAR
6 Income		
a. From Employment	________	________
b. From Investments and Other Sources	________	________
c. TOTAL	________	________
7 Basic Expenditures	________	________
8 Discretionary Expenditures	________	________
9 Taxes		
a. Federal	________	________
b. State	________	________
c. Employment	________	________
d. TOTAL	________	________
10 TOTAL Expenditures and Taxes	________	________
11 Amount Available for Long-Term Goals	________	________

File Under ACTION

Date: ____________

FORM 34 ACTION STEPS

List 10 specific steps you will take during the next year to implement your personal financial plan.

____

____

____

____

____

____

____

____

____

____

INDEX

L

M

N

O

P

SEND NOW FOR ADDITIONAL INFORMATION IN THE AREA OF FINANCIAL PLANNING AND MANAGEMENT

☐ **Yes–**I would like additional information on the TOUCHE ROSS PERSONAL FINANCIAL MANAGER and the TOUCHE ROSS PERSONAL FINANCIAL PLANNER, forthcoming IBM–compatible software packages being developed by Lumen Systems Inc.

☐ **Yes–**Please send me additional information on the full range of Touche Ross Personal Financial Planning Services.

To assist Prentice-Hall, Lumen Systems, and Touche Ross in better responding to your request, please take a moment to answer the following questions:

(a) Where did you purchase the Touche Ross Guide to Personal Financial Management?

____

(b) Do you presently own or are you planning to purchase an IBM–compatible personal computer? ______________________

(c) If you own a personal computer, please indicate your dealer and location. __________

____

(d) Income Level (PLEASE CIRCLE)

(1) Under $25,000
(2) $25,000–$50,000
(3) $50,000–$100,000
(4) Over $100,000

(e) Age Bracket (PLEASE CIRCLE)

(1) Under 30
(2) 30–40
(3) 40–50
(4) 50–60
(5) over 60

(f) Estimated Net Worth (PLEASE CIRCLE)

(1) Under $250,000
(2) $250,000–$500,000
(3) $500,000–$1,000,000
(4) Over $1,000,000

Name ______________________________

Address ____________________________

City ________________ **State** __________ **Zip** __________

RETURN TO:

Prentice-Hall, Inc.
Book Distribution Center
Department 4-R
Route 59 at Brook Hollow Drive
West Nyack, New York 10094

NOTES

NOTES

NOTES

NOTES

NOTES

NOTES

NOTES

NOTES

NOTES

NOTES

NOTES

NOTES